Jana Bressem
Repetitions in Gesture

Applications of Cognitive Linguistics

Editors
Gitte Kristiansen
Francisco J. Ruiz de Mendoza Ibáñez

Honorary editor
René Dirven

Volume 46

Jana Bressem

Repetitions in Gesture

A Cognitive-Linguistic and Usage-Based Perspective

DE GRUYTER
MOUTON

ISBN 978-3-11-126248-2
e-ISBN (PDF) 978-3-11-069790-2
e-ISBN (EPUB) 978-3-11-069799-5
ISSN 1861-4078

Library of Congress Control Number: 2021937512

Bibliographic information published by the Deutsche Nationalbibliothek
The Deutsche Nationalbibliothek lists this publication in the Deutsche Nationalbibliografie;
detailed bibliographic data are available on the Internet at http://dnb.dnb.de.

© 2023 Walter de Gruyter GmbH, Berlin/Boston
This volume is text- and page-identical with the hardback published in 2021.
Drawings by Mathias Roloff, www.mathiasroloff.de
Typesetting: Integra Software Services Pvt. Ltd.
Printing and binding: CPI books GmbH, Leck

www.degruyter.com

Contents

List of figures —— VII

List of tables —— IX

1 Setting the stage: Gestural repetitions in a multimodal corpus —— 1
    1.1   Introduction: Research topic, question, and aim —— 1
    1.2   Theoretical framework: Multimodality of language —— 4
    1.3   Data basis, annotation, analysis —— 12
    1.4   Forecast of the book —— 18

2 Building patterns in spoken and visual modalities —— 22
    2.1   The principle of iteration in spoken languages —— 22
    2.2   Repetition and reduplication in the visual modality of sign languages —— 31
    2.3   Means of creating gestural complexity —— 38
    2.4   Summary —— 44

3 Repeating gestures: Building (complex) units —— 46
    3.1   Iteration and reduplication: A cognitive-semantic classification —— 46
    3.2   A closer look: Repetitions and their structural and semantic characteristics —— 60
    3.3   Summary —— 84

4 Multimodal utterances I: Repetitive gestures affecting the semantics of speech —— 88
    4.1   The notion of multimodal utterances —— 88
    4.2   Repeating gestures: Emphasizing and altering speech —— 93
    4.3   Summary —— 111

5 Multimodal utterances II: Repetitive gestures interacting with the syntax of speech —— 114
    5.1   The notion of multimodal grammar —— 114
    5.2   Repeating gestures: Emphasizing or modifying the syntax of speech? —— 121
    5.3   Explaining the link: Multimodal constructions? —— 133
    5.4   Summary —— 151

6 **Cognitive functions of repetitive sequences: Attention and salience** —— 153
    6.1   Attention in Cognitive Linguistics and gesture studies —— 153
    6.2   Salience and gestural repetitions —— 158
    6.3   Reconsidering the nature of attention: New insights from gesture studies? —— 170
    6.4   Summary —— 174

7 **Closing the stage** —— 176
    7.1   Iteration as a basic principle of pattern-building in speech, sign, and gesture —— 181
    7.2   Implications for (Cognitive) Linguistics and further research perspectives —— 194

Appendices

A   **Notation conventions** —— 201

B   **Description of gestural form features** —— 203

C   **Excerpt from the excel sheet for the example "send back and forth"** —— 211

D   **Transcript example iteration "weapons of mass destruction"** —— 217

E   **Transcript example iteration "Arko"** —— 231

F   **Transcript example iteration "metal thing"** —— 233

G   **Transcript example reduplication "send back and forth"** —— 235

H   **Transcript example reduplication "single steps"** —— 237

References —— 239

Index —— 259

List of figures

Figure 1	Overview of the Methods of Gesture Analysis —— 13	
Figure 2	Extract from ELAN annotation file for the example 1 "weapons of mass destruction" —— 16	
Figure 3	Conceptual structure of reduplication (adapted from Stolz et al., 2011, p. 186) —— 28	
Figure 4	Fuzzy boundary between repetition and reduplication (adapted from Stolz et al., 2011, p. 147) —— 31	
Figure 5	Sign SICK and eight aspectual modulations (taken from Klima & Belugi, 1979, p. 265) —— 33	
Figure 6	Reciprocal form of HELFEN ('help') through backward reduplication (taken from Pfau & Steinbach, 2005, p. 573) —— 34	
Figure 7	Ungrammatical reciprocal form of GEBEN ('give') through back ward reduplication (taken from Pfau & Steinbach, 2005, p. 573) —— 35	
Figure 8	Plural marking in the sign KIND ('child') through sideward reduplication (taken from Pfau & Steinbach, 2005, Bressem & Ladewig, 2011, p. 580) —— 35	
Figure 9	Noun-verb pair (taken from Supalla & Newport, 1978, p. 102) —— 36	
Figure 10	Verb LOOK-AT (taken from Klima & Beluggi, 1979, p. 280) —— 37	
Figure 11	Ideal succession of gesture phases (taken from Bressem & Ladewig, 2011, p. 54) —— 39	
Figure 12	Constituent structure of gestural sequences with and without preparation phases (adapted from Fricke, 2012, p. 179) —— 40	
Figure 13	Cognitive-semantic classification of gestural repetition —— 47	
Figure 14	Example 1 iteration "weapons of mass destruction" —— 49	
Figure 15	Example 2 iteration "Arko" —— 50	
Figure 16	Example 3 iteration "metal thing" —— 52	
Figure 17	Example 4 reduplication "send back and forth" —— 56	
Figure 18	Example 5 reduplication "single steps" —— 57	
Figure 19	Overview of most frequent types of iterations and their forms, meanings, and functions —— 61	
Figure 20	Motivation of gestural forms —— 69	
Figure 21	Diagrammatic iconic relation in gestural reduplication —— 82	
Figure 22	Overview of iterations and reduplications and their form and meaning —— 87	
Figure 23	Continuum of co-expressivity between gestural and verbal meaning (adapted from Gut, Looks, Thies, & Gibbon, 2002, p. 9) —— 90	
Figure 24	Continuum of integrability of speech and gesture (adapted from Ladewig, 2012, p. 184) —— 119	
Figure 25	Overview of iterations and reduplications and their temporal and syntactil relation with speech —— 126	
Figure 26	Continuum of constructions in multimodal language use —— 142	
Figure 27	Types of multimodal constructions —— 143	
Figure 28	Types of verbo-kinesic constructions —— 144	
Figure 29	Example 6 iteration "big rain drops" —— 160	
Figure 30	Example 7 iteration "handles" —— 165	

https://doi.org/10.1515/9783110697902-203

List of tables

Table 1   Examples of full and partial reduplications —— 26
Table 2   Number of phonemes involved in cases of partial reduplication in Illocano language (examples taken from Rubino, 2005, p. 12) —— 26
Table 3   Criteria for prototypical cases of reduplication (adapted from Stolz, 2007a) —— 29
Table 4   Criteria for the distinction between repetition and reduplication (adapted from Gil, 2005, p. 33) —— 30
Table 5   Excerpt from transcript "weapons of mass destruction" —— 48
Table 6   Excerpt from transcript "Arko" —— 51
Table 7   Excerpt from transcript "metal thing" —— 53
Table 8   Excerpt from transcript "send back and forth" —— 55
Table 9   Excerpt from transcript "single steps" —— 58
Table 10 Distribution of iteration and reduplication in the corpus —— 63
Table 11 Overview of the length of repetition and parameter changes in iterations and reduplications —— 64
Table 12 Distribution of most frequent gestural modes of representation and their subtypes across iterations and reduplications —— 74
Table 13 Most frequent mimetic modes, gestural meanings and gesture types for iterations and reduplications —— 83
Table 14 Temporal positioning of gestural repetitions with the co-expressive speech —— 95
Table 15 Temporal relation of speech and gestures in examples 1–5 —— 96
Table 16 Examples of gestural repetitions occurring before the co-expressive speech —— 100
Table 17 Semantic relation of most frequent gestural repetitions —— 101
Table 18 Three most common syntactical categories and relations correlating with iterations and reduplications —— 122
Table 19 Characteristics of multimodal and verbo-kinesic constructions —— 148
Table 20 Iterations marking aspects of attention —— 159
Table 21 Characteristics of Figures and Grounds (based on Talmy, 2000, p. 315) —— 172

1 Setting the stage: Gestural repetitions in a multimodal corpus

1.1 Introduction: Research topic, question, and aim

Repetitive sequences play a significant role as a pattern-building device and are a basic syntagmatic linguistic means on all language levels in spoken and signed languages. In spoken languages, they are used for stylistic and pragmatic purposes when expressing viewpoints (Kotschi, 2001). Rhythmic structures arising from the doubling of syllables, such as in onomatopoeia (*oink oink* or *tick tock*), are a basic pattern for experiencing, embodying, and acquiring the phonological and prosodic structures of a language (Dressler, Dziubalska-Kołaczyk, Gagarina, & Kilani-Schoch, 2005). Syntactic repetition (*very very hot, fast fast*), recursive affixation (*Ur-ur-ur-großmutter* "great-great-great grandmother") or the repetition of a phrase (*A shark, a shark is behind you!*) are further examples of repetitions used for stylistic purposes (see Mattes, 2014; Schindler, 1991). On the morphological level, repetition is defined as the "systematic repetition of phonological material within a word for semantic or grammatical purposes" (Rubino, 2005, p. 11) and, as such, fulfills a multitude of functions in spoken and signed languages (Hurch, 2005). Reduplication is used in spoken languages for lexical purposes, such as the creation of nouns, indefinite pronouns or the expression of aspect, and achieves grammatical function when used for the expression of plural, number, and tense (Mattes, 2014). Similarly, reduplication in signed languages marks plural by varying the execution of the movement towards the body or horizontally to the side (Pfau & Steinbach, 2006). Furthermore, it may be used to derive adverbs from signs expressing temporal events, such as *week* or *month*. Repeating a sign slowly with a large and circular movement marks the duration (*for weeks and weeks*) (Meir, 2012).

In what follows, the discussion of repetitive sequences is expanded towards a multimodal perspective on gesture-speech relation in spoken language and poses the following questions:
- Do gestures exhibit different types of repetitive sequences?
- Do gestures build complex units based on these types and if so, how is the pattern building to be described?
- How is the interrelation of gestural and spoken units in such complex units?
- Is it possible to identify repetitive patterns that are comparable to spoken and signed languages and/or patterns specific to the gestural modality?

For answering these questions, the book takes a usage-based approach grounded in a cognitive-linguistic perspective and shows that gestures also form units of different complexity and functionality by using the same principles as spoken or signed languages. In particular, the book postulates that gestures constitute two categories of repetition: iteration and reduplication. These two forms of repetition differ concerning formational, structural, and semantic aspects and have specific semantic, grammatical, and cognitive relevance for the creation of multimodal utterances. The analysis indicates that gestures may develop structures comparable to spoken and signed languages, yet, at the same time, instantiate patterns that are specific to the gestural modality. Similar to spoken or signed languages, iterations are used for stylistic and prosodic purposes and may mark the focus of attention and Figure-Ground structures (Chafe, 1994). Gestural reduplications carry lexical and grammatical meaning by conveying iterativity and plural, and, as such, express similar verb-semantic and grammatical aspects of meaning as speech and signs. Characteristics specific to the gestural modality can be found, for instance, in the length of the repetitions, exhibiting a contrastive pattern documented for spoken, but not for signed languages. A further difference is to be found in the gestures' relation with the spoken utterance, leading to a difference in the semantic strength of the gestural reduplicative construction. By addressing questions of mediality and multimodality of language-in-use, the book thus contributes to the investigation of repetition as a fundamental means of sign and meaning construction (crosscutting modalities) and enhances the understanding of the multimodal character of language in use.

Repetitions have so far not yet been systematically addressed from a multimodal perspective. A corpus-based analysis, as presented in this book, which discusses the phenomenon on a broad empirical basis, is still a research desideratum. This research gap is particularly surprising because the phenomenon of repetitions poses a range of methodological and theoretical questions discussed controversially for the multimodality of language (e.g., segmentation, complexity, and functionality of gestural units, semantization, and grammaticalization of gestures). Such questions are, thereby, not only of relevance for "practical" decisions in the process of coding but, more importantly, also address fundamental characteristics of gestures and language. By adopting a cognitive-linguistic and form-based approach to gestures (Bressem, Ladewig, & Müller, 2013; Müller, Bressem, & Ladewig, 2013), the book gives an empirically sound and encompassing account of repetitive sequences addressing the form, semantics, and (cognitive) functions of these sequences. The distinction that repetitions in gestures are either used to create coherent units or may even serve as a means of meaning constitution underlines the linguistic potential of gestures. By doing so, the book contributes to a better understanding of how gestures' potential for language needs to be conceived and described and, thus, addresses core issues of present-day gesture studies.

Furthermore, the proposition argued for in the book, namely that repetitive structures as a fundamental means of sign constitution are also a basic principle for building patterns and units of different complexity and functionality in gestures, addresses a core notion of Cognitive Linguistics: the question of universal principles crosscutting modalities. By departing from the assumption that linguistic patterns and structures rest upon general cognitive principles that are not particular for spoken or written languages but can play out in the visual modality as well, the book grounds gestural processes of pattern building on general principles of conceptualization and explains their relevance and characteristics for a multimodal understanding of language use. This assumption is further strengthened by the book's aim of identifying factors of repetitive sequences that cut across modalities (verbal vs. visual) and semiotic systems (language vs. gesture). In comparison with the phenomenon of repetition in spoken and signed languages, the book explores, on the one hand, the specifics of gestures and of multimodal spoken language use. On the other hand, it attempts to identify fundamental principles for building patterns irrespective of the modality on which they are based. With this perspective, the book follows other approaches assuming that "language and gesture are dynamic, emergent systems, the product of a human expressive ability that is grounded in embodied cognitive abilities" (Wilcox & Nogueira, 2013, p. 107). Moreover, by taking up the notion of constructions as a framework for explaining the principles of pattern building in gestures alone and in relation with speech, the book joins in the strand of research on (Multimodal) Construction Grammar and tackles the question of how the interplay of speech and gesture can be accounted for from a usage-based and cognitive-linguistic perspective (Bergs & Zima, 2017). As such, it offers another piece of the puzzle on how "a new facility for understanding the grammar of multimodal meaning construction" (Steen & Turner, 2013, p. 19) can be modeled.

Considering all the aspects discussed above, the book addresses basic principles of Cognitive Linguistics, namely that "language is not an autonomous cognitive faculty, [that] grammar is conceptualization, [and that] knowledge of language emerges from language use" (Croft & Cruse 2004: 1). The book gives fresh impetus for cognitive linguistic research, both methodologically and theoretically, and demonstrates how linguistic phenomena can be accounted for against the notion of multimodality of language that considers gestures not only as an attachment but rather as an essential part of language. Therefore, the book has fundamental implications for the study of language because it supports the view that language use is inherently multimodal. It assumes it to be the natural form of spoken language and posits that other modalities, such as gestures, are indispensable for analyzing language in use and for understanding the nature of language itself. The book presents a cognitive-linguistic perspective on gestures that builds the basis for an adequate linguistic description of the visual modality (Bressem et al., 2013; Müller, Bressem, et al., 2013) and, thus, provides the theoretical frame necessary for an analysis of the multimodality of language.

Moreover, the book achieves particular methodological relevance due to its empirical foundation on a multimodal corpus and its elaboration on data elicitation, evaluation, and analysis. Analyses of multimodal language use based on multimodal corpora are scarce within Cognitive Linguistic research. Yet, considering present attempts at gathering large corpora for speech and gesture, as with the "The Distributed Little Red Hen Lab" (Steen & Turner, 2013), a linguistic perspective on multimodal data is needed.

Consequently, the book provides necessary information on the use of multimodal corpora focusing on the relation of speech and gesture. Finally, by addressing processes of building patterns on the level of gestures alone as well as concerning speech, the book offers a further facet in examining how the same linguistic processes, structures, and functions may manifest themselves in speech and gesture. By discussing the interaction and relevance of gestures for the semantics and syntax of speech, it examines possible areas of integrating speech and gesture. The following chapters thus contribute to a discussion of the general principles of linguistic multimodality from the perspective of gesture-speech relations (Cienki, 2012; Fricke, 2007, 2012; Mittelberg, 2006; Müller, 1998, 2008).

1.2 Theoretical framework: Multimodality of language

In recent years, an ever-growing body of research shows that human communication is fundamentally multimodal. Language is intertwined with other modalities in several ways and only seldom occurs isolated. Written language appears with static or moving images (Jewitt, 2014). Spoken language is used in connection with sound, music, or kinesic forms of expressions, such as gestures, facial expressions, or head movements. Accordingly, the notion of multimodality in current linguistic and semiotic approaches encompasses text/image as well as speech/gesture relations and defines multimodality as a) two linguistic media that are structurally and functionally integrated into one and the same code or b) as one code that manifests itself simultaneously in two different media (Fricke, 2012, 2014c).

From the range of media occurring with speech, kinesic movements in face-to-face communication assume a specific role. At the latest, since the works of

Kendon (1972, 1980) and McNeill (1985, 1992), it is evident that gestures play a prominent role in human communication. Research indicates that gesturing is not only a universal companion of spoken languages, but moreover that speech and gesture are "manifestations of the same process of utterance" (Kendon, 1980, p. 208). Gestures are "an integral part of language much as are words, phrases, and sentences – gesture and language are one system" (McNeill, 1992, p. 2). Evidence for the close connection of both modes is provided by a wealth of studies underlining gestures' close link with speech on the levels of semantics, syntax, and pragmatics. Due to their close temporal relation with the co-expressive speech segment, gestures embody elements of the verbal meaning, in particular, information about the size, shape, and location of objects, mark salient information, and highlight and foreground information in the flow of discourse (Müller & Tag, 2010). Cognitive-semantic approaches stress that processes of conceptualization in speech and gesture rest upon general principles of meaning making (see for instance Cienki & Müller, 2008; Mittelberg, 2006; Müller, 2008). Cross-linguistic studies on motion events emphasize this tight link of gestures with the semantics of speech, even showing a close connection with grammatical differences in the spoken utterance (Kita & Özyürek, 2003). Gestures are also essential when fulfilling communicative actions and show what kind of speech act the speaker is engaged at the moment of speaking. They regulate the behavior of others, express the speaker's attitude or mark focal aspects of the utterance (Kendon, 2004a; Müller, 1998; Streeck, 2009).

Apart from gestures' specific structural, functional, and cognitive relevance for spoken language, communicative movements of the hands possess medial and functional properties that make them stand out from other bodily resources. With reference to Bühler's functional language theory, gestures can be said to possess a basic potential for language because they can be used to make statements about objects in the world ("representation"), have the potential to regulate the behavior of others ("appeal"), and express the inner state of the speaker ("expression") (Müller, 1998, 2013). "As in language these functions are co-present dimensions of any sign and rather than characterizing alternative signs, their 'dominance' within one sign varies" (Müller, 2009, p. 501). In the absence of speech, this linguistic potential allows gestures to develop into full-fledged languages, as it is the case with sign languages of the deaf. At least two characteristics of movements of the hand enable this elaboration:

> A highly flexible articulation (the capacity for a high differentiation of movements is a prerequisite for a complex sign system) and a manifold instrumental use of the hands, which provides the functional grounds (and infinite sources) for the creation of gestural meaning. (Müller, 2013, p. 203)

Based on this potential for language, linguistic approaches to the study of multimodality argue that speech and gestures rest upon similar structural and semiotic principles and that an analysis of both modi provides insight into the nature of language itself. To reveal these principles, approaches concentrate on two aspects: First, discovering structures in gestures and giving an account of a "grammar" of gesture (Fricke, 2007, 2012; Müller, 1998; Müller, Bressem, et al., 2013; Müller, Ladewig, & Bressem, 2013). Secondly, describing the relation of speech and gesture in conjunction from the perspective of the multimodality of grammar (Cienki, 2012; Fricke, 2012; Kok & Cienki, 2016; Ladewig, 2012, 2020; Muntigl, 2004).

The formulation "grammar" of gestures thereby underlines two aspects:

> first, co-verbal gestures show properties of form and meaning which are prerequisites of language and which – in case the oral mode of expression is not available – may evolve into a more or less full-fledged linguistic system such as a sign language or an alternate sign language [. . .]. Second, when used in conjunction with speech, co-verbal gestures may take over grammatical functions, such as that of verbs, nouns, or attributes pointing towards a multimodal nature of grammar. (Bressem 2012; Fricke 2012; Ladewig 2012)
>
> (Müller, Bressem, et al., 2013, p. 711)

As such, gestures are not regarded as linguistic units in the full-fledged sense but are instead considered to take over functions of linguistic units either in collaboration or in exchange with vocal linguistic units. Possible similarities and differences between the two sign systems are aimed at while keeping the specifics, in particular of gestures, in mind (Bressem & Ladewig, 2011; Enfield, 2009). A perspective on a "grammar" of gesture thus directs at a systematic, form-based linguistic documentation of gestural patterns. It refers to the basic form properties of gestures, to their structures, and to revealing their potential for language. It is assumed that gestures follow principles of meaning creation, build units of different complexity, and show various degrees of lexicalization and grammaticalization. Considering the semiotic and symbolic nature of gestures, their ability to express meaning, for instance, is assumed to be grounded in particular processes of sign creation. The hands either mime or reenact actual manual activities ("acting") or embody an object as a whole, becoming a kind of manual sculpture ("representing") (Müller, 1998, 2009, 2010, 2013, 2014). These gestural modes of representation make up techniques of sign creation by which movements of the hands and arms become symbolic. They reconstruct the practices of gestural mimesis and provide the first step towards gestural meaning construction and the embodied basis of gestural movements (see chapter 3 for a detailed discussion). Gestural meaning, as indicated by the modes of representation, is thus considered to be motivated. Gestures make use of basic cognitive image-schematic structures and can be understood as forms of "exbodied" cognitive structures: They exploit motoric patterns of mundane actions, evoke geometrical or schematic patterns or Gestalts (e.g., circles, oval shapes, squares), and realize image-schematic structures (e.g., source-path-goal, container/containment) (e.g., Calbris, 2011; Cienki, 2005; Ladewig, 2011; Mittelberg, 2010; Müller, 1998; Sowa, 2005; Streeck, 2009). Hence, gestural forms carry abstract meaning independent from the verbal context. Through a dynamic process of meaning constitution (Kolter et al., 2012; Müller, 2008; Müller & Tag, 2010), the gestural meaning is indexically anchored within a given sequential structure and as such specified and enriched in relation with speech (Enfield, 2009). Moreover, gestures are motivated form Gestalts in the sense that they are internally structured. Gestures and gestural meanings are made up of formational features (handshape, orientation, movement, position) that may be meaningful for themselves[1] (Calbris, 1990, 2011; Fricke, 2010, 2012; Kendon, 2004; Müller, 2004; Webb, 1996). The use of these formational features is not considered to be random. For specific types of co-speech gestures, it is instead assumed that they recur across speakers and contexts whilst sharing stable form-meaning relations. Also, gestures may also systematically vary with regard to how and which formational features participate in meaning construction (Calbris, 2011; Fricke, 2012; Harrison, 2009; Kendon, 2004; Ladewig, 2014b; Müller, 1998) (see chapter 3 for a detailed discussion). Research has also shown that speakers draw on a repertoire of forms that they use recurrently (Bressem & Müller, 2014b; Brookes, 2004; Kendon, 1992; Payrato, 1993). Based on analyses of such recurrent gestural forms and meanings, studies have documented that gestures become semanticized as well as grammaticalized. They may be deployed with speech as markers of negation (Harrison, 2009; Kendon, 2004; Müller & Speckmann, 2002), "Aktionsarten" (Becker et al., 2011; Cienki & Iriskhanova, 2018; Ladewig, 2011; Müller, 2000) or plurality (Bressem, 2015, submitted). Yet, gestures are not only simultaneously complex. As movements, gestures are also structured in time and space and hierarchically organized. On the one hand, gestural movement sequences can be segmented into individual phases (e.g., rest position, preparation, stroke). On the other hand, gestures build units of different size and complexity, that may range from smaller "gestural phrases" to larger "gesture units" (Kendon, 2004). Research documents "how sequences of gestures are formally and functionally structured" (Enfield, 2009, p. 57), revealing gesture combinations of different complexity (Bressem, 2015; Müller, Bressem, et al., 2013). Moreover, gestural movements are coordinated with syntagms in speech:

---

[1] For the description of gestures' formational features, gesture research falls back on the notion of form parameters in sign languages (e.g., Battison 1974; Frishberg 1975; Stokoe 1960).

> sweeps of the arms or movements of the head may be sustained over larger linguistic units, such as phrases, while eye shifts, wrist and finger movements occur over smaller segments, such as syllables. (Kendon, 1972, p. 183)

Based on this structural relation, speech and gesture build a functional unit that is achieved by the speakers:

> In creating an utterance that uses both modes of expression, the speaker creates an *ensemble* in which gesture and speech are employed together as *partners* in a single rhetoric enterprise. (Kendon, 2004a, p. 127 emphasis in original)

The functional relation of both modes is focused on in the multimodality of grammar. Here, the perspective shifts from an investigation of gestures as a medium of expression to gestures as being structural and functional elements of spoken utterances. Gestures are obligatory elements for the use of particular verbal deictic expressions such as *so, here,* or *there* (Fricke, 2007; Kita, 2003; Streeck, 2002) and may even differ in the form depending on the intended reference object of the deictic expression (Fricke, 2007; Kendon, 2004a). They stand in close relation with different types of negation, such as morphological or implicit negation (Calbris, 1990; Harrison, 2009, 2018; Kendon, 2003, 2004a) and are influenced by the semantic and syntactic encoding of the verbal utterance. Differences in the marking of aspect, for instance, are reflected in the gestural forms, the timing of gestures relative to the verbal utterance, and in the information distributed across the modalities (Duncan, 2005; Kita & Özyürek, 2003; McNeill & Duncan, 2000; Müller, 2000). Locative expressions are not only expressed in gestures but rather establish the location of the lexicalized topological configuration in space (Tutton, 2015). Moreover, particular gestures are related to specific word classes or syntactic phrases. Gestures depicting concrete entities or events mostly correlate with nouns, verbs, and adjectives or noun phrases (Fricke, 2012; Hadar & Krauss, 1999). As such, they may achieve particular syntactic function as attributes, for example, when specifying the nucleus noun of the nominal phrase (Fricke, 2014c). When replacing speech, gestures may even form an utterance on their own or provide the semantic center of a multimodal utterance (Clark, 1996; Slama-Cazacu, 1976). In cases of syntactic gaps, for example, gestures are even structurally integrated into the syntax of speech by adopting syntactic positions of nouns and verbs (Ladewig, 2014a, 2020). Based on these results, studies concentrating on the multimodality of grammar contribute to understanding the interfaces of gesture-speech relations, different forms of integration of gestures on various linguistic levels, and a broader understanding of the nature of language (see chapter 5 for details on multimodal grammar).

With this growing body of evidence, proposals also include gestures, and even more generally the notion of multimodality, in grammatical models and theories. Within these efforts, different scopes of the argument and theoretical frameworks are discussed (Cienki, 2012; Fricke, 2012; Kok & Cienki, 2016; Ladewig, 2020; Lücking, 2013; Muntigl, 2004; Wilcox & Xavier, 2013). Fricke (2012, 2013, 2014a, 2014b) presents preconditions for the assumptions of a multimodal grammar: she argues for typification and semantization of gestures as potential syntactic constituents, a syntactic function of gestures as attributes in spoken noun phrases, and the display of recursivity based on gestures' linear and sequential complexity. With these characteristics, Fricke argues, gestures fall within the area of grammar and the grammar of a single language, such as German, must be considered multimodal. Apart from claiming this multimodality of the language system, two fundamental principles that not only take effect in gesture-speech relations but are also applicable to other semiotic sign systems, such as text-image relations, are proposed: a) two linguistic media are structurally and functionally integrated into one and the same code ("code-integration") or b) one code manifests itself simultaneously in two different media ("code-manifestation") (Fricke, 2012, 2014c). In addition, multimodality in the narrow sense (two different modalities, e.g., gesture-speech) and broader sense (same sense modality, e.g., text-image) are set apart. With this perspective, Fricke propagates an approach to the multimodality of grammar which "contributes to a description of language in all its structural, functional as well as medial and cognitive particularities" (Fricke, 2013, p. 751) and aims at a theoretical and methodological framework that allows for a unified description of linguistic multimodality.

A notion of multimodality that is, first of all, restricted to spoken language usage events and kinesic expressions is formulated by Cienki (2012, 2013, 2015a). Taking a cognitive-linguistic perspective, Cienki argues that gestures, for instance, achieve particular relevance for the grammar of a single language: "the degree to which gesture is part of language varies, both when we consider language as a system and with regard to the use of any language in real time" (Cienki, 2012, p. 154). Language, on the level of use and system, is thus not categorically multimodal. Instead, multimodality of language needs to be understood in terms of a prototype structure in which we find prototypical instances of multimodal language, such as when speech and gesture form rather conventional units (e.g., negation and deixis). Moreover, the degree and ways to which gestures may achieve linguistic status differs. "Thus while we might not be able to support a broad claim that grammar is multimodal, the evidence suggests that a flexible model of grammar is in order (Cienki 2012)." (Cienki, 2013, p. 681). Kinesic expressions that frequently co-occur with linguist units may become more entrenched signs and move towards the center of the grammar.

This position is also advocated by other studies, integrating gestures, in particular, co-verbal gestures, into the framework of Cognitive Grammar (Langacker, 1999): Gestures are conceived of as symbolic units and assumed to show conceptual archetypes of spoken language. Gestures reflect meaning construal by making use of schematization, reification, and scanning as a means for symbolization (Kok & Cienki, 2016; Ladewig, 2012, 2014a, 2020). "In adopting cognitive grammar [. . .], we suggest that all of the theoretical and analytic framework of cognitive grammar can be recruited to study gesture." (Wilcox & Xavier, 2013, p. 92)[2] Recently, also the framework of Construction Grammar is broadened to include kinesic expressions, such as gestures or body movements. Falling back on the notions of entrenchment and frequency, studies formulate basic premises for the application of the term "construction" and the nature of the constructions as multimodal signs (see Bergs & Zima, 2017 for an overview and chapter 5 for a more detailed discussion).

The present book takes up these two perspectives: Using repetitive sequences in co-speech gestures, and more generally, processes of building patterns and units as an example, it concentrates on describing the multimodality of language by describing the "grammar" of gesture and the multimodality of grammar. More specifically, it points at how both perspectives are connected and necessary for a deeper understanding of gestural and verbo-gestural signs and the multimodal nature of language use. The book thereby not only aims at setting verbal and gestural structures in relation but rather tries to identify fundamental means of signs and meaning construction crosscutting modalities. As such, it provides evidence for a shared conceptual basis of speech and gesture and the fact that "language and gesture are dynamic, emergent systems, the product of a human expressive ability that is grounded in embodied cognitive abilities" (Wilcox & Xavier, 2013, p. 107). The book thereby pursues a cognitive take on verbo-gestural meaning construction: It is considered to be fundamentally rooted in human experience and assumed that gestures display embodied facets and roots of language. Hence, in discussing repetitive sequences and their medial characteristics and relation with speech, the book pursues a focus on language use framed by the perspective of Cognitive Linguistics and Embodied Cognition:

---

[2] Drawing on Systemic Functional Grammar, Muntigl (2004) also argues that semiotic systems must be seen along a continuum between language and proto-language and that multiple semiotic systems, such as speech and gestures, may be functionally interrelated through elaboration, extension and enhancement, for instance. Accordingly, by adding textural, interpersonal and ideational meanings to speech, gestures are functionally integrated into speech and as such need to be considered part of the grammar of language (see K. Kok, 2016 for a further functional perspective.)

"a characterization of the general principles for language that accord with what is known about the mind and brain from other disciplines" (Evans, Bergen & Zinken, 2007, p. 4) and the rootedness of cognitive and conceptual knowledge in the bodily experiences with and in the world and the embodied roots of language and thought (Croft & Cruse, 2004; Gibbs, 2006). As such, the book concords with the assumption that language is not an autonomous faculty, that the basic principle in "grammar is conceptualization" (Langacker, 1999), and that knowledge of language emerges from language use through abstraction and schematization. As such language, and, in particular, the multimodality of language use, offers a window into general cognitive functions and processes. It provides evidence for the fact that the structure of our conceptual system is reflected in the patterns of language and that language, in general, is grounded in bodily experiences. "People's subjective, felt experiences of their bodies in action provide part of the fundamental grounding for language and thought." (Gibbs, 2006, p. 9). Processes of abstraction and pre-conceptual structures, such as image (Cienki, 1997; Mittelberg, 2010), action (Bressem & Müller, 2014a; Mittelberg, 2006; Streeck, 2008; Teßendorf, 2016), and mimetic schemas (Zlatev, 2005), are pertinent to the motivation of the form of gestures, and contribute significantly to the meaning of gestures. Evidence of multimodal metaphors highlights that gestures frequently embody the experiential source domain of the verbalized metaphoric expression and as such mediate between the concrete and the abstract world (Calbris, 2003; Cienki, 1998; Cienki & Müller, 2008; McNeill, 1992; Mittelberg, 2006; Müller, 2008; Sweetser, 1998). And metonymy is vital in gestural sign creation, thus illuminating "links between habitual bodily acts, the abstractive power of the mind, and interpretative/inferential processes." (Mittelberg, 2006, pp. 292–293)

Following the premise that the study of language is the study of language use, the book presents a usage-based and cognitive-linguistic analysis of repetitive sequences in gestures from a perspective of language use as being "inherently and variably multimodal" (Cienki, 2012; Fricke, 2007, 2012; Müller, 1998, 2008) and of grammar as being "potentially multimodal" (Cienki, 2012). Based on a corpus-analysis of multimodal usage-events, the book discusses gestural repetitions with regard to their structure, semantic, and syntactic relevance for multimodal utterances and cognitive saliency. It is concluded that an abstract process of copying along with diagrammatic iconicity is the general underlying structural principle that constitutes a modality-independent universal principle of repetitive sequences in the spoken and visual modality. As such, the book not only contributes to gesture studies and linguistics proper but also opens ways for "a comparative semiotics of kinesic expression" (Kendon, 2008, p. 360) and thus a deeper understanding of the nature of language in general.

1.3 Data basis, annotation, analysis

The argumentation presented in this book is based on a data set of 30 hours of video data containing different kinds of discourse types and interactional settings ranging from naturally occurring conversations, game shows, discussions, political discussions, debates from the German Bundestag to games, and experimental data.[3] As the occurrence of gestures differs greatly depending on the interactional setting as well as the type of discourse, a balanced data set is a prerequisite for a sound representation of the phenomenon under investigation. For this reason, a corpus of video data was built that would account for the phenomenon of gestural repetitions in its broadest way possible.

All in all, the corpus contains 182 gestural repetitions from 40 German speakers. In order to arrive at these instances, the video data were sifted for gestural repetitions, occurring within gesture phrases[4] (Kendon, 1980, 2004a) using the annotation program ELAN (Wittenburg, Brugman, Russal, Klassmann, & Sloetjes, 2006). At this point in the study, gestures were defined as similar when sharing a related handshape, orientation of the palm, and/or movement. The subsequent segmentation, annotation, and analysis followed a particular method that is grounded in a cognitive-linguistic approach to gesture-speech relations as outlined in the section above. The "Methods of Gesture Analysis" have been developed within research projects aiming at encompassing documentation of those properties of form that characterize the hand(s) as a medium of expression (Müller, Bressem, Ladewig, 2013). They offer a form-based method to systematically reconstruct the meaning of gestures by focusing on the fundamental properties and basic principles of gestural meaning creation in four successive and interrelated steps: 1) analysis of form, 2) analysis of the sequential structure of gestures in relation to speech and other gestures, 3) analysis of the gestures' local context of use, i.e., its connection to syntactic, semantic, and pragmatic aspects of speech, and 4) the gestures' distribution over different contexts use (see Figure 1) (Bressem et al., 2013; Ladewig & Bressem, 2013; Müller, 2004, 2010b). The "Methods of Gesture Analysis" assume that the meaning of a gesture emerges out of a fine-grained interaction of all four aspects (form, sequential

---

3 I would like to thank Silva H. Ladewig for allowing me to use parts of her video data corpus (see Ladewig 2020) for further information on the corpus) and the ToGoG project for sharing parts of their experimental data (see www.togog.org).
4 Following Kendon (1980, 2004a), gesture phrases are sequences of gesture phases that are not delimited by retractions or rest positions. See chapter 3 for more detail on the classification of gestural movement sequences.

structure, and (local and global) context of use). A gesture's meaning is thus determined in a (widely) context-free analysis of its form, which grounds the later context-sensitive analysis of gestures in relation to speech. Following this logic, the "Methods of Gesture Analysis" propagate a separate analysis of speech and gestures for gestures' form and its sequential structure.

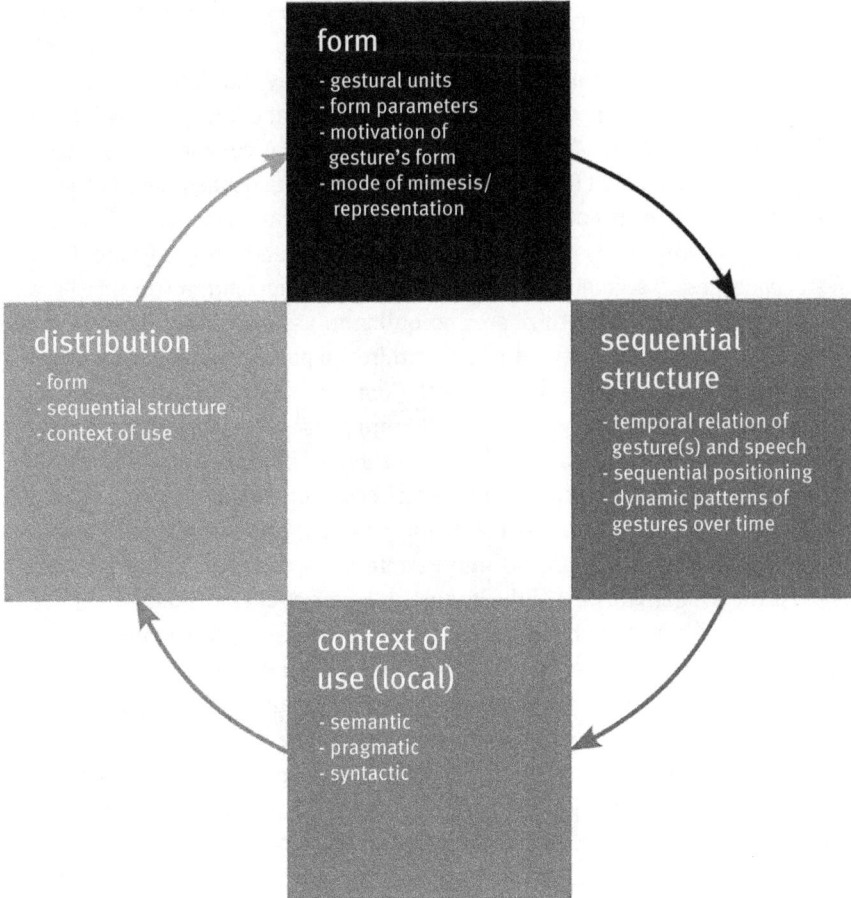

Figure 1: Overview of the Methods of Gesture Analysis.

The basic rationale of the "Methods of Gesture Analysis" is represented in the "Linguistic Annotation System for Gestures" (LASG), which transforms it into a format applicable in annotation software such as ELAN (Bressem, Ladewig & Müller, 2013).[5]

Based on the "Methods of Gesture Analysis" and the "Linguistic Annotation System for Gestures", the study presented in this book started out from an analysis of the gestures' form and, in particular, the determination of gestural units and an account of gestures as motivated signs by spelling out cognitive-semiotic properties of gesture creation. Here, it is addressed how gestures achieve meaning, how they function as signs, and what kinds of cognitive processes are at stake both in the mind of the speaker and the recipient. Specifically, the following questions were addressed: What are the boundaries of a gesture and how are they internally structured (combinatorics/simultaneity)? What kinds of complex connections of gestures can be identified (syntagmatics/ linearity)? What is the gestures' meaning independent of speech? For the determination of gestural units, the study followed a three-step-procedure: 1) identification of beginnings and ends of gestural movement sequences, 2) segmentation of movement into single movement phases, and 3) classification of movement phases according to gesture phases. Gesture units, "the moment the articulators begin to depart from a position of relaxation until the moment when they finally return to one" (Kendon, 2004a, p. 111), constitute the broadest level of gesture segmentation. Gesture phases, "in which the articulators reach points of furthest remove from the position of relaxation" (Kendon, 2004a, p. 112), constitute the lowest level of gesture segmentation and the referring unit for all following annotations. Following this procedure, sequences containing gestural repetitions were segmented into gesture units and then coded for gesture phases. The meaningful part of the gestures, i.e., the stroke, was then described in its form feature based on the four parameters "handshape", "orientation", "movement", and "position in gesture space", developed for the description of signs to gestures (Klima & Beluggi, 1979; Stokoe, 1960). Taking the four form parameters as the basis of a gestural form description aims at systematically addressing the form aspects of a gestural Gestalt. It allows for a fine-grained description of gestures and for detecting gestural patterns and structures. For this, the study used a notation system that focuses solely on the physical appearance of gestures and propagates a differentiation between an articulatory and taxonomic description of gestures' forms (Bressem, 2013). After focusing on gestural forms, the focus of analysis shifts to their motivation. Here, semiotic processes involved in gestural sign creation were addressed by concentrating on image schema, actions, and

---

[5] Gestures are always interpreted against the background of a particular theoretical frame. This frame determines the analytical steps taken in the process of annotation and coding. As such, the book presents one approach to the study of multimodal language use. For an overview of other approaches see (Müller et al., 2013).

modes of representations. Detecting the motivation of a gestural form is assumed to be a crucial step in tracing back and explaining gestures' characteristics of form, meaning, and function. In particular, by asking what the hands do when performing a gesture and by considering the ephemeral shapes, movements, and objects that are created, the first account of a basic meaning of gestures is aimed at. The gestural modes of representation thereby reconstruct the techniques of gestural mimesis, provide grounds for answering the question of how gestures become symbolic. As such, they provide access to the grounding of gestures in motor patterns, image and actions schemas which then, in turn, advance the understanding of the nature and meaning of gestural forms and, in particular, their embodied basis (Müller, 1998, 2009, 2010b, 2013, 2014). In addition, the number of strokes included in a gestural repetition was annotated (see Figure 2 for an impression of the ELAN template).

In the following steps, the study focused on analyzing gestural repetitions in relation to speech. In particular, the following questions were addressed: How are speech and gesture related temporally? What dynamic patterns over time are observable, that is how does meaning evolve over a longer stretch of discourse? What are the gestures' semantic, pragmatic, and syntactic functions? With these questions, the preceding context-free analysis is brought together with a context-sensitive analysis of gestures. Meaning is regarded here in its cognitive, functional, and interactive dimensions (Müller, 2010b). For answering these questions, the speech was transcribed and annotated. The segmentation of the verbal utterance was based on the concept of intonation units as proposed by Chafe (1994) for three reasons. First, it defines segments of spoken language on the basis of a variety of form-based criteria and is not primarily dependent on syntactical units of verbal utterances. Secondly, different than other accounts (cf. Ladd, 1996), intonation units can contain more than one primary accent, a feature that is of particular importance when considering sequences of gestural repetitions in relation to speech. Thirdly, intonation units make up a unit of mental and linguistic processing which "verbalizes the speaker's focus of consciousness at that moment" (Chafe, 1994, p. 63), such that each intonation unit verbalizes a different idea, event, or state, a factor which will be of crucial importance in explaining the function of gestural repetitions (see chapter 6). Based on the segmentation of intonation units, speech was transcribed according to the GAT conventions (Selting et al., 2009). Furthermore, gesture phases were aligned with the co-expressive segments of the verbal utterance, and phonological units (phone, syllable) of the verbal utterance being co-expressive with the coded gestures phases were annotated.

16 — 1 Setting the stage: Gestural repetitions in a multimodal corpus

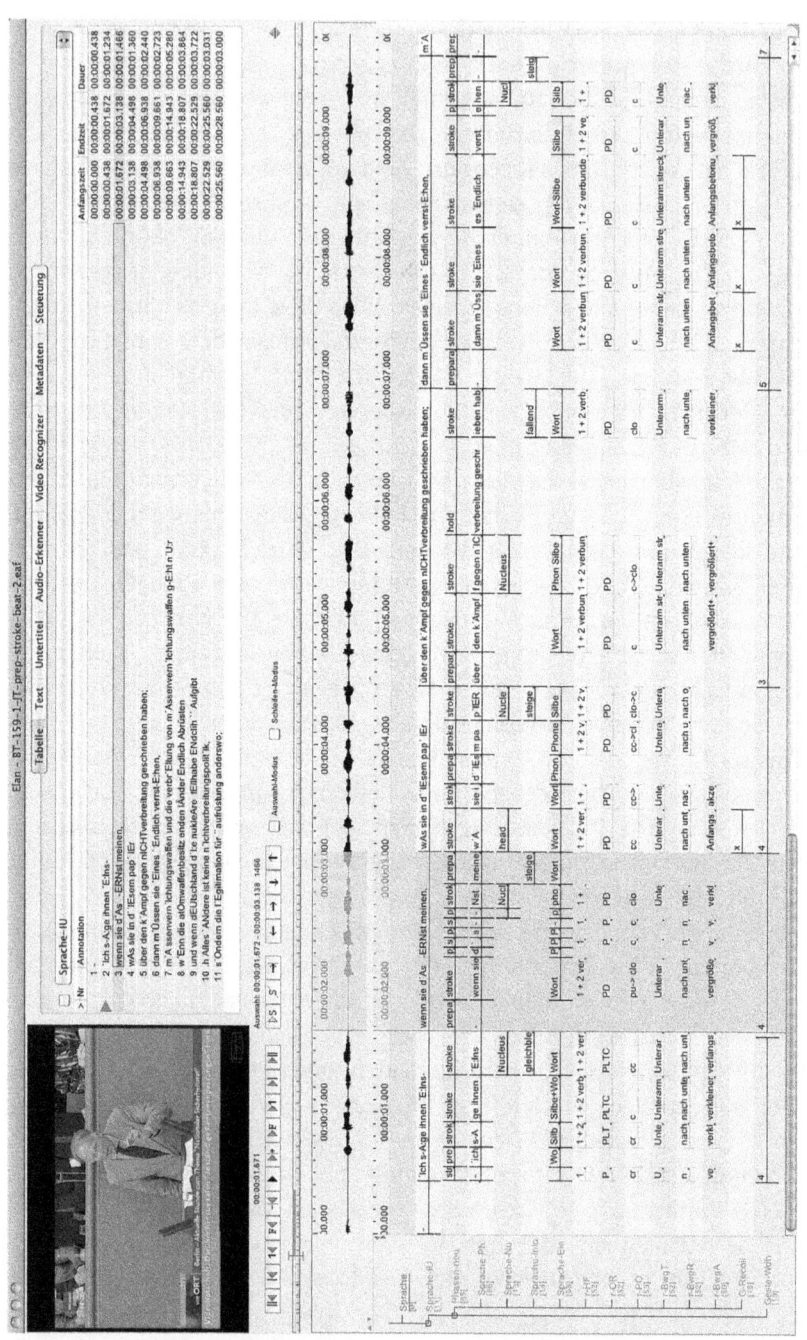

Figure 2: Extract from ELAN annotation file for the example 1 "weapons of mass destruction".

Next, the temporal and semantic relation of speech and gesture was annotated based on the notion of "co-expressiveness" (Engle, 2000; McNeill, 2005):

> To count as co-expressive, both the speech segment and the visible behavior had to be interpretable as collectively referring to the same thing. [. . .] It had to be possible to specify a single conceptual category [. . .] that the spoken and visible elements collectively referred to.
> (Engle, 2000, p. 26)

Specifically, the following questions were addressed: How are speech and gesture related temporally? How are speech and gesture related semantically? What are the gestures' semantic functions? The temporal position of a gesture in relation to speech determines its local meaning and is of core importance for establishing the local meaning of a gesture, as elements that are expressed simultaneously are also perceived as belonging together. The semantic relation not only highlights the verbal elements of meaning that are embodied in the gestures but also provides insights into salient and foregrounded information in verbo-gestural utterances. These aspects are further supported by addressing the gestures' relation with the syntax of speech. In particular, the following questions were posed: What is the gestures' position with regard to syntactic units? How are gestures integrated syntactically into the spoken utterances? What is the syntactic function of the gesture? These questions contribute to a close description of the gesture's linguistic context that is fundamental for determining the structural and functional relevance of gestures in language use and reconstructing their meaning. The gestures' interactive functions are addressed when examining their relationship with the pragmatics of speech and discourse. The following facets were considered: How is the gesture positioned within turns? Do they acquire interactive and discursive functions? What is their relation with the verbal speech act and their pragmatic function? Addressing these aspects adds information on the local context of the use of gestures and specifies further aspects of the local meaning construction in gestures.

After completing the annotation process in ELAN, the annotations were exported to an Excel database, which provided the grounds for a distributional analysis aiming at three main questions:

- Is it possible to differentiate gestural repetitions on the level of form? Are they characterized by particular successions of gesture phases, changes of form features, and a specific length?
- Is it possible to differentiate gestural repetitions based on semantic characteristics? Do they show a particular distribution of the gestural modes of representation and gesture types? Do they differ in the gestural meaning that is expressed?
- Is it possible to differentiate gestural repetitions based on functional aspects? Do they fulfill particular functions (cognitive, semantic, syntactic, and pragmatic) for the creation of the verbo-gestural utterances?

For answering these questions, it was first analyzed whether the strokes remain the same in their form aspects throughout the entire repetition or whether they show changes in particular form features. Furthermore, the number of strokes of the sequences and the amount within an intonation unit were counted. Also, the number of intonation units encompassed by a repetitive sequence were counted. Secondly, the repetitions were examined for their gestural modes of representation and whether they take over concrete or abstract referential function. Thirdly, using a semantic feature-based approach (Bergmann, Aksu, & Kopp, 2011), the semantic features of speech and gesture were coded, and the gesture's semantic function was specified. In the last step of the analysis, the results of the semantic analysis were brought together with an analysis examining the temporal alignment of the repetitions with syntactical categories and relations of the verbal utterance (Eisenberg, 1999/2001). The corresponding syntactical categories were determined for each stroke of the repetition as well as the complete repetition from beginning to end. The syntactical relations were coded for the entire repetition.

The combination of a bottom-up perspective grounded in a form-based cognitive-linguistic annotation of the gestures with the distributional analysis provided the means for a corpus study of gestural repetitions. Guiding all of the methodological and analytical steps presented above was the assumption that repetitions in gestures show different characteristics on the level of form, meaning and function, and that an analysis successively moving from form to function can unravel the systematics of gestural repetitions. As such, the study would contribute both to a perspective on the grammar of gestures but also the multimodal nature of grammar.

1.4 Forecast of the book

Chapter 2 of the book discusses the principles of building patterns in the spoken and visual modality (Hurch, 2005; Klima & Beluggi, 1979; Wilbur, 2005). It focuses on the role and function of repetitions in spoken and signed languages and examines modality-specific differences regarding the status of repetitions. Afterward, means of creating gestural complexity are presented and existing proposals arguing for the capability of gestures to build complex units are critically reviewed. It is concluded that existing research has not yet adequately addressed the question of repetitive sequences in gestures. Answering the question of how repetitions in gestures are used to build complex units and patterns calls for a usage-based perspective examining the phenomenon on the gestural level of form, semantics, and (cognitive) functions, as well as in relation to speech. Thus, the chapter introduces theoretical notions from spoken and signed languages, as well as gesture studies against which gestural repetitions are to be examined in the following chapters of the book. With this, a common methodological and theoretical frame is aimed at which not only allows for a comparative focus on the use of repetitions in speech, sign, and gesture but, more importantly, also contributes to an understanding of the multimodality of language.

The theoretical strands discussed in the second chapter are brought together in chapter 3. Based on a corpus-linguistic analysis, a cognitive-semantic classification of gestural repetitions is proposed: 1) Iterations, in which the repetition of gestural material results in the repeated recurrence of one and the same meaning and does not lead to the construction of complex gestural meaning. 2) Reduplications, in which the repetition of gestural material results in complex gestural meaning and a coherent reduplicative construction. The construction is understood as a complex sign schema which "possesses an independent meaning [. . .] that is describable as a 'potential for semiosis' also independently of particular contexts of utterances" (Schneider, 2015, translation JB). The chapter grounds the classification in specific structural and semantic aspects characteristic for iterations and reduplications, which sets them apart as distinct ways of building patterns in the gestural modality. Other than existing research on the notion of "multimodal constructions," which grounds the notion of construction in gestures solely on their co-occurrence and dependence on spoken constructions (e.g., Steen & Turner 2013), the book argues for the notion of a complex gestural unit in the sense of a construction that is to be found on the gestural level alone. Thereby, the chapter introduces a new aspect into present discussions on multimodal constructions, a topic that is discussed in more detail in chapter 5 of the book.

The twofold cognitive-semantic classification of repetitions that is introduced in chapter 3 is further explicated and supported in the following two chapters. After discussing what is known about multimodal utterances and the temporal and semantic relation of speech and gesture, chapter 4 shows that iterations and reduplications affect the semantics of the verbal utterance in particular ways. Similar to the spoken utterance, gestural reduplications express lexical or grammatical meaning and are used either to indicate iterativity or plural. They convey verb-semantic and grammatical meaning in a further modality and, thus, need to be described as supportive in their semantic function for the construction of a multimodal utterance meaning. However, iterations, the other type of gestural repetition, not only emphasizes the semantics of the utterance but also modify the verbal referent. When used to depict actions (e.g., scraping, hammering, beating) or objects (e.g., the shape of a bowl), iterations complement and specify the type of action expressed verbally regarding its manner and the object in terms of size and shape.

This different semantic integration also results in a different syntactic integration of the gestures, treated in detail in chapter 5. After discussing the notion of "multimodal grammar" (Cienki, 2012; Fricke, 2012), gestural repetitions are examined regarding their relevance for modifying the syntax of speech, and it is shown that they interact with it in specific ways. Iterations that describe objects concerning their size and shape are found to overlap temporally with nouns or nominal phrases of the spoken utterance. Accordingly, as Fricke (2012) has shown, they can be classified as gestural attributes because they specify and restrict the extension of the nucleus noun of the nominal phrase. Iterations that characterize actions in their manner overlap with verbs or verb phrases, modify the verb of the co-expressive speech segment, and, thus, are comparable to adverbial adjectives. Reduplications also show typical patterns of correlating with speech segments. When used to express iterativity, they usually correlate with verb phrases. When displaying plural, they tend to overlap not only with single phrases but rather whole utterances. However, unlike iterations, they do not take over the syntactic function of modification due to their semantic redundancy. Based on these findings, a notion of multimodal constructions is suggested that functions as a possible framework for explaining recurrent pairings of speech and gesture. Starting from a critical discussion of construction grammar (Fillmore, Kay, & O'connor, 1988; Goldberg, 1995; Lakoff, 1987) as well as new proposals for multimodal construction grammar (Zima & Bergs, 2017), and by picking up the discussion on gestural constructions introduced in chapter 3, chapter 5 proposes a new understanding of constructions in multimodal language use.

In chapter 6, repetitive sequences are examined with regard to their contribution to processes of attention and salience in language use. After discussing the concept of attention in Cognitive Linguistics and gesture studies (Croft & Cruse, 2004; Müller & Tag, 2010; Oakley, 2009), the idea of a multimodal nature of attention is introduced. The concept is based on the relevance of gestural repetitions for establishing salience in discourse and the possibility of gestural repetitions to detach themselves from Figure-Ground structures expressed in speech. The empirical findings of the study revealed that gestural repetitions provide insight into specific aspects of attention, such as scope, focus, and scale of attention, and that both types achieve particular importance. Whereas reduplications mark the focus of attention, iterations provide further information on specific aspects of the process of attention and display what is accessible in the periphery of attention, give a fine-grained view on particular scenes, events, and objects, and, therefore, contribute aspects missing in speech. Concluding, a new cognitive-linguistic understanding of repetitive sequences as embodied constructions with the potential of dynamically focusing the speakers' attention is proposed.

The final chapter (chapter 7) argues for the universality of repetitive sequences and postulates that repetitions are a fundamental principle of building patterns in speech, sign, and gesture. The empirical findings of the corpus-based study are brought together with findings from repetitions in spoken and signed languages discussed in chapter 2, and a general principle is formulated which accounts for the commonalities identified of gestural repetitions with the phenomenon in speech and sign: the abstract process of copying along with diagrammatic iconicity is the general structural principle that allows for similar structures in different modalities and languages. In addition, with reference to Gestalt theory and the principles of Gestalt perception (Köhler, 1935; Wertheimer, 1925), the relevance of gestural form features along with the length of gestural sequences is emphasized as being constitutive for building (complex) gestural units. The book concludes by spelling out further implications of the perspective taken in the book for analyzing multimodal language use from a cognitive linguistic point of view.

2 Building patterns in spoken and visual modalities

Repeating elements of speech is not only a common and frequent linguistic phenomenon – sounds, words, phrases, or sentences can be repeated – but affects spoken and visual signs equally and as such might even be a universal phenomenon across spoken and signed languages. The present chapter concentrates on the phenomenon of repetitions. It discusses principles of building patterns in the spoken and the visual modality and introduces notions from spoken and signed languages and gesture studies against which gestural repetitions are to be examined throughout the rest of the book. Particular emphasis will be put on possible modality-specific differences regarding the status of repetitions in spoken and visual modalities. The chapter aims at a concise outline of how repetitions are discussed in the particular fields of research as grounds for a usage and corpus-based classification of repetitions in gestures.

2.1 The principle of iteration in spoken languages

Quite early, the repetition of linguistic material is discussed as the most basic pattern to build complex units in speech (Pott, 1862). Whereas early studies assumed a holistic approach examining the repetition of sounds, words, and sentences as a whole,[6] today's studies usually distinguish two main areas of interest: repetition and reduplication. Both types reflect similar phenomena that arise through an analog principle, namely the repetition of linguistic material. Iteration is, next to recursion, a basic linguistic principle for sequentially arranging units, yet results in different kinds:

> Iteration involves repetition of an action or object, where each repetition is entirely independent of those that come before and after. Recursion involves the embedding of an action or object inside another of the same type, each embedding being dependent in some way on the one it is embedded inside. [. . .] Iteration allows for any repetition to be removed without the end result being altered. (Kinsella, 2010, p. 180)

While recursion builds structures of different depths of embedding, iteration results in flat structures and units on the same level that do not increase the depth of embedding. Six types of iterations, all sharing the characteristic that they "concatenate elements without additional depth-increasing structure building"

---

[6] For a historic overview see Stolz, Stroh, & Urdze (2011).

(Karlsson, 2010, p. 46ff) differentiating them clearly from recursion, can be distinguished:
1) structural iteration: most frequent type with no semantic function and the effect of coordinating units (syndetically and asyndetically),
2) apposition: repeating nominal phrases with shared co-reference,
3) enumeration: listing of, for instance, lexical taxonomies,
4) succession: particular type of enumeration (numerosity),
5) plain repetition: repetition of words or syntagms for reasons of speech planning and
6) (syntactic) reduplication: repetition of words to express intensification, augmentation, repetition, diminution, iterative, or continuative action.

Depending on the type of linguistic material that is affected, the principle of iteration thus assumes various functions on different linguistic levels. Whereas repetition (types 1–5 above) is usually assigned to the area of discourse, reduplication is generally allocated to the area of grammar and, even more restrictedly, understood as a morphological process (Stolz, 2007a).

In the course of acquiring a first language, repetitions are one of the most frequent processes on the phonological level. Through the doubling of (parts of) syllables, repetitions create rhythmic patterns. These patterns are an essential means for experiencing, embodying, and acquiring the phonological and prosodic structure of a language. A similar function can be attributed to early reduplications: "Their phonological play activity and experimentation enable them [the children] to discover phonological regularities in the organization of their mother tongue." (Leroy & Morgenstern, 2005, p. 475) Both repetition and reduplication allow children in the process of language acquisition to experience and produce multisyllabic productions and multiple-word utterances.

Also, in adult language, repetition and reduplication are central means for the creation of structures and units in language fulfilling a range of different functions. Repetition of words or phrases allows speakers to produce fluent speech and, as such, is closely linked not only with speech production processes and word searches (Gülich, 1994) but also to the narrative structure by fulfilling tying function, for instance (Tannen, 2007, p. 58ff). As a stylistic and pragmatic resource, they not only serve to express viewpoint (Kotschi, 2001) but also contribute to accomplish social goals or manage the conversation. Through repetitions, speakers may keep the floor, give listener feedback, or ratify contributions (Tannen, 2007, p. 60ff).

The repeated occurrence of natural sounds or other acoustic phenomena as in onomatopoeic formulations (e.g., *Kuckuck, Tamtam, Wauwau* in German), for instance, are also included among repetitions. As sound imitations, they represent the multiple occurrences of natural sounds or other non-linguistic acoustic phenomena.[7] Repetition of words (syndetic or asyndetic) such as in *He rode on and on* (Stefanowitsch, 2007, p. 35) as well as recursive affixation, that is the repeated application of a morphological process, for instance, in the German *ur*-prefixation for building *Ur-ur-großmutter* ('great-great-grand mother') (Mattes, 2014, p. 34) are means of creating complex syntactic expressions. A similar function is allocated to syntactic repetitions, for instance, *sehr sehr heiß* ('very very hot') *or schnell schnell* ('fast fast'), and repetitions of a word phrases (*Ein Hai, ein Hai ist hinter dir!* 'A shark, a shark is behind you!') or whole utterances (*Lebt wohl! Lebt wohl!* 'Farewell! Farewell!') (Schindler, 1991, p. 601). All of these repeated uses of words, phrases, or sentences fulfill pragmatic function by creating emphasis and focus of attention and, as such, are assigned to the class of repetitions.

The most productive process, however, is the repetition of elements of speech as a morphological device: Reduplication, the "systematic repetition of phonological material within a word for semantic or grammatical processes" (Rubino, 2005, p. 11), is a common morphological device used for a variety of functions in a number of spoken languages. Particularly in Austronesia, Australia, South Asia, parts of Africa, the Caucasus, and Amazonia, reduplication is a productive morphological device serving various functions. While not being used as systematically in Western Europe (Stolz et al., 2011), reduplication has been reported to be productive in a variety of Creole languages that have developed from Western European languages, such as Nigerian Pidgin English or Berbice Dutch Creole (Kouwenberg, 1994).

Due to its worldwide distribution and use in a number of languages, already Pott (1862) and Brandstetter (1917), pioneers in research on reduplication, considered reduplication as an elementary procedure for the creation of patterns and structures in human language. As one of the first, Pott (1862) put forward a formal and functional classification of doubling, which includes repetitions in sentences, words, syllables, individual phonemes, and grammatical as well as extragrammatical aspects of word formation. Similarly, Brandstetter (1917) accounts for reduplication within a holistic approach covering the full range of repetition. The first systematic study on reduplication in Indo-European languages providing a systematization of its distinct meanings is found in the work by Gonda (1950). After that, works on reduplication became rare (Moraycsik, 1978; Wilbur,

---

[7] Ideophones, i.e., sounds and things which have an effect in the visual sense, are discussed controversially regarding their classification. Whereas Niepokuj (1997) considers them to be results of reduplication processes, Stolz et al. (2011, p. 65), for instance argue, that "ideophones fail to meet the most important criterion and thus cannot be considered proper cases of reduplication unless it can be shown that ideophones are derived by reduplication from independently existing members of other word classes."

1973). Yet interest in the phenomenon has risen again over the past three decades (see edited volumes by Hurch, 2005; Kouwenberg, 2003).[8] Current accounts thereby fall within two positions: 1) formal and semantic/functional approaches considering reduplication to be a process of copying features from one constituent to another (e.g., Gil, 2005; Hurch & Mattes, 2005; Mattes, 2014; Rubino, 2005; Schindler, 1991; Stolz, 2007a; Stolz et al., 2011; Wiese, 1990) and 2) inherently semantic approaches, neglecting the transference of features while assuming general independence of the individual constituents (Inkelas & Zoll, 2005). The following overview on reduplication in spoken languages focuses on transference approaches as it is argued throughout the book, that a combination of form-based, semantic as well as functional characteristics not only offers a sound basis for the discussion of reduplication in gesture, but also the grounds for a comparative perspective of the phenomenon in spoken and visual signs.

Reduplication, which is the repetition of morphological bases (Haspelmath, 2002), is considered to be a process of word formation.[9] Two basic types of reduplication can be distinguished, i.e., full vs. partial reduplication.[10] "Full reduplication is the repetition of an entire word, word stem [. . .] or root." (Rubino, 2005, p. 11) In cases of partial reduplication, a part of the base is copied. Partial reduplication may involve consonant gemination, vowel lengthening, or an almost complete copy of the base (see Table 1).

For a more systematic classification, reduplicative morphemes are often distinguished by the number of phonemes, reduplicated syllables or morae involved in the copying[11] (Rubino, 2005, p. 14) (see Table 2).

Reduplicative morphemes occur in a number of positions, such as the beginning of the base, in medial or final position. Furthermore, reduplications differ regarding the direction in which the reduplicant is copied. It may be copied to the left as in Bikol **tu**~*tulohe*[12] ('exactly there'), to the right *dury*~*ry* ('is rolling') as in Kwaza, or the direction might be unspecified as in Bikol *bula*~*lakaw* ('shooting

---

[8] For an overview of major theoretical strands in research on reduplication see Mattes (2014) and Stolz et al. (2011).
[9] Many studies consider reduplication to be a special case of affixation (e.g., Marantz, 1982).
[10] A further distinction of reduplications is "simple" (matches the base), "complex" (differs in phonological material from the base) or "automatic" ("Automatic reduplication is reduplication that is obligatory in combination with another affix, which does not add meaning by itself to the overall construction" (Rubino, 2005).
[11] In newer studies, phonological units applied for the description of reduplications are being supple mented with prosodic features such as accent, quantity, and tone (Schwaiger 2011). Some even assume that prosodic differences suffice to speak of reduplication (e.g., Nguyen & Ingram, 2006).
[12] The copied morpheme is set in bold in order to highlight the direction of the copying process.

Table 1: Examples of full and partial reduplications.

Type of reduplication	Example	Language
Full	*laag* 'layer' > *laag laag* 'one layer after the other'	Afrikaans (Botha, 1988)
	xám 'gray' > *xám xám* 'grayish'	Vietnamese (Nguyen, 1997)
	orang 'man' > *orangorang* 'men'	Indonesian (Stolz, 2007b)
Partial	*bukú* 'cow' > *upugú* 'cows'	Tarahumara (Hurch, 2000)
	fille 'girl' > *fi~fille* 'little girl'	French (Scullen, 2002)
	ticken 'to tick' > *ticktack* 'ticktock'	German (Dressler, Dziubalska-Kołaczyk, Gagarina, & Kilani-Schoch, 2005)

Table 2: Number of phonemes involved in cases of partial reduplication in Illocano language (examples taken from Rubino, 2005, p. 12).

Shape of reduplicant	Function	Example, language
CV	plural argument, animate plurals	*laláki* 'male' > *lalláki* 'males'
CVC	imperfective aspect	*agbása* 'read' > *agbasbása* 'reading'
CVCV	lexical iterativity	*agtilmón* 'swallow' > *agtilmotilmón* 'swallow repeatedly'

star') (Mattes, 2014, p. 37). The reduplicated material may be furthermore adjacent to the base from which it is copied or nonadjacent because the reduplication is separated by a stem, for instance. In addition, reduplicative constructions may constitute contiguous sequences of segments as in the example *laag~laag* ('one layer after another') (Botha, 1988, p. 102) or noncontiguous sequences *muru~malisioso* ('somewhat malicious' as in Bikol (Mattes, 2014, p. 37).

Reduplication is used for the expression of a number of different categories and functions:[13] It creates new nouns (*mata* 'eye' > *matamata* 'spy' in Indonesian), denotes concepts such as plurality or numbers (*gogs* 'dog' > *gogogs* 'dogs' in Papago; *ténet* 'seven' > *ténetnet* 'seven each' in Tibeto Burman), reciprocity

---

[13] Some areas of grammar, such as gender, person or case distinction, seem not to be associated with reduplication (Stolz, 2007b).

(*balembales* 'avenge each other' in Austronasian) and distributivity (Rubino, 2005, p. 21). With verbs and adjectives, reduplication seems to be even more productive. It denotes number (plurality, distribution, collectivity) (*lawi* 'to make a hole' > *lawlawi* 'to make two holes, make a hole twice') and tense and aspect (continuity, iterativity, completion, inchoativity) (*lóca* 'to be black' > *lóoca* 'to be a black person' in Alabama) (Rubino, 2005, p. 1922). Cross-linguistically, however, the most frequent functions of reduplicative constructions are the marking of plurality,[14] diminution, and intensity (Mattes, 2014; Niepokuj, 1997; Uspensky, 1972).

> However, in a cross-linguistic comparative view, "typical" functions of reduplication can be found: The procedure is most frequently associated with the broader categories of plurality, diminution and intensity. In general, these can refer to all parts of speech and all major lexical classes, although there are often language-specific constraints and category-specific preferences (cf. also Stolz, 2007a, p. 320) In verbs or, if a language lacks such a word class, in lexemes expressing events, it is often tense-aspect categories such as continuity, imperfectivity etc. which are marked by reduplication ("verbal plurality"). In nouns or lexemes refer- ring to entities, reduplication often marks the plural ("nominal plurality"). (Mattes, 2014, p. 39)

Due to the fact that reduplications are cross-linguistically often associated with particular meanings, such as intensification or plurality, the discussion of reduplication is closely connected to the question of iconicity (see Stolz et al., 2011 for an overview). Full reduplication expressing intensification, for instance, signifies a multitude, or collectivity with nouns. With verbs, it marks an intense or repeated action. Adhering to the principle "more content requires more expression", iconicity seems a logical explanation for the nature of reduplication.

> It is an iconic device, i.e. it is always syntagmatically iconic, insofar as copying is concerned. [. . .] Often reduplication is also paradigmatically iconic, if the morphological meaning involves repetition or greater duration or higher intensity. (Dressler et al., 2005, p. 456)

Haspelmath (2008, p. 2) underlines that, in particular with plurality, the understanding of iconicity in reduplication is connected to the structure of experience. Thus "repeated forms signal repetition in experience" (see also Croft, 2002). However, reduplication also expresses counter notions, like diminution and reduction (see Hurch & Mattes, 2005). The seemingly missing semantic bond between the various linguistic categories expressed by reduplication (Abbi, 1992; Brandstetter, 1917; Inkelas & Zoll, 2005; Kiyomi, 1995; Pott, 1862) raises doubts about the principle of iconicity as a significant driving force in reduplicative

---

[14] Plurality is often also understood as a cover term for different uses of reduplication (creation of nouns, plurality of actors marked on verbs, reciprocal verbal actions, mark repeated or continuous actions) (Niepokuj, 1997, p. 67).

processes: "Iconicity is one factor determining the semantic of the process, but it is clearly not the only factor" (Niepokuj, 1997, p. 65). An attempt at bringing together the diverse range of reduplicative meanings is an understanding of iconicity that is not necessarily tied to the notion of "more X is more meaning":

> Iconicity is not tied to an increase in size of the entities referred to by the reduplicative construction. Iconicity applies if the semantic description of the quality encoded by reduplication is more complex than the one necessary for the description of the non-reduplicated pattern. (Stolz, 2007b, p. 317)

Accordingly, non-reduplicated types are understood as a kind of norm or prototype from which reduplications differ. Reduplicative constructions thus stand in opposition to the unmarked partner, which is represented by a morphologically simple word. Therefore, simple forms go along with simple concepts, and complex forms go along with complex concepts. In diminutive, attentuative, simulative, and imitative reduplications, for instance, more form is used to express less content. A given entity falls short of fulfilling the required criteria to pass as what is indicated by the non-reduplicated form. There is not enough of property X and this is highlighted in the reduplicative construction while using a complex and thus marked form. Accordingly, the nature of reduplicative meanings might be best discussed, as Stolz et al. (2011) propose, with reference to conceptual structure:

> In lieu of semantics, we prefer to talk about conceptual structure. The conceptual structure of plural and diminutive is clearly more complex than the conceptual structure of the categories represented by the non-reduplicated item. The same holds for the intensified and attenuated adjectives as opposed to their unspecified form (Stolz et al., 2011, p. 186)

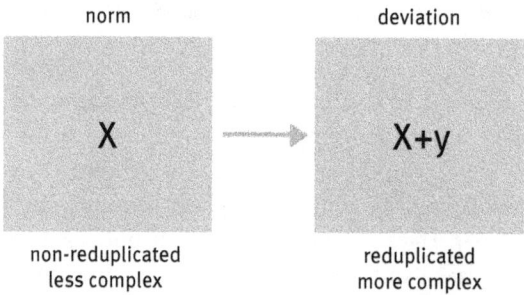

Figure 3: Conceptual structure of reduplication (adapted from Stolz et al., 2011, p. 186).

A further problematic aspect in studies on reduplications centers on the process in general and the linguistic units that are affected by it. A generally accepted understanding of what is considered to be reduplication proper and what not differs immensely in the literature due to dissimilar conceptions of the reduplicative process.

While some depart from an understanding of reduplication, which assumes formal accordance between the linguistic units, others attribute significance to the semantic accordance between the linguistic units. Furthermore, approaches differ in the question as to whether reduplication is an instance of copying or not. Whereas accounts assuming the transference of properties adhere to the concept of base and copy in reduplicative constructions, Inkelas & Zoll (2005) object to the transference of properties and assume an independency of the two reduplicative constituents. (For a detailed overview of the discussion see Stolz et al., 2011). Following Stolz (2007b) and others (Stolz et al., 2011), the present study assumes that the

> sole use of a single criterion for the identification of reduplication is completely insufficient. In doing so, it is of no importance if one adheres to the phonology or semantics. Both viewpoints are too one-sided. Especially, as they limit the view for recognizing the prototype. [. . .] Both form and meaning need to be involved for reduplication, without assuming 100% agreement on all levels.
> (Stolz, 2007a, p. 77, translation JB, highlights in original)

Accordingly, Stolz proposes a set of criteria to classify deviations from prototypical instances of reduplications (see Table 3).

Table 3: Criteria for prototypical cases of reduplication (adapted from Stolz, 2007a).

level A	level B	level C	level D
expression	word	identical chains of segments, same morphological status, and word class	asymmetry on suprasegmental level,
	construction	syntagmatic adjacent units, part of the same unit (constituency), dependency relation	
content		both parts are equal in meaning	

Based on these criteria, reduplications carry a central characteristic, which sets them apart from other similar yet different phenomena:

> Genuine reduplications build constructions that have a particular construction meaning, which is not identical with the meaning of the individual constituents of the reduplication. [. . .] Accordingly, it is suitable to principally distinguish: Repetitions cause changes on the connotative level, whereas reduplications go along with changes on the semantic level. Therefore, reduplications are assigned in the lexical and grammatical area, while repetitions rather fall within the stylistic area. (Stolz, 2007a, p. 57, translation JB)

In isolating languages, such as Riau Indonesian, for instance, a clear separation of repetition and reduplication based on the concept 'word', however, is not possible.

> In isolating languages, characterized by a paucity of morphological structure, there may not be enough morphology to support a robust and systematic distinction between morphological and syntactic structure. Accordingly, in isolating languages, there may be relatively little evidence for the existence of words as a viable unit of linguistic structure, as distinct from morphemes. (Gil, 2005, p. 31)

Resulting from this difficulty, Gil (2005) presents criteria allowing for a distinction between repetition and reduplication in isolating languages not exclusively based on words (see Table 4). Although not all criteria can be used for a clear-cut diagnostic, as only two are definitely characteristic for reduplication (unit of input and interpretation), the criteria offer a sound basis for differentiating repetition and reduplication not only in isolating languages but in spoken languages in general.[15]

Table 4: Criteria for the distinction between repetition and reduplication (adapted from Gil, 2005, p. 33).

criterion		repetition	reduplication
form-based	unit of input	greater than word	equal or smaller than word
	contiguity of copies	contiguous or disjoint	contiguous
	number of copies	two or more	usually two
	intonational domain of output	within one or more intonation groups	within one intonation group
semantic function	interpretation	iconic or absent	arbitrary or iconic
	communicative reinforcement	present or absent	absent

In repetitions, two or more segments are repeated, which may be contiguous or disjoint and occur within one or more intonation groups. In reduplications, however, copied segments are contiguous, usually consist of two segments and occur within one intonation group. Whereas repetitions either do not possess an independent or only an iconic meaning, reduplications carry arbitrary or iconic meanings. As such, reduplications are cross-linguistically used for marking of plurality, aspect, or intensification. Due to these characteristics, repetitions serve to produce particular effects and changes on the connotative level and are used for stylistic, textural, or pragmatic purposes. Tied to this is a different function of both

---

15 Moreover, as we will see in the following section, the proposed criteria are applicable to the repetitions in sign languages and also provide a basis for distinguishing iteration and reduplication in co-speech gesture.

patterns in spoken languages: For repetitions, the factor of communicative reinforcement, that is, the use of repetition to manage the focus of attention, is characteristic. This function cannot be attested to reduplications. Yet newer studies, in particular on total reduplication, show that this proposed clear-cut boundary between repetition and reduplication is best conceived of as a continuum with a fuzzy intersection (see Figure 4). Although particular functions can be clearly attested to either one of the phenomena, emphasis and intensification seem to be cases which stand between stools:

> There is a zone where phenomena can be interpreted in both ways. This could mean that elements which originally served purely pragmatic purposes may be taken for grammatical strategies. This happens most easily with those phenomena whose pragmatic use almost inevitably invites a semantic reading. This is the case with emphasis and intensification.
> (Stolz et al., 2011, p. 147)

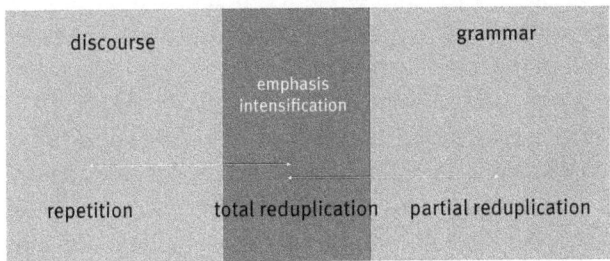

Figure 4: Fuzzy boundary between repetition and reduplication (adapted from Stolz et al., 2011, p. 147).

As a result, a grammaticalization chain can be assumed with partial reduplication being the most grammaticalized, repetition being the less grammaticalized, and total reduplication as the linking chain between both ends. (For a detailed discussion of reduplication and grammaticalization see Stolz et al., 2011)

2.2 Repetition and reduplication in the visual modality of sign languages

Contrary to the majority of spoken languages, in which reduplication is not an essential grammatical means, reduplication is highly productive in a number of different sign languages, such as American Sign Language (ASL) (Battison, 1978; Klima & Beluggi, 1979; Supalla & Newport, 1978; Wilbur, 1973), British Sign Language (BSL) (Sutton-Spence & Woll, 1998), German Sign Language (DGS) (Pfau &

Steinbach, 2005, 2006), Russian Sign Language (Kimmelman, 2018) and Swedish Sign Language (SSL) (Bergman, 1982).[16] For the majority of sign languages, reduplication is essential for expressing modulations of aspectual differences as well as inflectional variations of lexical units, such as number, person, distributional, or temporal aspects. Research has furthermore shown that reduplication in sign languages fulfills similar functions as in spoken languages: it is used to mark habitual, iterative and continuative aspects, plurality, reciprocity as well as noun-verb derivations and conversions (see below for modality-specific differences).

The process of reduplication in signed languages thereby generally affects verbs, adjectival predicates, and nouns. When operating on adjectival predicates, reduplication modulates signs for the expression of aspectual processes. Similar as in spoken languages, which have the ability to express different meanings such as *tend to get sick, get sick easily, sick for a long time*, sign languages have the means to express distinctions that indicate "aspects such as onset, duration, frequency, recurrence, permanence or intensity of states or events" (Klima & Beluggi, 1979, p. 247). For the modulation of signs, sign languages thereby predominantly use variations of the movement, such as circular reduplicated movements, elliptical reduplicated forms, or an accelerated movement (Bergman, 1982; Fischer, 1973; Klima & Beluggi, 1979; Pfau & Steinbach, 2005; Wilbur, 2005 see Figure 5).

Common types of reduplication in which the movement is modulated in its execution are "slow reduplication" and "fast reduplication". By changing the speed as well as the evenness of the movement in ASL and SSL, for instance, this modulation of the signs correlates with the continuation of some kind or the indication of some kind of habituality, i.e., iterations over time[17] (cf. Fischer, 1973, p. 480). However, reduplication processes and, in particular, aspectual modulations do not occur with any lexical unit. As in the case of adjectival predicates, signs that may be modulated refer to incidental or temporary states (e.g., SICK, ANGRY, DIRTY),[18] while signs referring to inherent characteristics (e.g., PRETTY, INTELLIGENT, TALL) may not be modulated to express aspectual differences. Thus

---

16 In the following, reference to particular sign languages will be made by using their acronym.
17 Using this distinction between slow and fast reduplication, Fischer introduces the distinction between stative and durative verbs in signs. Durative verbs denote an action which can last some amount of time, such as sleep, walk, watch, while stative verbs or non-durative verbs denote an action of little duration as in kill, win, leave (Fischer, 1973, p. 473).
18 Following the standard conventions within sign language linguistics, the glosses for signs are given in capitals.

2.2 Repetition and reduplication in the visual modality of sign languages — 33

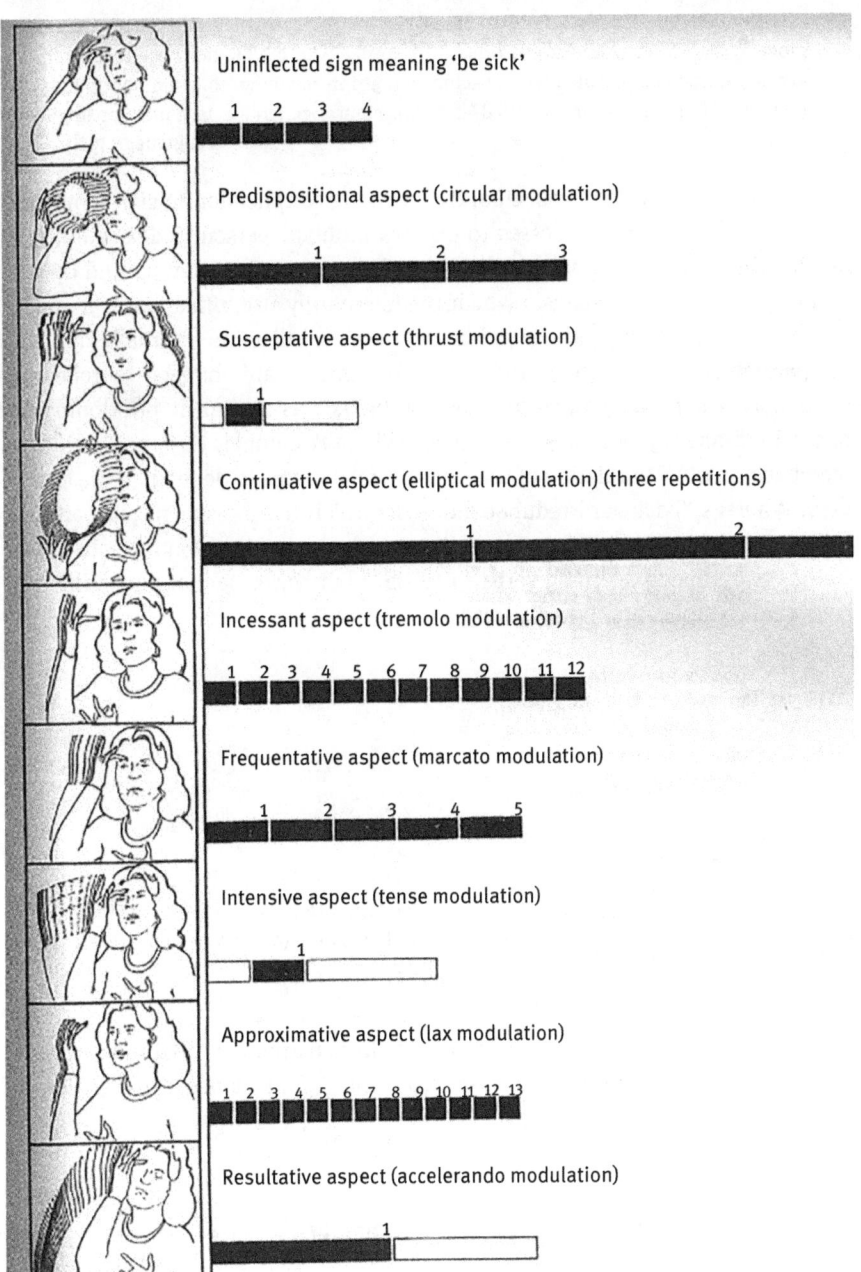

Figure 5: Sign SICK and eight aspectual modulations (taken from Klima & Belugi, 1979, p. 265).

aspectual modulations on adjectival predicates in ASL represent a rich set of grammatical processes marking subtle distinctions in meaning. The modulations are regular formational variations associated with specific changes in meaning; they are not optional expressive additions but are required and consistently generated in particular linguistics contexts.   (Klima & Beluggi, 1979, p. 271)

Apart from modulation of aspectual differences, reduplication in sign languages is used for inflectional processes to express number, person, indexicality, reciprocity, distribution, temporal aspect, and focus as well as manner and degree. Contrary to spoken languages, which predominantly use affixation to modify a lexical unit morphologically, sign languages mark inflection internally by using the parameters of movement and space: Movements are changed by repeating them along the horizontal, vertical, or sagittal axis as well as by positioning the hands in different places in gesture space (Klima & Beluggi, 1979, p. 274; Pfau & Steinbach, 2005). Modulation of the signs thereby seems to depend on the type of verb. Whereas "backward reduplication", in which the movement path and the orientation of the hands may change, is a common phenomenon for both one as well as two-handed agreeing verbs[19] in DGS, plain verbs cannot be modified by backward reduplication (see Figures 6, 7).[20]

$_x$WIR_BEIDE$_y$ $_x^x$HELF$_y^y$HELF$_x^x$
we.two   help:REC
'We are helping each other.'

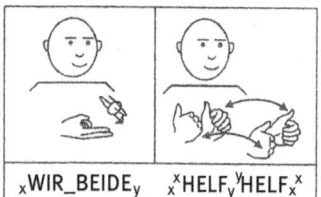

Figure 6: Reciprocal form of HELFEN ('help') through backward reduplication (taken from Pfau & Steinbach, 2005, p. 573).

Similar constraints seem to be at work in the plural marking in DGS, in which non-body anchored lateral nouns, such as KIND ('child'), for instance, exhibit sideward

---

19 In agreeing verbs, the hand "moves from the position of the source argument towards the position of the goal argument", while plain verbs have a "lexically fixed beginning and end point of the path movement" (Pfau & Steinbach, 2005, p. 571ff).
20 Because path of movement and orientation are lexically fixed in plain verbs, plain verbs "neither permit sequential backward reduplication nor simultaneous backward reduplication" (Pfau & Steinbach, 2005, p. 547).

* ₓWIR_BEIDEy   BLUME++   ₓGEByGEBₓ
   we.two   flower:PL   give:REC
   'We are giving flowers to each other.'

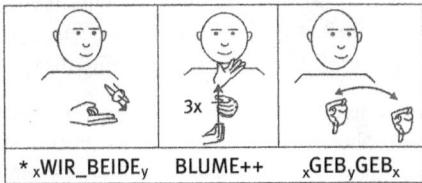

Figure 7: Ungrammatical reciprocal form of the GEBEN ('give') through backward reduplication (taken from Pfau & Steinbach, 2005, p. 573).

reduplication of the whole sign (see Figure 8), while non-body anchored signs, such as BUCH ('book'), only exhibit simple reduplication. Thus, the "output form crucially depends on phonological and/or morpho-syntactic features of the underlying noun/verb sign." (Pfau & Steinbach, 2005, p. 588)

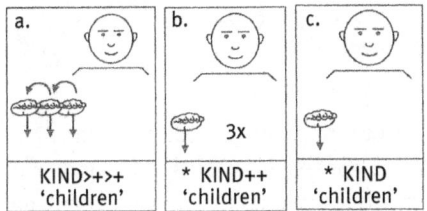

Figure 8: Plural marking in the sign KIND ('child') through sideward reduplication (taken from Pfau & Steinbach, 2005, p. 580).

As seen in Figure 8, sign languages use modulations of the parameter movement not only for inflectional or aspectual processes but also for pluralization. Moreover, reduplication is highly productive in derivational processes. In the nominalization of verbs, as in the case of the noun COMPARE in ASL, for instance, the movement is modulated such that it is usually smaller than in their related verbs (Klima & Beluggi, 1979, p. 290ff).

Although signed and spoken languages show a great number of commonalities regarding the process of reduplication itself and its meaning and use, the two modalities differ immensely in two aspects, namely a) the number of repeated segments and b) the type of reduplication. Whereas segments in speech are generally repeated once, signs in ASL are repeated "at least twice (so that the sign occurs at least three times), with the number of repetition greater than two indeterminate" (Fischer, 1973, p. 470, see also Battison, 1978). Accordingly, signing CHAIR for instance (see Figure 9), three, four, or five times does not result in meaning differences because signs do not mark lexical differentiation through the number of repeated beats. Similarly, Pfau & Steinbach (2006) underline that

> pluralization in DGS does not involve reduplication but rather triplication, i.e., the base is not repeated once but twice. [. . .] In DGS triplication is a very productive process. It is not only used for pluralization but also for aspectual modification. [. . .] DGS does not draw a clear functional distinction between reduplication and triplication, which are usually similar in meaning. (Pfau & Steinbach, 2006, p. 144ff)

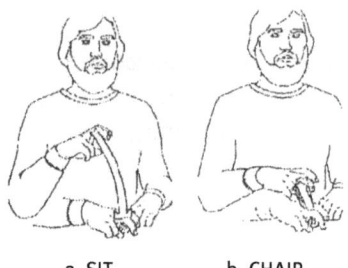

a. SIT   b. CHAIR

Figure 9: Noun-verb pair (taken from Supalla & Newport, 1978, p. 102).

In spoken languages, however, the number of repetitions is usually contrastive, creating meaning differences. Thus, while in spoken languages the number of repetitions is a characteristic criterion for reduplication, it is not in sign language. The difference in sign languages is rather between signs with two and more iterations and signs without iterations. Furthermore, "it is not clear whether the number of repetitions is random (with presumably a strong bias toward the most efficient production, that is a minimal number of repetitions) or whether it is predictable" (Channon, 2002b, p. 56). Instead, research seems to suggest that "certain differences in the number of repetitions appearing in different inflectional patterns may be correlated with (and predictable from) features of size, tension, and rate." (Klima & Beluggi, 1979, p. 307) The number of repetition might increase due to stressing of signs (Coulter, 1990; Wilbur & Nolen, 1986), to the position within a sentence, or to increasing attention (Holzrichter & Meier, 2000).

Another significant difference between signed and spoken languages concerns the overall Gestalt of the reduplicative construction: While reduplications

2.2 Repetition and reduplication in the visual modality of sign languages — 37

in spoken languages exhibit to a large extent irregular patterns,[21] sign languages seem to use overwhelmingly rhythmic patterns (Channon, 2002a,b). In rhythmic repetitions,[22] which is comparable to total reduplication in spoken languages, "all the segments of a word can be temporally sliced to form at least two identical subunits, with patterns like aa, abab, and ababab." (Channon, 2002b, p. 52) The sign TEACH, in which the hands move out from the face, then back in several times creating an out-in-out-in movement pattern, instantiates such a rhythmic pattern. The compound sign TEACHER is an example for irregular repetition, as the hands first move in the same way as in the verb TEACH and are then moved down in parallel lines down the side of the person to create the noun. The sign TEACHER thus creates an irregular movement pattern (out-in-out-in-down) (Channon, 2002b, p. 53).

While in the majority of literature on sign languages, the repetition is not distinguished from the grammatical process of reduplication, Wilbur (2005) argues for a separation between repetition and reduplication in sign languages. While she defines repetition as "a single repetition of the lexical movement with a (non-meaningful) return/transition movement in between" (Wilbur, 2005, p. 596) (see Figure 2.6 for the sign CHAIR in ASL), reduplication consists of at least three repetitions of the lexical form of the predicate and the movements between the lexical stems are meaningful (Wilbur, 2005, p. 598f) (see Figure 10 for the verb LOOKAT in ASL). Contrary to repetition, which may be used in the creation of nouns, for instance, but seems to be most importantly lexically or prosodically determined (Channon, 2002b; Wilbur, 2005), reduplication serves clearly grammatical functions.

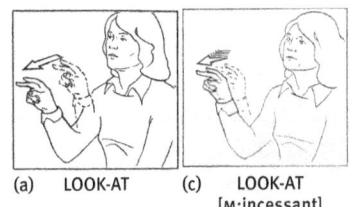

(a)   LOOK-AT   (c)   LOOK-AT
                          [M:incessant]

Figure 10: Verb LOOK-AT (taken from Klima & Beluggi, 1979, p. 280).

---

21 Bear in mind that Stolz et al. (2011, p. 565), for instance, point out that research on reduplication has mainly focused on partial reduplication and in particular neglected the frequency and role of total reduplication in European languages. Channon's statement considering the frequency of regular and irregular repetitions in spoken languages might thus have to be cautiously considered by further studies.
22 Channon (2002, p. 57) uses the term rhythmic repetition "to allow a modality-neutral comparison between speech and sign."

2.3 Means of creating gestural complexity

Current research on co-speech gestures treats the question of whether gestures have the potential to build units of different complexity from two perspectives. Departing from an understanding that ascribes speech and gesture fundamentally different properties, David McNeill (1992, 2005) argues that gestures do not build complex units. Since co-speech gestures, contrary to speech, are found in the moment of speaking, do not show standards of form and have no code, and furthermore convey meaning only as holistic Gestalts, they are non-combinatoric and non-hierarchic in principle. As a result, "two gestures produced together don't combine to form a larger, more complex gesture. There is no hierarchical structure of gestures made out of other gestures" (McNeill, 1992, p. 21). In contrast to the McNeillian view, Adam Kendon and works following his line of thought support the position that gestural movement patterns are structured in time and are hierarchically organized (Kendon, 1972, p. 190). In addition, form features of co-speech gestures may be conventionalized so that gestures may systematically vary as to how form features take part in creating gestural meaning (Kendon, 2004b, p. 248ff). These properties allow gestures to construe units of different complexities and sizes: simultaneously and linearly.

Similar to sign languages, co-speech gestures are articulated with the hands: The hands are shaped and oriented in particular ways, moved and positioned freely in the space around the body. Sign language linguistics captures this simultaneous complexity of signing hands with the help of phonological parameters, bundles of meaning differentiating features, made up of handshape, orientation, movement, and position in space (Klima & Beluggi, 1979; Stokoe, 1960). Gesture studies have adapted these parameters because they allow the identification and segmentation of simultaneously occurring hand shapes, orientations, movements, and positions in co-speech gestures (see Bressem, 2013 for an overview of notational systems). Furthermore, they show that gestural forms recur, appear with stable form-meaning relations across speakers and contexts, and that changes in individual features may result in meaning differences (e.g., change of palm orientation or movement) (Kendon, 2004a, p. 248ff; Müller, 2004). The occurrence of such kinesthemes, "a set of intersubjectively semanticized movement tokens whose similarity on the form level correlates with a similarity on the meaning level" (Fricke, 2014b, p. 1622) is proof of emerging proto-morpho-semantic structures in co-speech gestures (see also Kendon, 2004b, p. 224; Müller, 2004).

However, co-speech gestures are not only simultaneously complex but also structured in time and hierarchically organized. On the one hand, the gestural movement can be segmented into individual phases. When people gesture, they move their hands and arms in a particular succession. Starting from a relaxed position, such as on their lap or on a table, they move the hands to a place in front of their body, where they may perform further movements, and then back to a relaxed position again. These successions, first defined by Kendon (1980), are referred to as gesture phases and describe the different movement phases observable in the execution of gestures. In an "ideal" succession of gesture phases, the speaker's hands progress from a rest position to a preparation, then execute the meaningful part of the gestures, namely the stroke, and afterward progress via a retraction to a rest position again (see Figure 11).[23]

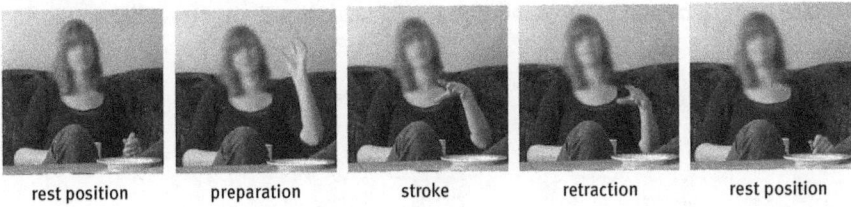

   rest position   preparation   stroke   retraction   rest position

Figure 11: Ideal succession of gesture phases (taken from Bressem & Ladewig, 2011, p. 54).

On the other hand, gestures build units of different sizes and complexities that range from smaller gestural phrases to larger gesture units. In addition, gestural movement units are coordinated with syntagms in speech (Kendon, 1972, 1980): "sweeps of the arms or movements of the head may be sustained over larger linguistic units, such as phrases, while eye shifts, wrist and finger movements occur over smaller segments, such as syllables" (Kendon, 1972, p. 183).

Picking up on Kendon's central idea of the linear and hierarchical structure of co-speech gestures, in her proposal for a multimodal grammar, Fricke (2012) develops the idea that gestures can be assigned constituent structures and, due to the property of recursion, build units of different complexities and depths of embedding. Of particular interest for Fricke's conception are gestural movement sequences that are not build based on self-embedding but, in principle, may build infinite gestural chains through iteration and coordination (Fricke, 2012, p. 165ff). Two types of sequences with the ability of building units of different

---

[23] In longer sequences, however, such as in gestural repetitions, gestures are produced immediately following each other without exhibiting easily definable boundaries between the individual strokes. "In many cases, for example, rest positions are missing, meaning that the hand after executing a stroke or a retraction does not return to its rest position, but rather sets off in order to perform a new preparation or even a stroke. Also, preparations are quite frequently missing, so that strokes follow each other immediately without exhibiting preparational phases in between." (Bressem & Ladewig, 2011, p. 76)

complexities due to articulatory features (see also Kita, van Gijn, & van der Hulst, 1998) can be distinguished. First, sequences in which the meaningful parts of the gestures (strokes) are separated by preparation phases. Such sequences can be observed in the depiction of actions (e.g., hammering, scraping) or in gestures that follow the rhythmic structure of the spoken utterance (e.g., beats [McNeill, 1992]). In these cases, strokes are separated by upward movements necessary for their articulation (see Figure 12). Secondly, sequences in which the individual strokes follow each other immediately without inserted preparation phases, as it can be observed in the depiction of objects (e.g., a square picture frame) or movement patterns (e.g., iterativity) (see Figure 12).

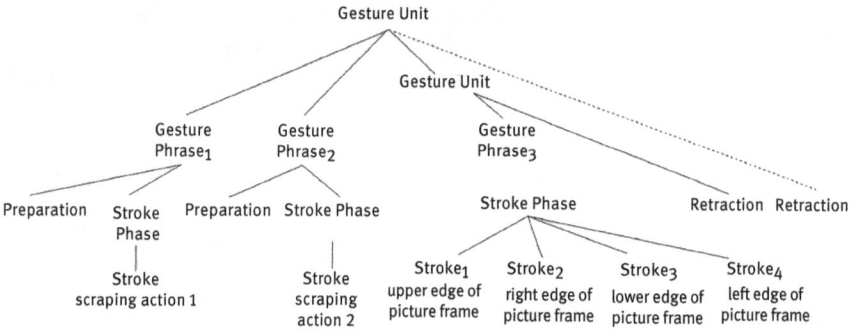

Figure 12: Constituent structure of gestural sequences with and without preparation phases (adapted from Fricke, 2012, p. 179).

Due to these characteristics of form, both sequences not only constitute different units on the level of gesture phases that are characterized by different degrees of unity but also functionally. Stroke-phases are usually considered to be the most meaningful part of a gestural movement because they carry the semantic value of the gesture and are typically coordinated with the lexical affiliate of the spoken utterance (Kendon, 1972, 1980; McNeill, 1992). As a result, sequences of strokes without inserted preparation phases show a stronger degree of unity and thus a more complex gestural meaning than strokes that are separated by preparation phases. Both types also correspond to different kinds of constituent structures that reflect the various degrees of unity in Fricke's proposal: Whereas preparation-stroke sequences are dominated by other nodes and as such are constituents of different gesture phrases (GP) (see Figure 12 example "scraping"), stroke-stroke sequences build complex stroke phases. As a result, they are constituents of the same gesture phrase and thus dominated by the same node (see Figure 12 example "picture frame"). For stroke-stroke sequences, Fricke (2012) furthermore proposes three basic types: 1) repetitions, in which the individual strokes do not vary in their form features and all strokes instantiate the same form parameters, 2) reduplications, in which the individual strokes differ in one form feature, namely position in gesture space[24] and 3) variations, in which only the hand shape remains constant across the sequence, yet all other form features change (Fricke, 2012, p. 167ff).

Whereas Fricke is mainly interested in the kind of complexity arising from the repeated execution of gestures, other proposals within gesture studies concentrate on questions of segmentation and coding of gestural repetitions (Gut, Looks, Thies, & Gibbon, 2002; Kipp, 2004; Kita et al., 1998; Latoschik, 2000; Lausberg & Sloetjes, 2009; McNeill, 2002; Seyfeddinipur, 2006; Sowa, 2005; Sparhawk, 1978). Sequences of gestural movements pose problems in the coding process because the identification of boundaries between gestures becomes difficult. With missing preparation phases, the beginning and end of a stroke may be difficult to recognize. Moreover, in gestures depicting iterative actions, such as stamping, cutting, or waving, it needs to be decided whether the individual movements are part of the iconic depiction of the action.

> Gestural movements that were repeated several times (e.g., gestures depicting hammering, sawing, an object rolling down a hill or a gesture which repeatedly traced the outline of a room) posed the problem of whether to segment the movement as a single stroke or as a series of multiple strokes. (Seyfeddinipur, 2006, p. 108)

With this focus in mind, Kita, van Gijn & van der Hulst (1998), for instance, distinguish two types of gestural sequences: 1) Multi-segment phases, that is, a two-segment movement without a velocity profile discontinuity (e.g., a depiction of reaching and pulling), and 2) repetitive phases, that is, the repetition of a movement without any hold in between (e.g., a gesture in which hammering actions are enacted). Contrary to the multi-segment phase in which each gestural movement phase is considered to be a distinct segment, in repetitive phases, the entire duration of repetition is classified as one phase (Kita et al., 1998, p. 29f)). Similarly, Seyfeddinipur (2006) proposes two ways of separating and coding repetitive sequences: 1) Symmetrical movements, which are uniform in trajectory, velocity, and hand configuration (e.g., tracing the outline of a room) are coded as a single stroke and thus one gestural unit. 2) Movements not uniform in trajectory and velocity are coded as sequences of preparations and strokes and thus

---

24 Lücking (2013) also considers change of position as a central parameter for differentiating sequences of iconic gestures (change in position marks a new gestures).

considered to be individual gestural units. Successions of such preparation-stroke sequences can be observed in beats (McNeill, 1992) or batons (Efron, 1972), gestures used to mark rhythmical aspects of speech. In these cases, "the velocity profile of preparation versus stroke differed in speed: one was deployed faster than the other" and thus considered to be individual phases of gestural movement (Seyfeddinipur, 2006, p. 108). Sowa (2005) offers a comparable focus on articulatory aspects of gestural repetitions and distinguishes a) the exact reversal of the movement in which the hand configuration is kept from b) a "repetition of a stroke movement with a succeeding, more relaxed, rewinding movement phase leading the hand(s) back to the start point of the stroke" (Sowa, 2005, p. 89).

In addition to questions of segmentation and coding, the study of gestural repetitions has long focused on the meaning of such gestural sequences. As one of the first gesture researchers, de Jorio (1832/2000) discusses the meaning and functional potential of gestural repetitions in his treatise on gestures in Naples. Stating that "gestures are not only adopted to express isolated ideas, but also ideas connected together" (de Jorio, 1832/2000, p. 398), he examines three different ways in which gestural repetitions are used for various functions:

i. Gestures can be repeated because they are parts of a single action, such as in swearing or praying.
ii. They may be used in order to deliberately connect one idea with the other and for altering the verbal meaning either through the context in which they are performed or through a modification of their execution. The precision grip, in which the thumb and index finger form a ring, or gestures expressing vagueness, for instance, may function as particles having the force of adverbs, prepositions, or conjunctions, thereby altering the meaning of verbal utterance (de Jorio, 1832/2000, pp. 180, 398).
iii. Gestural repetitions may be used to express grammatical notions. Modifying the gestures through enlargement, increase, or amplification of its qualities expresses the superlative.[25] Reducing the movement conveys the diminutive (de Jorio, 1832/2000, p. 389).

Similar functions of gestural repetitions are also accounted for in modern gestures research. McNeill (1992), for instance, states that repetitions either mark the contrast between gestures by enhancing their quality or, in cases of no contrast, function as diminution. Moreover, he observes that in repeated gestures, the second gesture is rarely a repetition of the first. Instead, the second one seems to be about half of the

---

[25] Apart from the repeated succession of gestures, de Jorio also mentions both-handedness as an indicator for intensification (see also Müller, 2004).

size of the first. Apart from marking contrast, gestural repetitions are often used to tie together thematically related parts of discourse (see also Kendon, 1972). The recurrence or continuation of a theme is signaled in catchments, that is, recurring gestural form features in at least two (not necessarily consecutive) gestures. "The logic is that recurrent images suggest a common discourse theme, and a discourse theme will produce gestures with recurring features. [. . .]" (McNeill, 2005, p. 117). The recurrence of gestural forms functions as a "visiospatial imagery" connecting immediately following but also separated parts of the discourse. The repetition of the gestures, and, in particular, the repetition of form features, thus functions not only as an iconic representation. Instead, the expressional potential connected with the gestural forms is overlaid with a meta-communicative function operating on and signaling the discourse structure.[26]

Others pick up on the meaning potential mentioned by de Jorio and identify four main semantic areas for gestural sequences: durativity, iterativity, plurality, and intensification. Examples for gestural repetitions used to indicate durativity and iterativity are the repetitions of enacted actions (e.g., Andrén, 2010; Brookes, 2005; Ladewig, 2011; Müller, 1998, 2000), the repetition of cyclic or spiral movements (Calbris, 1990, 2011; Ladewig, 2010, 2011, 2014b) or repeated paths of movements in motion events used for the expression of aspect or Aktionsart (Becker et al., 2011; Boutet, Morgenstern, & Cienki, 2016; Cienki & Iriskhanova, 2018; Ladewig, 2011; Müller, 1998, 2000). Gestural movements, such as the successive positioning of the individual strokes in different regions of the gesture space, may be used to express the meaning 'element, in detail' (Calbris, 1990, p. 58) or highlight the separation of topics of talk (Fricke, 2012). Most often, gestural repetitions are linked with the notion of intensification:

> By increasing the amplitude of the stroke, increasing the number of movements in the stroke or placing the gesture further away from and higher in relation to the body and therefore in a more prominent position, gestures can also intensify quantity or degree.
> (Brookes, 2005, p. 2037)

Using modifications of movements, gestures make an assertion, convey a strong request (Brookes, 2005), or intensify its degree (Müller & Tag, 2010). "If greater emphasis is desired, the entire stroke may be repeated, and in this case, the effect is increased by raising the hand slightly higher on each succeeding repetition." (Mosher, 1916, p. 29)

---

[26] A similar function is noticed by Fornel (1992). Return gestures are repetitions of gestures in a usually abbreviated manner. Return gestures are either grounded in the repeated mentioning of a topic of talk or in interactive reasons when gestures are picked up by another participant of the interaction (see also Cienki, 2015; Furuyama, 2002; Yasui, 2013 for similar phenomena).

2.4 Summary

The present chapter has shown that repeating elements is a common and frequent linguistic phenomenon in spoken and sign languages that plays a significant role on different levels of the language system. Depending on the linguistic material affected, repetitive sequences assume various functions. Whereas repetitions, that is, the mere recurrence of words or signs for prosodic or stylistic reasons, for instance, is usually assigned to the area of discourse, reduplications, that is, the recurrence of units of speech or signs for morphosyntactic reasons is allocated to the area of grammar. Although both modalities make use of the underlying principle of iteration, the chapter has shown that repetition as a grammatical process is a much more common device in sign languages. Moreover, sign languages show a greater preference for rhythmic repetitions than spoken languages. Despite these modality-specific differences, repetition and reduplication in spoken and signed languages show a range of functional similarities. Both modalities use reduplication to mark plurality, aspect, intensification, and quantity, for instance, cross-linguistically widespread functions of reduplicative constructions. Although spoken and signed languages use different modalities (auditory vs. visually) and thus dispose of other articulatory capabilities and conditions, they show apparent similarities in the use and function of repetitions and reduplications. Repetitive sequences in gestures have so far been only selectively investigated from particular perspectives. Accounts focus on descriptions of possible types and describe them generally on the level of gesture phases, rudimentary on the level of gestural form parameters, and only selectively with respect to their meaning potential and functions. Studies thereby identify basic repetitive patterns with different semantic and functional relevance. On the one hand, successions that need to be ascribed to the level of discourse. On the other hand, sequences that carry grammatical meaning themselves and covering semantic fields of durativity, iterativity, plurality, and intensification. These findings emphasize that gestural repetitions are a promising object of research, not only for gesture studies but even more so for cognitive-linguistic studies on language. Existing results point towards possible basic and fundamental characteristics of the principle of iteration that play out irrespective of the modality. A systematic and corpus-based investigation of the phenomenon is yet missing. Why?

Present-day research on gestures is primarily dominated by a research paradigm focusing on psychological aspects of gesture production and use and gestures as "'window' onto thinking" (McNeill & Duncan, 2000, p. 142).[27] Research

---

[27] See Fricke (2012, p. 9ff) for a more detailed discussion of McNeills theory and its implication for a linguistic perspective on gestures.

within this paradigm assumes gestures to be idiosyncratic inventions of speakers, global and synthetic in meaning, and never combinatoric nor hierarchical (McNeill, 1992, see the section above). "Repetition in these cases is plausibly due to priming, catchments and/or recurring references. A gesture is born each time anew." (McNeill 2007) Gestural repetitions are of interest because of their underlying imagery and not as structures themselves. Although a newly risen interest in gestural structures and patterns within the field of gesture studies has resulted in a large body of analyses on the recurrent use of forms and meanings in gestures, patterns and functions of linear structures in gestures are still only rarely explored (Andrén, 2010; Fricke, 2012; Müller, 1998; Müller, Bressem, & Ladewig, 2013). A systematic description of gestural repetitions and with it the question of whether gestures build units of different complexities is, therefore, still a desideratum for research. Gestural complexity, as shown in the previous section, arises on the level of gestural form parameters, on the one hand, and in the linear succession of gesture phases, on the other hand. However, co-speech gestures are not articulated alone but most often with speech, interact and are prosodically, semantically, and pragmatically closely connected with spoken syntagms. Besides, speech and gesture relate to each other syntactically. Co-speech gestures are obligatory for the use of verbal deictics such as *so* 'like', *son* 'like this', or *hier* 'here' (Fricke, 2007; Streeck, 2002), stand in close relation with verbal negation (Harrison, 2009) and word classes (e.g., nouns, verbs, adjectives) (Hadar & Krauss, 1999) or replace speech in syntactic gaps (Ladewig, 2014a, 2020). In addition, co-speech gestures may specify the nucleus noun in nominal phrases and function as gestural attributes (Fricke, 2012, 2013). In these cases, speech and gesture occur simultaneously or are temporarily displaced at which gestures more often precede the spoken affiliate than vice versa. Speech and gesture also stand in different semantic relations. Co-speech gestures may replace, modify, or complement spoken utterances. As a result, through the interplay of both modalities, a multimodal meaning arises in which gestures assume particular relevance.

Consequently, answering the question of how repetitions in gestures are used to build complex units and patterns calls for a usage-based perspective examining the phenomenon on the gestural level of form, semantics, and (cognitive) functions, as well as in relation to speech. The following chapters will show that an investigation considering all of these aspects not only makes the assumption possible that, based on the principle of iteration, co-speech gestures build two main classes of repetitions but also that commonalities and differences of gestural repetitions with repetitive sequences in spoken and signed languages can be uncovered.

3 Repeating gestures: Building (complex) units

Following the premise of cognitive-linguistics, that the study of language is the study of language use, an empirical investigation of gestural repetitions needs to pursue a usage-based perspective because patterns of language can only be found in the actual use so that the "type can only be found in the tokens themselves" (Fricke, 2012, p., 81, emphasis in original, translation JB) (see also Stetter, 2005). Token or type frequency determines the degree of entrenchment of units (Croft & Cruse, 2004; Langacker, 1987, 2008) and is an indicator for the salience of structures and patterns in language use. Following Langacker's assumption that any type of behavior may become entrenched as a symbolic structure (Langacker, 1987) and based on the assumption by Fricke (2014, p. 734) that "gestures are capable of being typified and semanticized independently of the simultaneously accompanying vocal utterance" (see also Andrén, 2010, p. 67ff), the chapter introduces a cognitive-semantic classification of gestural repetitions. This classification is grounded in specific structural and semantic aspects characteristic of these gestural patterns, which set them apart as distinct ways of building (complex) units in the gestural modality.

3.1 Iteration and reduplication: A cognitive-semantic classification

Using a cognitive-linguistic method to study gesture-speech relations and a corpus-driven analysis of repetitive sequences in gestures (see chapter 1), the present study distinguishes two types of gestural repetitions: iteration and reduplication.

In the following, the terms 'iteration' and 'reduplication' label the identified gestural patterns. The book thus distinguishes between the underlying principle of iteration (see chapter 2) and the emerging patterns as they have been introduced above by definition.

The proposed classification of gestural repetitions is grounded in classifications of repetitive sequences in spoken and signed languages (see chapter 2). As a result, it is assumed that iterations predominantly fall within the area of discourse, produce particular effects and changes on the connotative level, and are used for stylistic, textural, or pragmatic purposes. Thus, iterations reinforce the utterance, highlight the focus of attention and Figure-Ground structures (see chapter 6). Contrary to iterations, in which the repetition is a means for creating complex gestural units, reduplications are considered to be processes of gestural meaning-making. The repetition creates complex gestural units in which the meaning of the unit as

Cognitive-semantic classification of gestural repetitions

Iterations	Reduplications
are sequences of at least **two preparation-stroke** or **stroke-stroke phases**, in which none or the realization of the parameter **direction, quality of movement** or **position** changes. The individual strokes repeat one and the **same gestural meaning**, and do not create a complex gestural meaning. Iterations **represent concrete objects** and **actions** or **refer to abstract events and facts**. Iterations fulfill **prosodic functions** and take over a **modifying function**, because they add complementary semantic information to the meaning expressed in speech.	are sequences of at least **two stroke-stroke phases**, in which the realization of the parameter direction of movement and position changes. Reduplications of **type A** are sequences of at least two stroke-stroke phases, in which the realization of the parameter **direction of movement** and **position** changes. Reduplications of **type B** are sequences of at least two stroke-stroke phases, in which the realization of the parameter **position** changes. The individual strokes instantiate discrete gestural meanings and thus create a **complex gestural meaning**. Reduplications **represent** or **refer to abstract states, events** or **facts**. They take over an **emphasizing function,** because they express redundant semantic information to the meaning expressed in speech.

Figure 13: Cognitive-semantic classification of gestural repetition.

a whole is different from the meaning of the individual segments. This semantic change inherent to the reduplicative construction is used to express lexical or grammatical meaning in the gestural modality. Five examples will shortly illustrate the proposed classification before the chapter addresses the structural and semantic characteristics of both types in more detail.

In the first example ("weapons of mass destruction"), taken from a debate of the German Bundestag (Federal Parliament), Jürgen Trittin, Chairman of Bündnis 90 / Die Grünen in the German Bundestag, comments on the proposed constitution of a national security council as presented by the parliamentary group of CDU/CSU on May 7 2008.[28] While expressing his position against Germany's nuclear partaking, Trittin moves his hands up and down in almost parallel synchrony to the strongly accented verbal utterance and produces a rather long succession of enlarged, reduced as well as accented recurrent gestures.[29]

---

[28] For further information on the debate see http://www.bundestag.de/Mediathek/(Plenarsitzungen).
[29] Recurrent gestures are gestures that show stable-form meaning relationships, are partly conventionalized, shared within a particular culture or speech community, and often fulfill pragmatic functions (see chapter 4 for more details and Ladewig [2014b], Müller, Bressem, & Ladewig, [2013]. Examples of German recurrent gestures include the Palm Up Open Hand, the sweeping away gesture or the ring gesture (Bressem & Müller, 2014b).

Table 5: Excerpt from transcript "weapons of mass destruction".

		'Ich s-A:ge ihnen 'E:Ins-					wenn sie d'As -ERNst meinen,							
utterance	i	'ich	s-A	ge ihnen	'E:Ins	-	wenn sie	d	'A	s	-	'En	Nst	meinen,
translation		i tell you one thing					if you take this seriously							
	i	i	te	ll you	one thing	-	if you	t	hi	s	-	seriou	sly	take
gesture phases	stroke	prep	stroke	stroke	stroke	prep	stroke	prep	stroke	prep	stroke	prep	stroke	prep
form parameter — hand shape	1+2 touched		1+2 touched	1+2 touched	1+2 touched		1+2 touched		1+2 touched		1+2 touched		1+2 touched	
orientation	PLTC		PLTC	PLTC	PLTC		PD		PD		PD		PD	
position	cr		cr	cr	cc		clo		clo		clo		clo	
movement-type	straight		straight	straight	straight		straight		straight		straight		straight	
movement-direction	down		down	down	down		down		down		down		down	
movement-quality	accentuated ending		accentuated ending	reduced	decelarated		accentuated ending		reduced		reduced		reduced	
number of strokes	4						4							

For instance, while uttering *wenn Sie das ernst meinen* ('if you take this seriously'), Trittin produces a series of four ring gestures of which the first is articulated with an enlarged and accented movement, while the following three strokes are reduced in size.³⁰

Figure 14: Example 1 iteration "weapons of mass destruction".

Conveying the semantic theme of "exactness, making something precise, or making prominent some specific fact or idea" (Kendon, 2004b, p. 240), the ring gestures act upon speech by metaphorically grasping and holding discursive objects (Kendon, 1995; Müller, 2014; Streeck, 2005; Teßendorf, 2016). Due to their meta-communicative function on the verbal utterance, the ring gestures mark focal aspects of Trittin's utterance against the national security strategy of the CDU/CSU party and underline the preciseness and correctness of his arguments. In addition, variations in the movement (reduced or enlarged size, differences in intensity) prosodically mark the gesture. The movement is not part of the gestural representation of preciseness but, similar to accents in spoken languages, is used to accentuate and place emphasis on the meaning of the recurrent gesture. Accordingly, iterations referring to abstract states or events, as illustrated in example 1, predominantly fulfill a prosodic function. Together

---

30 Iterations of this kind are usually described as a particular type of gesture referred to as batons, beats, or superimposed beats (e.g., Efron, 1941; Ekman & Friesen, 1969; McNeill, 1992; Loehr, 2007; McClave, 1991). However, in the present book, beats are not considered to be a separate gesture type. Rather, the characteristics of beats, namely straight downward movements with different qualities (changes in size, acceleration and intensity) are understood as forms of prosodic marking in gestures (see also chapter 6).

with the verbal utterance, the gestural repetition contributes to the creation of a multimodal prosodic structure through which specific parts of the verbo-gestural utterance are highlighted. Example 1 demonstrates the most frequent function of gestural iterations documented in the corpus, namely recurrent gestures with abstract referential function and prosodic marking.

Figure 15: Example 2 iteration "Arko".

Example 2 exemplifies another frequent type of iteration: the depiction of action or objects. In the example "Arko", a woman tells a story about a particular behavior of the family dog. After introducing her upcoming narration by saying *Wie er bellt und Oma animiert alles zu tun* ("how he barks and animates grandma to do it all"), speaker SU explains the sequence of actions the dog fulfills to initiate a particular reaction of the grandmother. After having finished her turn, speaker MO sets in and, in addition to SU's explanation, notes that the dog barks because a box is not moved (*und bellt, weil die Kiste nicht vorkommt* ["and barks because the box does not move"]). Already in temporal overlap with *weil die Kiste nicht vorkommt* ("because the box does not move"), speaker SU starts off to specify the utterance of MO and says *Nee nee da kratzt er. Dann rennt er in den Flur, rennt er in Flur, kratzt. Oma muss die Kiste vorschieben und das war's* ("no no, then he scrapes, runs into the hallway, runts into the hallway, scrapes. Grandma has to push forward the box and that was it"). While saying *rennt er in Flur, kratzt* ("runs into the hallway, scrapes"), speaker SU produces a gestural iteration consisting of three strokes. Using a flat hand, palm oriented downwards, a straight movement downwards and the acting mode "action only"[31]

---

[31] See chapter 4 for a detailed discussion of gestural modes of representation.

(Müller, 1998, 2014), speaker SU gesturally depicts the scraping action of the dog (see Figure 15 and Table 6).

Table 6: Excerpt from transcript "Arko".

utterance			rennt er in flur, krAtzt,					
utterance-intonation unit		rennt	er in flur	r,	kr	A	A	tzt,
translation		runs	into the hallway	y	scr	a	a	pes
gesture phases			prep	stroke	prep	stroke	prep	stroke
form parameter	hand shape			flat hand		flat hand		flat hand
	orientation			PD		PD		PD
	position			c		c		c
	movement-type			straight		straight		straight
	movement-direction			down		down		down
	movement-quality			–		–		–
number of strokes per repetition			3					

Through the repetitive movement sequence, in which the hand acts as if they would perform an actual action, speaker SU not only emphasizes the verb *kratzen* ("scrape") but more importantly offers a bodily depiction of the way how dogs scrape. In temporal overlap with the predicate of the sentence, the gestural iteration fulfills an emphasizing function by gesturally underlining a particular action and manner of action already specified by the verbal utterance.[32] Accordingly, speech and gesture together create a multimodal impression of the scraping dog. What is of particular importance with respect to the depicted scraping action, and moreover for the majority of actions depicted in the present corpus, is the fact that the repeated gestural execution is an integral part of the imitated action:

---

[32] The present corpus also documented a large number of instances in which the gesturally depicted actions express complementary semantic information and specify the manner of the action (see chapter 4).

The action itself is repetitive. Accordingly, in order to give the impression of the action of scraping, a repetition and thus an execution more than once is necessary. Otherwise, it is not possible to evoke the iterativity of the action scheme.[33]

Example 3 illustrates the third most frequent type: Iterations in which the repetition of movement is not part of the depiction but a necessary means for the depiction of concrete objects. In the example "metal thing", taken from the German TV show "Genial Daneben", in which five comedians face questions sent in by viewers,[34] a series of strokes is used for the representation of a concrete object. Speaker MB tries to come up with the right answer to the question *Was ist ein Bügeltrunk?* ('What is a holder drink?'). Shortly after a few of the other comedians suggest that such a "holder drink" might be used in the field of gastronomy, MB begins with his explanation. After uttering *ich glaube dass es ja so beim Italiener* ('I think that in an Italian restaurant'), MB starts to produce an iteration consisting of three strokes. While saying *wo die Flasche Wein da in som Metallding drinne is* ('where the bottle wine is in such a metal thing'[35]), MB then models the shape of holders for wine bottles, which, according to him, are often used in Italian restaurants (see Figure 16 and Table 7).

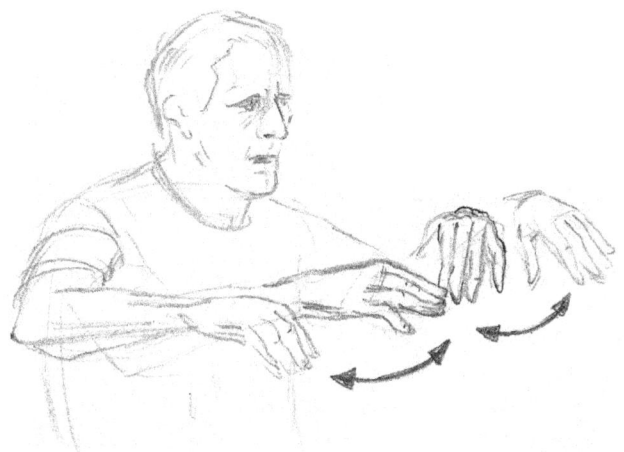

Figure 16: Example 3 iteration "metal thing".

---

33 See example "send back and forth" for the expression of iterativity in movement events by gestural repetitions.
34 For more information on the show, see http://www.genialdaneben.de/.
35 See Appendix for transcript.

3.1 Iteration and reduplication: A cognitive-semantic classification — 53

Through the threefold execution of strokes with arced movements going inwards and outwards, along with the bent hands facing downwards, the gesturally-mimed object, a bottle holder, emerges. Using the acting mode "action with specified object" (Müller, 2013), MB molds a three-dimensional object through a repetitive movement. This gestural iteration is one example of many in the corpus, in which speakers use movement to "outline an object or depict its extension" (Ladewig, 2020). By gesturally modeling the object, the repetition specifies the shape of the object that is described in speech. Through the gestural repetition, the concept of the metal thing is enriched to mean "bent metal thing". Following Fricke (2012, 2014), the gesture can be said to function as a gestural attribute. By providing a qualitative description of the object specified by the noun, the gestural repetition modifies the nominal nucleus. Summarizing, it can be stated that the gestural iteration expresses complementary semantic information, specifies and modifies the semantics of the spoken utterance, and, as a result, contributes essential aspects to the creation of a multimodal utterance meaning.

Table 7: Excerpt from transcript "metal thing".

utterance		wo die flasche w´Ein da in som metAllding drinne is,				
utterance-intonation unit		wo die	flasche w ´Ein	da in som	metAllding	drinne is,
translation		where the	bottle wine	in such a	metall thing	is
gesture phases		preparation	stroke	stroke	stroke	retraction
form parameter	hand shape		1–5 bent	1–5 bent	1–5 bent	
	orientation		PD	PD	PD	
	position		c	c	c	
	movement-type		arced	arced	arced	
	movement-direction		inwards	outwards	inwards	
	movement-quality		–	–	–	
number of strokes per repetition				3		

Example 3 is one of many examples documented in the corpus, in which the repetition of movement is a necessary prerequisite for the gestural depiction of objects. It is not, as was shown in example 2, part of the represented event or action scheme. Rather, repeating the movement is needed to gesturally depict the shape of the object and is thus solely a means to an end.

Examples 2 and 3 exemplarily show the most frequent uses of gestural iterations in the present corpus: the depiction of concrete actions or objects. It is emphasized that in both examples, iterations consisting of preparation-stroke sequences (example 1) and iterations consisting of stroke-stroke sequences (example 2), likewise depict actions and objects. The potential to represent actions or objects is not linked to a particular sequence type but is a characteristic of both types of iterations.

All of the examples given above illustrate characteristics of form, meaning, and functions of gestural repetition on which the definition of iteration given at the beginning of this chapter is based:

1) The examples are composed of different gestures phase sequences. Example 1 and 2 are characterized by preparation-stroke sequences. Example 3 illustrates stroke-stroke sequences.
2) The examples differ in their referential function. Whereas the gestures in example 1 express abstract meaning, examples 2 and 3 exemplify concrete referential functions of gestures.
3) The examples vary in their form characteristics. Either form features remain constant (example 2) or particular form features are changed, namely manner of movement (example 1) and direction of movement and position in gesture space (example 3).
4) The examples fulfill different functions. Iterations expressing abstract meaning take over prosodic functions (example 1), whereas iterations expressing concrete meaning either emphasize the meaning expressed in speech by carrying the same semantic information (example 2) or modify the verbal utterance by adding complementary semantic information (example 3).

Despite these differences, all examples share an essential characteristic: In all of them, the repetition results in the repeated recurrence of one and the same meaning. As a result, a complex gestural unit is created in which the meaning expressed by the individual repetitions remains the same across the whole unit. This is different in reduplications. Here, the repetition of gestural material results in a complex gestural meaning and coherent reduplicative construction. The construction is understood as a complex sign schema which "possesses an independent meaning [. . .] that is describable as a 'potential for semiosis' also independently of particular contexts of utterances" (Schneider, 2015; translation JB) (see chapter 5 for more detail). Two examples will give the first illustration.

In the example "send back and forth", also taken from the German TV show "Genial Daneben", the participants have to find the answer to the question *Was*

3.1 Iteration and reduplication: A cognitive-semantic classification — 55

ist Haus zu Hausverkehr? ('What is house to house transit?'). As one of the first among the participants, speaker BS starts off to give an explanation. According to her, house to house transit could be the name for the exchange of letters in offices. After introducing this possible explanation *ist es nich vielmehr so dass man diese Briefumschläge hat, die Hauspost oder wie das heißt* ('isn't it rather that you have those envelopes, this internal mail or how you call it'), she goes on to further explain the concept of internal mail. While doing so, BS produces a series of three strokes co-occurring with the verb phrase *zwischen zwei Ämtern hin und herschickt* ('send back and forth between two offices').

Table 8: Excerpt from transcript "send back and forth".

utterance		dInge immer zwischen zwei ÄMtern hin und hErschickt;				
utterance-intonation unit		dInge immer	zwischen zwei ÄM	mtern hin und	hErschi	ickt;
translation		always things	between two off	ices back	and fourth	send;
gesture phrases		prep	stroke	stroke	stroke	retraction
form parameter	hand shape		2 stretched	2 stretched	2 stretched	
	orientation		PLTC	PLTC	PLTC	
	position		cc	cc	cc	
	movement-type		arced	arced	arced	
	movement-direction		away body	towards body	away body	
	movement-quality		–	–	–	
number of strokes per repetition			3			

Using a stretched index finger and an arced movement away from the body (*zwischen zwei Äm* ['between two off']), towards the body (*mtern hin und* ['ices back and']) and once more away from the body (*herschickt* ['forth send']), BS gesturally represents the iterativity of the movement event expressed in the verb *hin und herschicken* ('send back and forth'). Accordingly, the iterativity of the movement event is expressed by the repeated execution of strokes. Thus, "repetition as a temporal process is verbally and gesturally conceptualized as a repeated movement sequence." (Müller, 2000, p. 221 translation JB) Moreover, the gestural repetition indicates that the movement event unfolds between two points: Because the beginning and endpoint of the represented movement event become visible in clear endpoints of the individual strokes,[36] the movement sequences are articulatory marked as individual and separate phases of movement. In combination with the change in the movement direction and position in gesture space, the single strokes become visible as individual and separate phases.

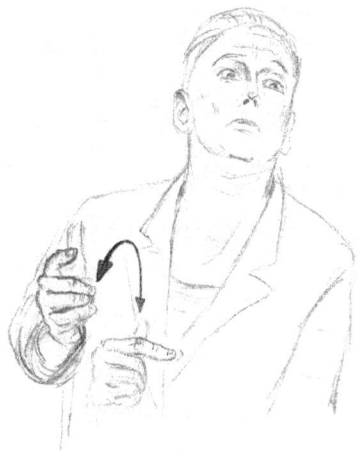

Figure 17: Example 4 reduplication "send back and forth".

However, the representation of iterativity and the meaning expressed in example 4 is not only based on the depiction of the concrete movement event visible in the individual movement sequences. Rather, the meaning of the reduplicative construction refers to the abstract notion of movement and, in particular, to iterativity expressed gesturally in the movement unfolding between two endpoints (Müller, 2000). Accordingly, contrary to the example 3, in which changes in the direction of movement and position are a necessary means for the depiction of objects, in example 4, they are semantically motivated: Each stroke refers to the abstract notion of the movement and as such carries semantic relevance for the creation of the meaning of iterativity expressed in the stroke sequence. Accordingly, the repetitive sequence in example 4 builds a complex gestural meaning, a reduplicative construction. Yet, although the individual strokes create a complex gestural meaning , the gestural meaning only emphasizes the semantics of the verbal utterance. Contrary to example 3, in which the sequence adds to the semantics

---

[36] Endpoints as well as transition points of gestural movements sequences become visible in clear picture frames (Seyfeddinipur, 2006) (see also Müller, 2000).

3.1 Iteration and reduplication: A cognitive-semantic classification — 57

expressed in speech, example 4 emphasizes the semantics expressed in speech. As such, example 4 offers insight into the embodied basis of the lexical concept of iterativity. Considering the expression of iterativity in sign languages (see chapter 2), commonalities with example 4 become visible. Sign languages express "aspects such as onset, duration, frequency, recurrence, permanence or intensity of states or events" (Klima & Beluggi, 1979, p. 247) by modulating the movement of the sign (circular or elliptical reduplicated forms, acceleration). Although sign languages clearly have greater variability in the modulations of movements (see section 2.2), example 4 illustrates that speech and gesture use similar structural means. Example 5 underlines this assumption.

In this example, which is taken from a corpus of naturally occurring conversations,[37] speaker ME and SI talk about a seminar for hairdressers in which ME has recently participated. After uttering *und dann fing der halt an zu texten* ('and then he started to babble'), speaker ME explains to her interlocutor that haircuts and their compositions are also explained in textbooks *oder steht och steht ja in den Büchern kannste ja* ('or it is written well in textbooks you can'). While saying *kannste dir ja immer die einzelnen Schritte durchlesen* ('well you can read through the single steps'), ME produces a series of three strokes co-occurring with *einzel* ('single'), *nen schritte* ('steps') and *durch* ('through'). Using a hand shape with fingers 2–5 flapped down and a palm down orientation, ME executes three strokes with an arced movement away from the body. The hands thereby successively move from a position in the upper periphery to periphery to center upper.

Figure 18: Example 5 reduplication "single steps".

---

37 I would like to thank Silva H. Ladewig for allowing me to work with the data. See Ladewig (2010, 2011, 2020) for further information on the data.

Through the arced movements, executed in different positions of the gesture space, the abstract concept of single steps is gesturally represented as different regions in front of the speaker's body. Using the "representing" mode, in which the hands are employed to represent something other than themselves (Müller 1998; 2010b), objects are "put in a particular spatial relation" (Müller, 2014, p. 1698). Yet, the position in gesture space is not used for the representation of perceived spatial relations between objects in the world. Rather, it is used for creating structural relations between gestures (Müller, Bressem, & Ladewig, 2013): The singe strokes mark individual spaces around the speaker's body, which are used to represent the single steps. Taken together, all strokes mark a sequence of individual spaces around the speaker's body, which, as a result, create a sequence of strokes representing the entirety of steps necessary for the creation of a haircut. Because the strokes are produced in spatial and temporal proximity and furthermore are marked as belonging together through constant form features, the impression of a sequence of similar yet different

Table 9: Excerpt from transcript "single steps".

utterance	kannste dir ja immer die Einzelnen schritte d´URCHlesen,				
utterance intonation unit	kannste dir ja immer die	Einzel	nen schritte	d´U	URCHlesen,
translation	*you can always the*	*single*	*steps*	*read*	*through*
gesture phases	preparation	stroke	stroke	stroke	retraction
form parameter	hand shape	2–5 flapped down	2–5 flapped down	2–5 flapped down	
	orientation	PLTC	PLTC	PLTC	
	position	pu	p	cu	
	movement-type	arced	arced	arced	
	movement-direction	away body	away body	away body	
	movement-quality	–	–	–	
number of strokes per reptition		3			

points in space arises. In combination with the co-expressive verbal utterance, the meaning of the gestural form is enriched (Enfield, 2009, p. 15) such that the notion of plurality emerges.

Comparable to example 4, the repetition results in the creation of a complex gestural meaning. The strokes are thus not just mere repetitions of each other. Rather, the repetition of the same gesture in different spaces around the speaker's body results in semantic change (one space vs. several spaces) and thus the creation of a constructional meaning. The different positions in gesture space are not used for the representation of perceived relations but take over structural function. The individual spaces marked by the strokes indicate the notion of a multitude and, as such, can be understood to serve a grammatical purpose in marking plurality. Here, a further commonality in the structural properties of both sign and gesture becomes visible:[38] Example 5 bears resemblance with the plural marking as observed in sign languages. As shortly discussed in section 2.2, sign languages express pluralization by repeating movements along the horizontal, vertical, or sagittal axis as well as by positioning the hands in different places in gesture space (Klima & Beluggi, 1979; Pfau & Steinbach, 2005). When signing *Kinder* ('children') in German Sign Language (see Figure 8), for instance, the flat hand with a straight movement downwards is horizontally moved to the side three times. The execution of the sign KIND ('child') in different spaces around the speaker's body thereby results in the indication of more than one child and thus the expression of plural. In Example 5, change of position is used for a similar functional purpose: The hands are positioned in different spaces around the speaker's body to indicate the multitude of the gesturally represented concept. Example 5, therefore, seems to share with sign languages the same structural principle (change of the position in gesture space) for a similar purpose (indication of plurality). Gestural reduplications, as illustrated in examples 4 and 5, thus indicate a range of possible commonalities between the two expressive modes.

The examples above gave a first impression of the cognitive-semantic classification of gestural repetition as they were documented in the study. The description and discussion of the examples demonstrate that repetitions are a pattern-building device in co-speech gestures. Consequently, repetition is clearly a means for building units of different complexities in co-speech gestures. Moreover, the patterns suggest structural and functional commonalities with the phenomenon in spoken and signed languages. As a result, in chapter 7 the argument is put forward that repetition is a basic means of linguistic pattern building that needs to be characterized as

---

38 See chapter 7 for a detailed discussion of repetitions across modalities.

modality-independent, cross-cutting visual and verbal modalities, yet while showing modality-specific characteristics. Following Stolz (2008), it is furthermore assumed that the abstract principle of multiple settings via copying in reduplications is a basic semiotic means that lays the ground for similar form-based and semantic structures in the verbal and visual modality. Accordingly, reduplication in speech, sign, and gestures is considered to rest upon the principle of diagrammatic iconicity (Peirce, 1960, p. CP 2.277). Overlaps in the spoken and visual modality are thus grounded in a general principle that is based on the copying of segments, their structural arrangement, and the iconicity arising from it (see chapter 7 for a detailed discussion). This argument is supported by the characteristics of gestural repetitions both on the level of the gestural modality alone and in relation to speech. The preceding section has already given a short overview of their form, meaning as well as functional variants. These aspects will be discussed in more detail in the following sections of this book by first focusing on "a 'grammar' of gesture" (Müller, Bressem, & Ladewig, 2013) and secondly of grammar as being "potentially multimodal" (Cienki, 2012; Fricke, 2012). The following section of this chapter concentrates on a 'grammar' of gesture and discusses structural and semantic characteristics of gestural iterations and reduplications. Chapters 4 and 5 further explicate and support the perspective of grammar being potentially multimodal. Chapter 4 discusses the semantic relevance of iterations and reduplications for the creation of verbo-gestural meaning and underlines that both types affect the semantics of the verbal utterance in particular ways. This different semantic integration also results in a different syntactic integration of the gestures, treated in detail in Chapter 5.

Figure 19 provides an overview and outlook of these aspects. It represents the most frequent types of repetitions along with their characteristics on the level of form and meaning, which contribute to a better understanding of the structural properties of gestures in general. It also presents the most frequent characteristics in relation to the syntax and semantics of speech contributing to a better understanding of the multimodal character of language in use.

3.2 A closer look: Repetitions and their structural and semantic characteristics

In chapter 2, different means of creating gestural complexity have been discussed and it has been illustrated that gestures construe units of different complexities and sizes in two different ways: linearly on the level of gestural movements and simultaneously on the level of form parameter. The following overview of gestural repetitions follows these two ways of creating gestural complexity. First, results from the corpus study will be discussed addressing the linear level, and in

3.2 A closer look: Repetitions and their structural and semantic characteristics

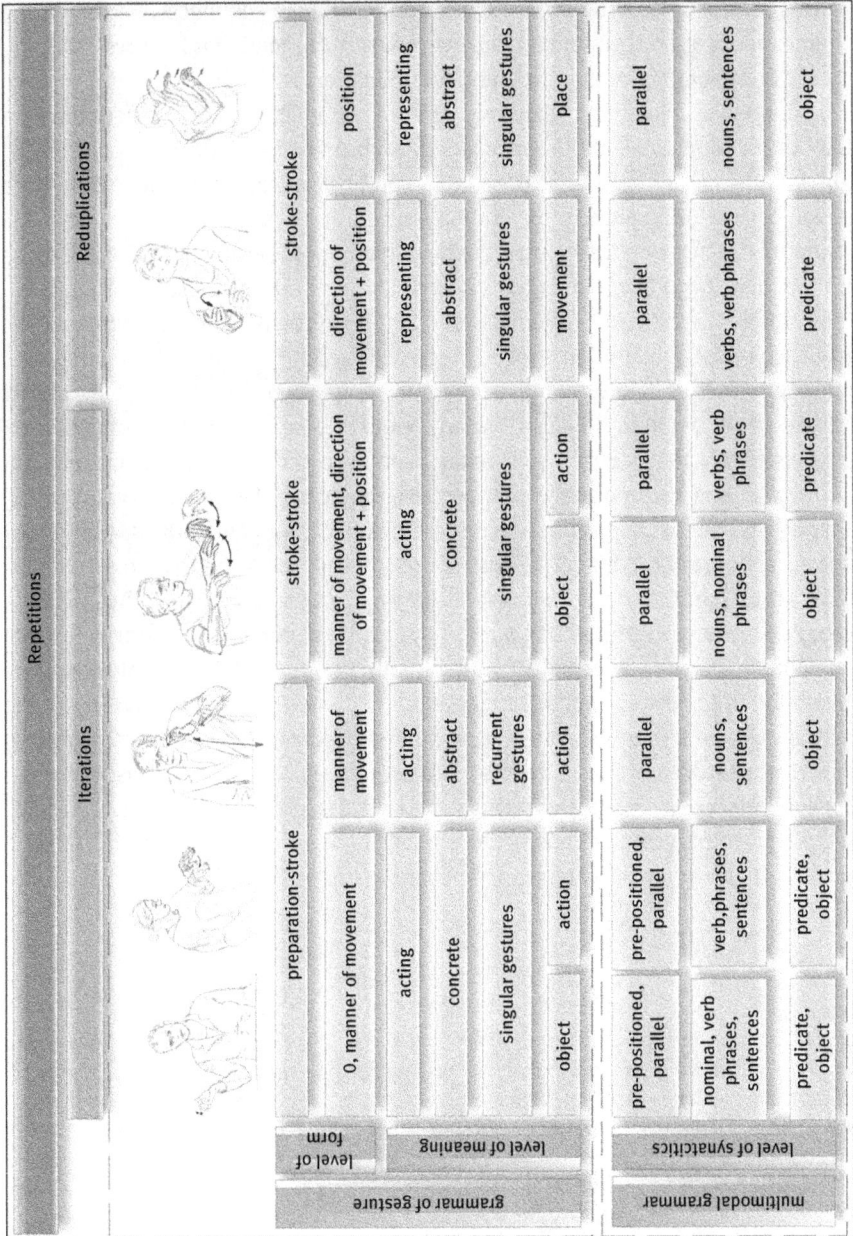

Figure 19: Overview of most frequent types of iterations and their forms, meanings, and functions.

particular, the types and lengths of gestural movement sequences. Secondly, the chapter focuses on the simultaneous complexity (formational features) and discusses the semantics of iterations and reduplications.

Altogether, the study analyzed 921 strokes, which are distributed across a total of 182 repetitions and 42 speakers (for more details on the corpus see chapter 1). Considering the complexity of the repetitive movement sequences in more detail, a clear preference in the corpus for iterations can be attested. Out of 182 repetitions, 144 repetitions are of this type. With 90%, iterations, therefore, make up the largest group documented in the study (see Table 10). Moreover, in iterations, expressive (stroke-stroke) as well as non-expressive movement phases follow each other (preparation-stroke), whereas in reduplications, solely expressive, namely meaningful gestural movement phases are produced in linear succession (stroke-stroke). Due to this distribution, both types of repetitions show different degrees of coherence. Stroke-phases are usually considered to be the most meaningful part of a gestural movement because they carry the semantic value of the gesture and are usually coordinated with the lexical affiliate of the spoken utterance (Kendon, 1972, 1980; McNeill, 1992). As a result, sequences of strokes without inserted preparation phases show a stronger degree of unity and, thus, a more complex gestural meaning than strokes that are separated by preparation phases (see chapter 2.3 for a more detailed discussion). Consequently, gestural repetitions create different gestural units both structurally as well as functionally: Iterations may either consist of several gesture phrases (preparation-stroke sequences) or single gesture phrases (stroke-stroke sequences). Reduplications, however, solely construct single gesture phrases consisting of several strokes.[39] Accordingly, repeating gestures in order to merely repeat a gestural meaning several times is the most common type documented in this study, whereas the use of rep-

---

39 The classification presented in this book differs from the one by Fricke (2012) discussed in chapter 2 in two major aspects: First, it includes preparation-stroke and stroke-stroke sequences. This distinction is based on differences in the velocity and acceleration of the movement execution observable in preparation-stroke sequences. The present study thus distinguishes iterations, which are characterized by differences in the velocity (preparation-stroke sequences) and iterations, which are not characterized by differences in the velocity (stroke-stroke). Fricke, however, based on the feature of gravity, argues that no preparation phase is necessary as no decline of gravitational force during the execution is observable (Fricke, 2012, p. 168). (For a discussion of articulatory features of gestures see Bressem & Ladewig, [2011]). Secondly, the present classification does not include the type 'variation'. This type of repetition had to be excluded from the study, because it was not possible to identify an adequate number of instances allowing a sound empirical investigation.

3.2 A closer look: Repetitions and their structural and semantic characteristics

etitions to create a reduplicative construction, namely a complex gestural meaning, as in the case of reduplications, is a less frequent use of gestural repetitions.

Table 10: Distribution of iteration and reduplication in the corpus.

Type of Repetition	Gesture phase sequence	Number of repetitions	Number of strokes
Iteration	prep-stroke	70 (39%)	487 (53%)
	stroke-stroke	74 (41%)	322 (35%)
Reduplication A	stroke-stroke	21 (12%)	65 (7%)
Reduplication B	stroke-stroke	17 (41%)	47 (5%)
		n= 182 (100%)	n= 921 (100%)

This difference in gestural movement phases is also reflected in the length of the sequences, which is how many strokes a repetitive sequence is composed of. The majority of repetitions is built up of a succession of two strokes (32%) followed by repetitions composed of three strokes (25%). Repetitions consisting of four strokes (11%) and five strokes (8%) were documented, yet, in comparison, much more rarely. Accordingly, in 57% of the cases, the gestural repetitions investigated in this corpus were composed of two or three strokes (see Table 11). Only iterations showed a greater range in their length of up to 9 strokes and more.[40]

These results reveal commonalities with repetitions in spoken and signed languages. On the one hand, gestural repetitions seem to mirror a preference documented for speech, namely that segments are usually repeated twice. At the same time, however, they show similarities with sign languages as well because "the sign occurs at least three times, with the number of repetition greater than two indeterminate" (Fischer, 1973, p. 470). Whereas in spoken languages, the number of repetitions is usually contrastive, research on sign languages supposes that number is not contrastive but rather dependent on stressing the sign or increasing attention (see chapter 2). Whether gestures also dispose of a similar functional distribution remains an open question until now. However, if

---

[40] The fact that gestural repetitions generally showed a length of two strokes is not surprising, because two is the minimum amount required to be considered a repetition. Yet, the overwhelming preference for sequences to not exceed three strokes, and thus the preference for relatively short sequences of repetitions across all types of repetitions, is interesting with respect to the internal structure of gestural repetitions. See chapter 7 for a detailed discussion of these empirical findings in relation to the question of gestural units.

Table 11: Overview of the length of repetition and parameter changes in iterations and reduplications.

Type of Repetition	Gesture Phases		Level of Form – Gesture Only			
			Changes of Parameters			Length of Repetitions
			yes/no	Number of Parameters	Type of Parameters	
Iteration	prep-stroke	487 (53%)	x	1 (71%)	manner of movement	2–3 (53%)
	stroke-stroke	322 (35%)	x	1, 2 (69%)	manner of movement, direction of movement	2–3
Reduplication A	stroke-stroke	65 (7%)	x	1, 2 (95%)	direction of movement, direction of movement + position	2–3
Reduplication B	stroke-stroke	47 (5%)	x	1 (78%)	position	2–3
				n= 921 (100%)		

3.2 A closer look: Repetitions and their structural and semantic characteristics — 65

one examines the scope of repetitions in gestures documented in the study, it seems to be likely that at least for reduplications, the number of repetitions is limited because only for this type, the study did not document longer sequences. Both types of gestural repetitions (iteration and reduplication) thus clearly show preferences and a particular distribution on the linear level. A similar effect also appears on the simultaneous level marking both types as distinct patterns.

In chapter one, it has been shortly discussed that, within a cognitive-linguistic approach to gestures, it is assumed that gestures are motivated form Gestalts in the sense that they are internally structured. Gestures and gestural meanings are made up of formational features that recur (handshape, orientation of the palm, movement, position in gesture space),[41] appear with stable form-meaning relations across speakers and contexts, and become semanticized and grammaticalized (Calbris, 2011; Fricke, 2012; Harrison, 2009; Kendon, 2004b; Ladewig, 2014b; Müller, 2004, 2010b; Webb, 1996). These formational features are also important for the creation of gestural units. For gestural sequences to be perceived as repetitions, form features of the sequence need to remain constant, as the maintenance of form marks the connection of gestural units: "Instantiations of the same parameters through the same features causes a connection comparable to the congruence between units of spoken language." (Fricke, 2012, p. 146). The study documented a predominant change in only one form parameter (66%), considering the total number of repetitions. Changes in more than one parameter occurred but were seldom (two parameters 8%, three parameters 2%). However, the rather unbalanced distribution of the particular types of repetitions in the corpus makes a general statement on the number of changing form parameters across all repetitions problematic. In order to arrive at a conclusive picture for the individual types of repetitions, a look at the distribution across iterations and reduplications is necessary. As such, it becomes clear that both types of repetitions differ in the type and number of formational features that change and remain constant.

In iterations, a large number of instances does not show a change in form parameters. The study documented 24% of iterations with preparation-stroke sequences and 30% of iterations with stroke-stroke sequences in which all of the form parameters remain constant throughout the succession. However, in

---

41 For the description of these formational features, gesture research falls back on the notion of form parameters in sign languages (e.g., Battison, 1974; Frishberg, 1975; Stokoe, 1960). However, whereas the parameters are understood as categories of the phoneme inventory of the respective language in sign language linguistics (see Crasborn, 2001; Johnson & Liddell, 2010 for a discussion of their phonological nature), in gesture studies "the four parameters are mainly understood as a grid for notating gestural forms and hardly as categories of the phoneme inventory." (Ladewig & Bressem, 2013, p. 204)

the majority of cases, changes in formational features do occur, and more importantly, only in particular ones. Iterations either most frequently change in one parameter (71%, preparation-stroke) or in more than one parameter (62%, stroke-stroke sequences). All reduplications of type A documented in the corpus change in two parameter realizations (95%). Reduplications of type B change most frequently in one parameter (73%) (see Table 3.7). If changes in parameters occurred, these were restricted to the direction and manner movement of the hands and their positioning in gesture space regardless of the type of repetition. Out of these changes, variations in the manner of movement occurred most frequently (51%).[42] Moreover, these changes were particularly distributed: For iterations, changes in the manner of movement are typical (see example 1 "weapons of mass destruction" in which the individual strokes differed in their size and speed of movement, Figure 14). Iterations with stroke-stroke sequences frequently showed changes in the direction and manner of the movement as well as the positioning of the hands in gesture space (see example 3 "metal thing", Figure 16). Similar changes were documented for reduplications of type A. However, contrary to iterations like example 3, in which these changes were frequent, in reduplications of type A it is almost the only change possible (95%). This was demonstrated in example 4 ("send back and forth"), in which speaker BS produced three strokes with arced movements, which differed in their direction of movements (towards vs. away from the body) as well as their position in gesture space (see Figure 17). Reduplications of type B, as illustrated in example 5 "single steps" (see Figure 18), most frequently change only in the positioning of the hands in gesture space. In 69% of all cases, the hands are positioned in different spaces around the speaker's body.

Summarizing the above-presented results, it can be stated that if gestural repetitions differ in parameter instantiations they do so in a small number (not more than two) and only in particular ones (movement and position). Moreover, changes in hand shapes and orientations of the hand did not occur. The results confirm the assumption that the instantiation of the same features across sequences of gestures causes a connection between the gestural units (Fricke 2012) and is thus necessary to mark the sequence of strokes as belonging to one gestural repetition.[43] With these results, gestural repetitions as documented in the present study bear a striking resemblance with repetitive sequences in sign languages:

---

[42] Changes in the direction of movement occurred in 11% of all cases and position was affected in 8% of all cases.
[43] See chapter 6 for a discussion of this aspect in relation to Gestalt principles.

3.2 A closer look: Repetitions and their structural and semantic characteristics

> Hand shapes seem to change rarely during the articulation of a sign and seem to remain quite stable. The ideal of a prototypical, one-handed, not composite sign corresponds with the conception of a sign with only one hand shape. Even if several movements are produced in succession (as for instance in so called classifying verbs), the used hand shape often remains the same. (Wrobel, 2007, p. 47, translation JB)

Moreover, sign languages predominantly use movement variation, such as circular reduplicated movements, elliptical reduplicated forms, or acceleration for the modulations of signs in reduplicative processes. Signs differ in their speed as well as the evenness of the movement and, moreover, are repeated along the horizontal, vertical, or sagittal axis as well as by positioning the hands in different places in gesture space (Bergman, 1982; Fischer, 1973; Klima & Beluggi, 1979; Pfau & Steinbach, 2005; Wilbur, 2005). Accordingly, gestural repetitions seem to show a similar use of movement and position. Akin to sign languages, gestures use modifications of movements (direction and manner) as well as positions in gesture space for differentiating types of repetitions.

After concentrating on the linear and simultaneous complexity of gestures, the focus now shifts to semantic aspects of both types of repetitions. In particular, the section will focus on how and what kind of meaning iterations and reduplications may express. As introduced in chapter 1, the study presented in this book is based on a cognitive-linguistic approach to gestures. Considering the semiotic and symbolic nature of gestures, their ability to express meaning, for instance, is assumed to be grounded in particular processes of sign creation. "The basis for gestural meaning constitution is – provided that gestures don't point – mimesis" (Müller 2010a, translation JB).

Building upon Aristotle, Müller (1998, 2009, 2010a) characterizes gestural mimesis according to the "media" (articulators), the "objects" (the range of gestural referents such as actions, parts of actions, object etc.) as well as the "modes" (how mimesis is achieved) and distinguishes four modes of representation: acting, representing, drawing, and molding (Müller, 1998, 2009, 2010a, 2013, 2014b).[44] In the acting mode, the hands either mime or re-enact actual manual activities. When representing, the hands embody an object as a whole, becoming a kind of manual "sculpture". In the drawing mode, the hand, and in particular the index finger, traces the contour or outline of an object. When molding an object, the hands mold a three-dimensional sculpture. The ability of gestures to refer to objects, actions, or processes in the real world lies in an abstraction process on the part of the speaker.

---

[44] See also Andrén (2010, p. 112ff), Calbris (1990, p. 111ff), Kendon (2004b, p. 160) and Streeck (2009, p. 119ff) for further proposals of gestural process of depiction.

> Gestures are forms of visual thinking in a manual modality. They come with specific perspectives on the world they depict, perspectives that are individual and subjective views of the world. Gestures are conceptualizations of perceived and conceived experiences that merge visual and manual ways of thinking through and in movement.
>
> (Müller, 2014, p. 1689)

Depending on the reference object, particular traits of objects, actions, or processes are extracted.[45] In cases of acting gestures, speakers may either focus on a) the outline of an object as in drawing with an index finger or b) its shape, position, and even movement when molding the object with the whole hand. Moreover, actions can be represented through actions, aspects of actions, or actions with objects. Objects can be represented through objects, their characteristics as well as the movement and localization of objects (Müller, 2010a, 2014a).

> In the absence of a specific dynamic characteristic, an animated being or object may have a distinctive static trait, reproduced (1) statically or (2) dynamically. The entire surface of a dome might be depicted by (1) a hand held convex, face down, with the fingers spread, or (2) by drawing a semi-circle from left to right with the surface of a hand, or else two symmetric quarter-circles with both hands. To evoke a small round object, one has the choice between joining the thumb and forefinger in a ring or drawing the circumference with the forefinger.
>
> (Calbris, 1990, p. 113)

Whether a gesture refers to the action itself or the involved object is thereby not resolvable through the gesture alone because a gesture often evokes the user, the action, or the tool (Calbris, 1990, p. 111ff; Ladewig, 2011; Müller, 2014; Teßendorf, 2016). Gestures thus do not just mirror perceived objects.

> The gesture that depicts an object or process of any kind offers a *construal* or *analysis* of the signified, an "active" organization. It does not mirror but analyzes the object. The gesture *is* not like its referent, but rather shows *what the referent is like*.
>
> (Streeck, 2008, p. 286 emphasis in original) (see also Calbris, 1990; Müller, 1998, 2010a)

And moreover, as Cienki and Müller (2008, p. 1689) point out, with reference to Slobin's concept of "thinking for speaking", speakers orient their thinking to the modality in which it is expressed, choosing particular ways of expression that suit, for instance, in cases of gestures, the manual modality.

Gestural modes of representation thus make up techniques of sign creation by which movements of the hands and arms become symbolic. They reconstruct the practices of gestural mimesis and provide a first step towards the embodied basis of gestural meaning and such are vital both for the producing and perceiving

---

45 Gestural depiction thereby essentially rests upon metonymic processes (Mittelberg, 2006, 2010b, 2014; Mittelberg & Waugh, 2009; Müller, 1998b).

gestures. Gestural meaning, as indicated by the modes of representation, is thus motivated: Gestures make use of basic cognitive image-schematic structures and can be understood as visible forms of cognitive structures: They exploit motoric patterns of mundane actions, evoke geometrical or schematic patterns or Gestalts (e.g., circles, oval shapes, squares), and realize image-schematic structures (e.g., source-path-goal, container/containment) (e.g., Calbris, 2011; Cienki, 2005; Hassemer, Joue, Willems, & Mittelberg, 2011; Ladewig, 2011; Mittelberg, 2010a; Müller, 1998; Sowa, 2005; Streeck, 2009). Hence, gestural forms carry abstract meaning independent from the verbal context.[46] In cases of gestures depicting objects, for instance, a round handshape may transmit the information of a round profile. A flat hand may represent a flat object in a particular orientation. Hands that are loosely shaped and moved downwards, for instance, may evoke the impression of a round object, such as a bowl (see Figure 20 for some examples).

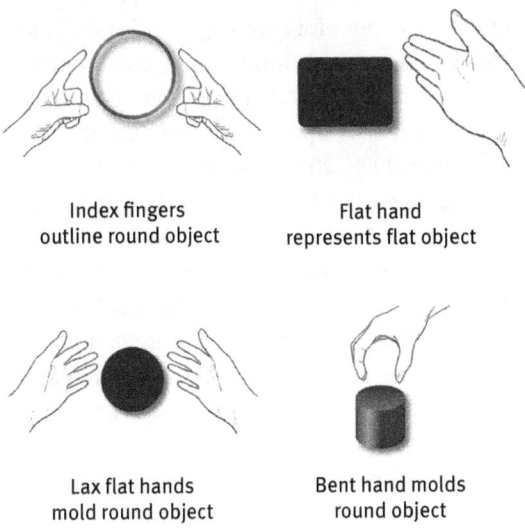

Index fingers
outline round object

Flat hand
represents flat object

Lax flat hands
mold round object

Bent hand molds
round object

Figure 20: Motivation of gestural forms.

---

46 Accordingly, a growing number of studies assumes gestures referring to actions, objects, or events to have "inherent content" (Kopp, Tepper, & Cassell, 2004), "inherent meaning" (Ladewig, 2011; Ladewig & Bressem, 2013), "underspecified meaning" (Lascarides & Stone, 2006), "context-independent meaning" (Müller, 2010b) or "internal imagery" (Sowa, 2005). With regard to recurrent or emblematic gestures notions such as "semantic theme" (Kendon, 2004b; Müller, 2004) or "semantic core" (Ladewig, 2011, 2014a; Teßendorf, 2014, 2016) are proposed (see below for a discussion of gesture types).

Gestural modes of representation thus

> spell out, how a schematized meaning of gesture form is motivated, a meaning which remains rather vague, when considered out of context, but is meaningful: We can recognize without problem that somebody is molding a shape, completely out of context. We need context to re-construct the local, the indexicalized meaning of the gesture and to establish a particular kind of reference for the gesture. But the form of the gesture is meaningful in itself. (Müller, 2014, p. 1693)

In relation to speech and through a dynamic process of meaning constitution, this abstract and decontextualized meaning of gestures is specified and enriched (see Enfield, 2009, p. 14).

Even though the gestural modes of representation address the iconic motivation of gestures, they are not only the basis of iconic gestures but rather of gestures in general (see Müller 2014, p. 1691). As basic techniques of gestural meaning creation, they allow the hands to represent in different ways. In particular, based on the assumption that gestures possess medial and functional properties similar to language and, with reference to Bühler's functional theory of language, gestures can be said to make statements about objects in the world ("representation"), have the potential to regulate the behavior of others ("appeal") and express the inner state of the speaker ("expression") (Müller, 1998, 2013). Gestures' appealing function may become visible when fulfilling interactive functions, for the organization of turns at talk (Bohle, 2007; Streeck & Hartge, 1992), for instance. Gesture's expressive function is visible in different qualities of gestural movement indicating, for example, degrees of emotional attitude. Their representational function is evident when gestures depict events or objects in the world. On this representational function not only rests the "gestural potential for a language analogous communication" that "even allows for a development of gestural languages to sign languages" (Müller 1998: 17) but also a common characteristic of language and gestures: "As in language these functions are co-present dimensions of any sign and rather than characterizing alternative signs, their 'dominance' within one sign varies" (Müller, 2009, p. 501). As such, these three functions play out in different types of gestures in particular ways.[47]

Based on the degree of conventionalization, two basic types of gestures may be distinguished: singular and recurrent gestures (Müller, 2009, 2010a, 2010b, 2013, 2017). Singular gestures are movements of the hands, which co-occur with

---

[47] The following discussion of gestural types and functions is not aimed at completeness but rather focuses on those relevant for the discussion of the empirical results in this book. For a detailed overview of existing gesture classifications systems see Bohle (2014), Fricke (2007, p. 156ff), Kendon (2004b, p. 84ff) and Müller (1998, p. 91ff).

speech and acquire a local, indexicalized meaning. They are found in the moment of speaking and are closely connected with cognitive, affective, and interactive processes. Singular gestures are not conventionalized. As embodied conceptualizations and felt experiences, they "are created on the spot" (Müller et al., 2013, p. 719). They are typical elements of spoken utterances and affect the proposition of the verbal utterance in a number of ways because they semantically complement and profile verbalized parts of utterances. An example is the drawing of a line to indicate the form of a concrete or abstract path (Müller, 2010b).[48] With their low degree of conventionalization, singular gestures stand in sharp contrast to recurrent gestures: Recurrent gestures are "used repeatedly in different contexts and [their] formational and semantic core remains stable across different contexts and speakers." (Ladewig, 2011; see also Müller, 2010b) These gestures are not found in the moment of speaking but rather make up a conventionalized repertoire of gestures. A very well-known example of recurrent gestures is the gesture of the Palm Up Open Hand. The gesture is characterized by a stable form meaning pairing through which ideas, arguments, or other discursive objects are presented on the open hand, and others are invited to take on a shared perspective on this object in everyday communication (Kendon, 2004b; Müller, 2004). Variations in the movement pattern (e.g., downwards, circular motion) associated with the kinesic core of the gesture result in meaning variations (Müller, 2004). Recurrent gestures are conventionalized; however, they have not yet reached quite the same degree of conventionalization as emblems,[49] and although they might be used without speech, they are characterized by a tight relationship with speech (Ladewig, 2014b). They group into families and build up culturally varying repertoires (Bressem & Müller, 2014a, 2014b; Brookes, 2001; Calbris, 1990, 2011; Fricke, Bressem, & Müller, 2014; Harrison, 2009; Kendon, 1995, 2004a; Ladewig, 2011, 2014a, 2014b; Müller, 2004; Teßendorf, 2014, 2016). Contrary to singular gestures, which primarily rest upon visual perception, recurrent gestures are, to a large part, derived from everyday

---

48 Singular gestures encompass what is referred to by other researchers as idiosyncratic gestures (iconic or metaphoric gestures) (McNeill, 2005) or (concrete or abstract) referential gestures (Müller 1998).
49 Emblems, such as the thumbs-up gesture or the headshake for instance, are kinesic movements, which, similar to words in spoken languages, possess a stable form-meaning relationship, are translatable into single words or phrases, and are used frequently without speech. Furthermore, they are compositional in that an emblem can consist of more than one gestural form as and emblems may be combined with each other (e.g., head shake with a particular facial expression). Emblems are thus highly conventionalized movements, which are culture and language specific and can be collected in dictionaries (for an overview see Efron, 1941/1972; Ekman & Friesen, 1969; Morris, 1979; Payrató, 2014).

actions from which aspects of actions are exploited for the constitution of gestural meaning. The basis of recurrent gestures on everyday actions is thereby often attributed to being a major factor for their primary pragmatic use, namely their ability to fulfill communicative actions and meta-communicative functions (Beavin, Chovil, Lawrie, & Wade, 1992; Bressem & Müller, 2014a; Brookes, 2004, 2005, 2015; Kendon, 1995; Ladewig, 2010, 2011, 2014a; Müller, 1998, 2010b, 2017; Müller & Speckmann, 2002; for an overview see Payrató & Teßendorf, 2014; Streeck, 2005, 2006; Teßendorf, 2016).

> The functions gestures have as they contribute to or constitute the acts or moves accomplished by utterances, are referred to as *pragmatic* functions. In the terminology proposed, gestures which show what sort of a move or speech act a speaker is engaging in are said to have *performative* functions. Gestures are said to have *modal* functions, if they seem to operate on a given unit of verbal discourse and show how it is to be interpreted. Gestures may serve *parsing* functions when they contribute to the marking of various aspects of the structure of spoken discourse. (Kendon, 2004, p. 225, emphasis in original)

Recurrent gestures may thus either "display the communicative act of the speaker and act upon speech as 'speech-performatives'" or they may "aim at a regulation of the behavior of others as 'performatives'" (Teßendorf, 2014, p. 1544). By holding off possible objections, they regulate the behavior of others and perform speech acts. By presenting or brushing aside arguments, they meta-communicatively operate on the verbal utterance expressing the speaker's attitude or mark focal aspects of the utterance.

The ability of gestures to mark focal aspects and to structure and organize the verbal utterance ("parsing function" [Kendon, 2004]), "discursive function" [Müller, 1998]), is thereby usually attributed to a particular type of gestures: batons (Efron, 1941/1972; Ekman & Friesen, 1969) or beats (McNeill, 1992; McNeill & Levy, 1982). These are gestures that coincide with the prosody of speech and beat out the rhythm of the verbal utterance by marking verbal accents and pitch through gestural movements. They function like "a yellow highlighter – beats emphasize what is important in some larger context, and this is why they coincide with prosodic emphasis as well." (McNeill, Levy & Duncan, 2015, p. 274) Beats are considered to carry no semantic content unless they are superimposed on other gestures, such as singular gestures, for instance. Their main function, apart from visually highlighting prosodic features of speech, is to signal narrative shifts in discourse (Alibali & Kita, 2010; Efron, 1941/1972; Ekman & Friesen, 1969; Kendon, 1983; Kettebekov, 2004; Krahmer & Swerts, 2007; Loehr, 2004; McClave, 1991, 1994; McCullough,

2005; McNeill, 1992; McNeill & Levy, 1982; Renwick, Shattuck, & Yasinnik, 2004; Schegloff, 1984; Sowa, 2005; Tuite, 1993).[50]

As shown in the preceding section, a cognitive-linguistic approach to gestures assumes that gestures follow principles of meaning-making and are motivated form Gestalts that express a range of meanings and fulfill a variety of functions. The following section will address these aspects in the gestural repetitions investigated in the present study. The main question that will be addressed now is: What modes of representation and gesture types can be identified in both types of gestural repetitions and what kinds of conclusions can be drawn from this for the meaning expressed by the gestural repetitions?

For the gestural modes of representation, a rather clear-cut distribution of both modes across iterations and reduplications can be noted: While iterations predominantly use the acting mode (75%), reduplications are generally depicted in the representing mode (85%).[51] Iterations, therefore, seem to be overwhelmingly used for re-enacting actions of the hand, which conceptualize and depict kinesthetic perceptions and thus are more directly associated with bodily experiences. Reduplications, on the other hand, represent something other than the hand: They re-enact or depict primarily visual perceptions and seem to go along with other and more complex kinds of processes of abstraction. These differences in the sign constitution process led to the assumption that both types of gestural repetitions carry particular and distinct meanings and functions. This assumption is supported by a closer look at the distribution across iterations and reduplication and by taking the gestural meaning into account.

First of all, the gestural modes of representation give insight into meaning differences within iterations. As was mentioned previously in the chapter, iterations were classified into preparation-stroke and stroke-stroke sequences. These different types of gesture phase sequences now also show a distinct distribution of the gestural modes. While for both types of repetitions, the acting mode is most frequent, a closer look reveals differences in the subtypes of the modes and, as a result, the kind of gestural meaning created. As shown in Table 3.8, both

---

[50] Contrary to notion of beats as a separate gesture type, proposals also consider the modulations of gestural movements (size, tension and type of movement) observed in gestures so far classified as beats, as a function that can be ascribed to singular or recurrent gestures (McCullough, 2005, see also chapter 6).

[51] The presentation of the empirical results for gestural modes of representation, gestural meanings, and gesture types will first of all concentrate on the most frequent types documented. The following section will thus not discuss the gestural mode "representing" in iterations or "acting" in reduplications.

Table 12: Distribution of most frequent gestural modes of representation and their subtypes across iterations and reduplications.

Type of Repetition	Gesture Phases		Gestural modes of representation			
		Type	Subtype	Meaning		Example
Iteration	prep-stroke 487 (53%)	acting (85%)	unspecified object (83%)	abstract (100%)	action	"Weapons of mass destruction"
			specified object (11%)	concrete (61%)	action	"put it in"
			action only (6%)	concrete (100%)	action	"Arko"
	stroke-stroke 322 (35%)	acting (86%)	specified object (67%)	concrete (83%)	action/object	"Metal thing", to fill out forms
			unspecified object (25%)	abstract (100%)	action	"no chance to be realized"
			action only (6%)	concrete (100%)	action	"run the hand over something"
Reduplication A	stroke-stroke 65 (7%)	representing (71%)	motion and path (81%)	abstract (100%)	movement	"send back and forth"
Reduplication B	stroke-stroke 47 (5%)	representing (97%)	spatial relation only (86%)	abstract (100%)	place	"single steps"
			objects in spatial relation (24%)	abstract (100%)	place	"different villages"
			n= 921 (100%)			

types of iterations use "action only" for the depiction of instrumental actions (see example 2, Figure 15 in which a speaker depicts the scraping action of a dog). In these cases, the hands act as if they perform an actual action. The corpus documents iterations for the depiction of pounding, scratching, and stroking, for instance. Yet, as can be seen in Table 12 with only 6% in each case, "acting only" makes up only a small portion of iterations. The corpus most often documents "acting with specified object" or "acting with unspecified object" and, more importantly, an opposing distribution of both modes. For iterations with preparation-stroke sequences, the mode "acting with unspecified object" (83%) (see example 1, Figure 14) followed by "acting with specified object" (11%) is documented. For stroke-stroke sequences, the predominant use of "acting with specified object" (67%) (see example 3, Figure 16) followed by "acting with unspecified object" (25%) is noted.

Based on this distribution, first conclusions on the gestural meaning can be drawn: Due to the overwhelming use of "acting with unspecified object", iterations with preparation-stroke sequences primarily express abstract meaning, whereas iterations with stroke-stroke sequence mostly express concrete meaning.

> When considering *en-acting of actions* as a base for meaning construal in gestures three different types of manual actions are to be distinguished: the hands may enact actions such as waving or drawing, they may enact actions where the hand shape specifies a particular object (holding a knife, turning a car key), or they enact actions which do not involve a specific hand shape, such as showing, giving, or receiving objects on the open hand. (Müller, 2013, p. 1697)

Example 1 ("weapons of mass destruction", see Figure 14) illustrates the mode "acting with unspecified object". Here, the politician Trittin articulates his position against Germany's nuclear partaking and produces a series of ring gestures. The ring gesture, a recurrent gesture, is derived from the action of holding small objects between the tips of fingers (Kendon, 2004b; Morris, 1979; Müller, 2014; Neumann, 2004). The necessary precision for holding objects between the fingers is projected to communicative objects so that arguments are marked as precise. By operating on the verbal utterance, the ring gestures fulfill meta-communicative functions and graduate and qualify the content of an utterance, and guide its interpretation. A further frequent example in the present corpus is the use of the Palm Up Open Hand gesture (PUOH). The PUOH is derived from the action of giving, showing, offering an object to another person by presenting it on the open hand (e.g., pleading for money). In discourse, arguments and ideas are treated as they were objects lying on the palm up the hand and are presented as visible and obvious, offered for joint inspection and propose a common perspective on it (Kendon, 2004b; Müller, 2004). What is foregrounded from the acting mode in a PUOH is the action itself, namely the presenting and offering the discourse object. In one example from the corpus, a speaker tries to explain an instruction on a plate (*das ist eine Informationstafel, da ist ne Info drauf* ['it is an information board, it has an information on it']) and produces a series of PUOH gestures by which the information on the board is presented as it were laying on the palm of the hand. Through this abstract action, it is presented as visible and obvious and offered for joint inspection. Both examples above illustrate that iterations with preparation-stroke sequences show an overwhelming use of recurrent gestures, that is gestures with a partly conventionalized stable form-meaning relationship.[52] Moreover, they fulfill pragmatic function: They meta-communicatively comment on the verbal utterance and have a prosodic function by marking various aspects of the structure of spoken discourse. Through up and down movements, which vary in their quality of movement (e.g., accelerated, enlarged, reduced), the verbal utterance is visually highlighted. As such, these gestures have a similar function as accent and pitch in spoken language, for instance. Accordingly, sequences of gestures using the mode "acting with unspecified object" express abstract, metaphoric meaning, while at the same time visually highlighting parts of the verbal utterance.

Although a similar use of recurrent gestures with prosodic function is documented for iterations with stroke-stroke sequences, the corpus revealed a different predominant mode of representation: For this type, the mode "acting with specified object" is predominant. As a result, these iterations do not depict abstract meaning but rather concrete meanings and, in particular, objects and actions. Example 3 (see Figure 16) illustrates this use. Here, the speaker molds the shape of an object by a succession of three strokes going inwards and outwards. Through the movement of the hand along with a bent hand shape with the palm facing downwards, the speaker molds the shape of the object. Accordingly, the concrete object, namely a bent metal thing in which wine bottles can be placed, is depicted through handling it and its shape and extension are created in space. A similar use is documented is the example "handles", in which speaker BS describes a particular type of handles often used in bathtubs in hotels (see Figure 30). While uttering *dass du in den Badewannen diese Griffe hast* ('that you have those handles in the bathtubs'), BS produces two gestural iterations consisting of six strokes in which she moves her right hand down up

---

[52] This frequent use of recurrent gestures is typical for particular discourse types such as speeches, argumentations, and discussions. The majority of iterations with abstract meaning were documented in video data taken from German parliamentary debates and the football talk show "Doppelpass". They were less frequent for the TV-show "Genial Daneben" and face-to-face communication (see appendix for more information on the data).

3.2 A closer look: Repetitions and their structural and semantic characteristics — 77

and down in small, accented straight movements, in parallel to *in den* ('in the'), *Badewanne* ('bathtub'), *diese* ('those') and *Griffe* ('handles'). By using a lax flat hand shape with the fingers curled in and a palm up orientation, speaker BS is able to show how the object "handles" is used, namely by holding on to them from underneath. Accordingly, using the mode "acting with specified object", she visually represents the handles in bathtubs by handling them.

Both of the examples given above are exemplary cases of gestural iterations in which a gestural repetition is used for the depiction of objects. Yet, depicting objects by handling them is only one option. Another one is the depiction of actions with objects. In the example "shoplifters", speaker HF talks about shoplifters and what kinds of tricks they may use to hide the stolen goods (*ein Fuchspel (-) pelz den sich Ladendiebinnen umlegen um da die Sachen reinzustecken* ['a fox fur that shoplifters put on to put in the things']). In parallel to the phrase *um da die Sachen reinzustecken* ('to put in the things') and using a hand shape with the fingers 1–5 bent, a palm lateral towards body orientation, and an arced movement to the left located in the upper center of the gesture space, HF produces a gestural iteration consisting of two strokes by which he depicts the action of putting something in a jacket. The gestural repetition not only represents the action of "putting in" but also, by maintaining a particular hand shape, transports the idea of an object that is put in the jacket. The gesture thus depicts an action along with a particular object involved in the action. A similar use is documented in the following example: Speaker SU talks about how to fill out a form. While doing so, she depicts the writing action and holding of a pen. While saying *Protokolle wo man dann per Hand der IM ausfüllt* ('protocols which are filled in by hand by the IM'),[53] speaker SU produces an iteration consisting of seven strokes aligning with *dann per Hand der IM ausfüllt* ('which are filled in by hand by the IM'). The strokes depict the action of writing by imitating the holding of a pen in one hand and moving it in a wavy line from left to right.[54] In all of the examples given, the gestural repetition depicts actions with objects. Whereas in the examples "metal thing" and "handles" the focus is on the object itself, in the examples "putting in" and "fill out" it is on the action.

Summarizing it can thus be stated that in iterations with stroke-stroke sequences concrete meanings predominate and most frequently a) actions, b) objects through handling them, and c) actions with objects are depicted. Accordingly, the

---

[53] The acronym IM stands for "inoffizieller Mitarbeiter" (unofficial employee) and refers to people in the former GDR that voluntarily gave or were forced to give information to the ministry of state security.
[54] See chapter 4 for a more detailed discussion of both of the examples.

principal use of singular gestures depicting concrete objects or actions was documented. Iterations with preparation-stroke sequences, however, although also depicting instrumental actions, primarily express abstract meanings due to the prevailing use of the mode "acting with unspecified objects" and recurrent gestures. Both types of iterations (preparation-stroke and stroke-stroke sequences) thus show a clear differentiation in the gestural modes of representation, the meaning that is created and the gesture types used.

Contrary to iteration, which depicts actions of the hands (with or without objects), in reduplications, the hands turn into something they are not. For both types of reduplications, the representing mode is characteristic. As a result, in these sequences, the hands become a sculpture for things in the world; they move and place things in space and as such depict objects, events, states, or processes. Although both types of reduplications (type A and B) make use of this mode, they differ in the distribution of the specific subtypes and thus show a clear distribution of meaning and function (see Table 3.8). Whereas reduplications of type A primarily use the mode "motion and path" (81%), reduplications of type B show the mode "spatial relation only" (86%). Consequently, they create different types of meanings. Let us first consider reduplications of type A in more detail.

As already mentioned above, reduplications of type A are most often used with the representing mode "motion and path". In these repetitions, motion events, and, in particular, the motion along with its path are depicted. Reduplications of type A embody thus frequently the iterativity of movement events. Moreover, they depict the spatial and temporal basis of *Aktionsarten*, thus giving insight into the conceptualization of lexical concepts (Becker et al., 2011; Boutet, Morgenstern, & Cienki, 2016; Duncan, 1996; Müller, 2000). This use is illustrated in the example "send back and forth" (see Figure 17), in which a woman depicts how internal mail is sent back and forth between offices by producing a succession of strokes going towards and away from the body. By doing so, she gesturally depicts the motion and path of the motion event. A further example of the depiction of iterativity of motion events is given when a speaker talks about how a bed is repeatedly being moved up and down (*der ganze Schnickschnack, Bett rauf runter* ['all of the gadgets, bed up and down']). Using a flat hand with the palm turned upwards, speaker WB moves his hand in a straight movement upwards (*Bett* ['bed']), downwards (*rauf* ['down']) and upwards (*runter* ['up']), depicting the motion as well as the path of the moving bed. A similar example is given when speaker HEB talks about doctors quickly going in and out of a patient's room in a hospital. Using a lax flat hand and a bent movement, speaker HEB moves his hand to the right (*Arzt rein* ['doctor

3.2 A closer look: Repetitions and their structural and semantic characteristics

in']) and to the left (*raus* ['out']) depicting the iterativity of the movement event "going in and out".

In all of the examples discussed above, the iterativity of the movement event is expressed by the repeated execution of strokes. Thus, "repetition as a temporal process is verbally and gesturally conceptualized as a repeated movement sequence." (Müller, 2000, p. 221, translation JB): Arced or straight movements are repeated by changing the direction of movement, either away and towards the body ("send back and forth") or up and down ("bed", "in and out"). Accordingly, through a particular type of movement, along with changes in the direction of movement causing different positions in gesture space, the motion and path of a motion event are created. Moreover, the individual strokes are marked by clear endpoints and, as such, highlight and make visible the individual endpoints of the movement sequence.[55] Although all instances of reduplications refer to concrete movement events, following Müller (2000), it is argued that a depiction of the movement event alone cannot account for the meaning of the gestural reduplication. Rather, the meaning refers to the abstract notion of iterativity, expressed gesturally in the movement unfolding between two endpoints.

> In all examples of verbo-gestural realizations of the concepts ingressivity, egressivity and iterativity, the boundary orientation of the path of movement is emphasized by a particular gestural form: the holding or the freezing of the gestures at the apex (which represents an endpoint of movement). (Müller, 2000, p. 226, translation JB)

For the reduplications of type A documented in the corpus, the unfolding of the movement between two endpoints becomes visible in the transition point between the successive movements (Seyfeddinipur, 2006). Accordingly, reduplications of type A documented in the corpus express iterativity and are thus a means for the conceptualization of 'Aktionsarten' in gestures. This is achieved through a succession of strokes that differ in the movement direction and position. Accordingly, the gestural repetition is not, as it was the case in the example "metal thing", solely a

---

[55] Although reduplications primarily use the representing mode, iterativity is also expressed by using the mode "acting with unspecified object" and holding and placing objects in different regions of the gesture space. This is exemplified in cases in which a speaker moves a lax flat hand in arced ways to the side, depicting how people drive from their home to a vacation house (*man fährt von zu Hause in sein Ferienhause und wieder zurück* ['you drive from home to your vacation house and back again']). Another example is given in description of how people drive from the work place to the apartment (*fahren die Leute von zu Hause zur Arbeit und wieder zürück* ['people drive from their home to work and back again']) by placing the hand palm downwards in different regions of the gesture space. The difference in the mode of representation thereby has no effect on the creation of the gestural meaning: in both cases the iterativity of the described motion event is depicted by the gestural repetition.

means for depiction but rather carries semantic relevance itself and contributes to the verbo-gestural meaning of iterativity.

In reduplications of type B, however, movement takes over a different role: Similar to iterations like example 3 "metal thing" (see Figure 16), in which the movement was a necessary means for the depiction of the shape of an object, in reduplications of type B movement itself does not carry semantic relevance in itself. The majority of reduplications of type B mime objects in spatial relation ("spatial relation only" 54%, "objects in spatial relation" 25%). The difference in both modes lies in the specificity of the object mimed in spatial relations: For "objects in spatial relation", the object itself is specified in the gestural forms. The hands may hold and place objects in different regions of the gesture space. This use is illustrated in a case in which speaker DA talks about the story of a film (*1914 spielt der wo zwei dörfer sich bekriegen aber die Enkel sich in einander verlieben aus den unterschiedlichen Dörfern* ['it is set in 1914 where two villages fight against each but the grandchildren fall in love with each other from the different villages']). While saying *aus den unterschiedlichen Dörfern* ('from the different villages'), speaker DA produces a gestural reduplication consisting of three strokes. By rotating the wrist three times and by using a 1–5 bent hand shape with a palm upwards orientation, the different villages are successively placed in different positions of the gesture space and thus represented as similar yet points in gesture space.

In the representing mode "spatial relation only", the gesture itself does not mark specific aspects of the objects, which are set in spatial in relation. This is illustrated in example 5 "single steps" (see Figure 18), in which speaker ME talks about the necessary steps for the composition of a haircut (*oder steht och steht ja in den büchern kannste ja kannste dir ja immer die einzelnen Schritte durchlesen* ['or it is written well in text books you can well you can read through the single steps']). In temporal overlap with *einzel* ('single'), *nen schritte* ('steps'), and *durch* ('through') and using a hand shape with fingers 2–5 flapped down and a PD orientation, ME produces a series of three strokes with an arced movement away from the body. By successively positioning the hands in different regions in front of her body, ME gesturally represents the single steps as different regions in gesture space. Similar as in the example "villages", the gestural repetition creates similar yet different points in gesture space by maintaining all the form features throughout the succession except the position in gesture space. Another example for this type of reduplication is taken from the parliamentary debate of the German Bundestag on July 3rd 2015, in which the parties discuss retirement age in Germany. The politician Markus Kurth from the German Party "Bündnis 90/Die Grünen" explains a proposal submitted by his party on how to create more flexibility

3.2 A closer look: Repetitions and their structural and semantic characteristics — 81

for employees to retire at different ages while allowing part-time jobs. This proposal, Kurth points out, allows employees to be more flexible and self-determined in designing the last years of their career and, in particular, allows for employees to work past the usual retirement age. Thus, the proposal includes 'also those employees that are healthy and fit and would like to work past the retirement age and can do so' (*auch die Beschäftigten die tatsächlich das Glück haben fit zu sein, die über die Regelaltersgrenze hinaus arbeiten möchten und das auch können*). While uttering *auch die Beschäftigten* ('also those employees'), Kurth produces a gestural reduplication consisting of three strokes during which the right flat hand with a lateral orientation moves along the horizontal axis from left to right in small arced movements (see Figure 21; Bressem, submitted).

A similar move along the horizontal axis is illustrated in an example in which the mathematician Christian Hesse tells the story of the inventor of the chess game, a wise Brahmin, who thought the game to his maharajah. As a reward, the maharajah granted the Brahmin one wish. The Brahmin demanded 'one grain of wheat for the first field of the chessboard, two for the second, four for the third, and always the double amount' (*ein Weizenkorn für das erste Feld auf dem Schachbrett, zwei für das zweite, vier für das dritte und immer die doppelte Anzahl*). When mentioning the individual numbers, Christian Hesse produces a series of pointing gestures through which he visually highlights the amount specified in the verbal utterance. Subsequently while uttering 'and always the double amount' (*und immer die doppelte Anzahl*), he executes a gestural reduplication in which the flat right hand with a palm lateral orientation is moved along the horizontal axis from left to right in three arced movements. The three strokes of the repetition align with the conjunction 'and' and the first and the second syllable of the adverb 'always' (Bressem, submitted).

Regardless of whether reduplications of type B are produced with the modes "objects in spatial relation" or "spatial relation only", in both cases, different regions in gesture space are used to depict the relation of objects or states to one another. In all these cases, the position in gesture space does not have a concrete meaning: Different areas in front of the speaker's body do not mime perceived relations between objects in the real world but are used for creating structural relations between gestures (Müller, Bressem & Ladewig, 2013; Sowa, 2005). As such, reduplications exemplify a non-mimetic use of gesture space (Müller, Bressem & Ladewig, 2013). Due to the fact that the parameter "position" does not represent relations in the real world, it is semantically free and can be charged with other functions. The semantic unloading of the form parameter "position" thus allows for a structural function in the case of gestural reduplications: Through spatial cohesion, perceived spatial relations and structural relations between the successive strokes emerge (Sowa, 2005, p. 115ff). As such, the different regions in gesture space are used to mark plurality. The individual strokes in the reduplication solely mark individual areas in gesture space. These are understood as different yet similar areas in space based on particular form characteristics (gestural form features, length of the unit) through which temporal and spatial contiguity and similarity between the individual strokes become apparent and thus a coherent structure or Gestalt arises (see chapter 6 for a more detailed discussion). Moreover, a diagrammatic iconic relation between the different strokes arises in which relations of forms are mapped onto relations of meanings: More of the same gestural form leads to a change in the semantic complexity (Jakobson, 1966; Peirce, 1960). Consequently, the gestural sequence is iconic in relation to quantity and complexity: one space vs. many spaces (see Figure 21). In combination with the verbal utterance, the meaning of the gestural construction is enriched (Enfield 2009). In all instances documented, speakers refer to multiple instances of the same aspect (e.g., single steps, each house, different villages, employees, double amount). As a result, the meaning of gestural sequence is enriched and the notion of multitude and plurality emerges. Due to all of these aforementioned characteristics, repetitions of this kind can be considered as a coherent and complex gestural unit, a gestural reduplication. The repetition of gestural material results in the creation of a complex gestural meaning: the conceptualization and construal of plurality as different areas in gesture space (see chapter 7 for a more detailed discussion).

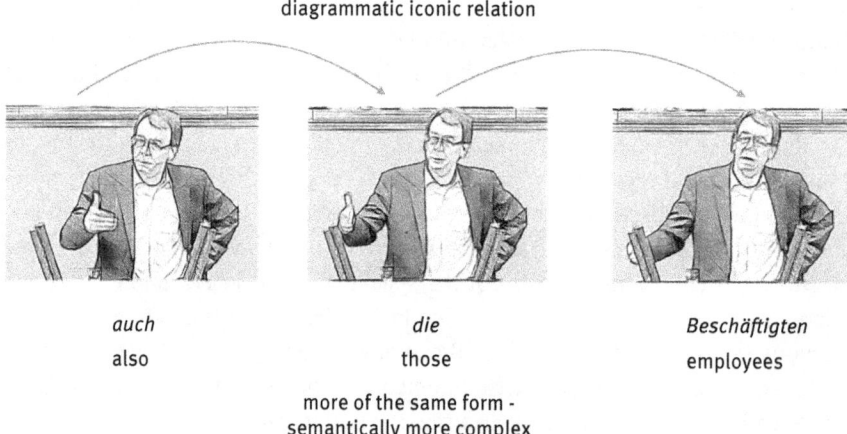

Figure 21: Diagrammatic iconic relation in gestural reduplication.

3.2 A closer look: Repetitions and their structural and semantic characteristics — 83

Contrary to other cases of non-mimetic uses of gesture space, in which the hands are successively moved upwards in gesture space to express intensification (Müller, Bressem & Ladewig, 2013, p. 725), for instance, in reduplications of type B documented in the present corpus, the hands are either moved downwards (e.g., example 5 "single steps") or in the lateral dimension while maintaining the same height in gesture space (examples "same schema", "different villages" or "employees"). Accordingly, although both grammatical notions, namely intensification and plurality, make use of the parameter "position", the characteristics in the use of the gesture space differ.

The preceding section has shown that the gestural repetitions documented in the corpus differ in the processes of sign creation (gestural modes of representation), the types of gestures (recurrent gestures vs. singular gestures), and thus in the gestural meaning expressed (concrete vs. abstract meaning) (see Table 13). Accordingly, the present chapter was able to empirically support the assumption presented in chapter 1 of the book, namely that repetitions in gestures show different characteristics on the level of form and meaning and that characteristics of form are grounded in differences in meaning.

Table 13: Most frequent mimetic modes, gestural meanings and gesture types for iterations and reduplications.

Type of Repetition	Level of Meaning – Gesture and Speech			
	Gesture Phases	Mimetic Mode	Gestural Meaning	Gesture Type
Iteration	prep-stroke	487 (53%) acting	abstract (action, prosodic)	recurrent gestures
	stroke-stroke	322 (35%) acting	concrete (action, object)	concrete referential gestures
Reduplication A	stroke-stroke	65 (7%) representing	abstract (movement)	abstract referential gestures
Reduplication B	stroke-stroke	47 (7%) representing	abstract (place)	abstract referential gestures
		n= 921 (100%)		

3.3 Summary

Based on a corpus-linguistic analysis, a cognitive-semantic classification of gestural repetitions was proposed in this chapter: 1) Iterations, in which the repetition of gestural material results in the repeated recurrence of one and the same meaning and does not lead to the construction of a complex gestural meaning. 2) Reduplications, in which the repetition of gestural material results in a complex gestural meaning and coherent reduplicative construction. The construction is understood as a complex sign schema which "possesses an independent meaning [. . .] that is describable as a 'potential for semiosis' also independently of particular contexts of utterances" (Schneider, 2015, p. 133 translation JB). The chapter grounded the classification in specific structural and semantic aspects characteristic for iterations and reduplications, which sets them apart as distinct ways of building patterns in the gestural modality.

Picking up on means of creating gestural complexity introduced in chapter 2, the chapter has first discussed how gestural repetitions construe complexity on the linear level, and, in particular, focused on the types and lengths of gestural movement sequences. It was shown that gestural iterations and reduplications show commonalities as well as differences in their gesture phase characteristics. Whereas iterations either consist of preparations-stroke sequences or stroke-stroke sequences, reduplications solely consist of stroke-stroke sequences. As a result, sequences of strokes without inserted preparation phases show a stronger degree of unity and, thus, a more complex gestural meaning than strokes that are separated by preparation phases. Moreover, in iterations and reduplication different structural and functional gestural units are created: Iterations may either consist of several gesture phrases (preparation-stroke sequences) or single gesture phrases (stroke-stroke sequences). Reduplications, however, solely construct single gesture phrases consisting of several strokes. Based on the distribution in the corpus, it was concluded that repeating gestures in order to merely repeat a gestural meaning several times is the most common type, whereas the use of repetitions to create a reduplicative construction, namely a complex gestural meaning, as in the case of reduplications, is a less frequent use of gestural repetitions. Furthermore, it was shown that this difference in gestural movement phases is also reflected in the length of the sequences, which is how many strokes a repetitive sequence is composed of. Here, both types of gestural repetitions (iteration and reduplication) clearly show preferences and a particular distribution on the linear level: The majority of repetitions were composed of two-three strokes. Only iterations showed a greater range in their length of up to 9 strokes and more. Based on this distribution, it was concluded that for reduplications the number of repetitions seems to be limited.

Following the complexity on the linear level, the chapter focused on the simultaneous complexity (formational features) and discussed the semantics of iterations and reduplications. Here, the clear preferences and particular distribution that was identified on the linear level was also attested, thus marking both types as distinct patterns: Firstly, it was shown that gestural repetitions, in general, do not change in more than two parameters at a time. Furthermore, iterations and reduplications differ in the number of changing parameters. Whereas in iterations, gestural forms remain constant or change in one or two parameters across the sequence, in reduplications form features always change. Depending on the type of reduplication either one or two parameters are affected. If form features change, they occur only in particular parameters, namely movement and position. These changes are thereby particularly distributed: 1) In iterations, the quality and direction of the movement as well as the position in gesture space change. 2) In reduplications of type A, only the direction of the movement and the position in gesture space change. And 3) in reduplications of type B, only the positioning of the hands in gesture space varies. The analysis of the form features has thus shown that if repetitions differ, they do so in a small number and only in particular parameters. Moreover, the distribution of changes in a parameter is distinctive for the different types of repetitions. It was concluded that the instantiation of the same features across sequences of gestures causes a connection between the gestural units (Fricke 2012) and is thus necessary to mark the sequence of strokes as belonging to one gestural repetition.

In the following, the chapter questioned whether the afore documented differences in form result in meaning differences. Based on the assumption that gestures are motivated form Gestalts, it was addressed how and which kind of gestural meaning is created in repetitions, whether iterations and reduplications show common as well as different meanings, and how these differences in meaning may be reflected in the distribution across gestures types. Based on the gestural modes of representation, iterations and reduplications were analyzed in their basic techniques of meaning creation. Here, a rather clear-cut distribution across iterations and reduplications was stated: Whereas iterations predominantly use the acting mode, for reduplications the representing mode is most frequent. Moreover, for iterations with preparation-stroke sequences "acting with unspecified object" and frequent use of recurrent gestures was noted. As a result, in these sequences, abstract meanings prevail. For iterations with stroke-stroke sequences, however, "acting with specified object" and singular gestures were most frequent. These sequences primarily depict a) objects through handling them, b) actions with objects, and c) actions. Accordingly, in iterations with stroke-stroke sequences, concrete meanings are most common. For reduplications, overwhelming use of representing mode and singular gestures depicting abstract objects, events, states, or processes was documented. Furthermore, the chapter demonstrated that reduplications of type A and B differ in the specific modes of representation as well as in the meaning expressed. For reduplications of type A primarily the mode 'motion and path' was documented. Accordingly, it was concluded that these sequences embody the spatial and temporal basis of the "Aktionsart" 'iterativity' and recreate the lexical basis of a grammatical concept. The majority of reduplications of type B however mime 'spatial relations only' and through the use of different regions in gesture space depict the relation of objects or states to one another. It was concluded that these repetitions exemplify a non-mimetic use of gesture space by which the gestural conceptualization and construal of plurality as different areas in gesture space arises.

Based on these results, it was concluded that in iterations the same meaning is repeated in reduplications. However, a new and complex meaning is created. Regardless of whether the ring gesture in example 1 ("weapons of mass destruction") is repeated two, ten, or twenty times: each stroke expresses marks arguments as precise. The same is true for the depiction of objects or actions illustrated example 2 ("Arko") and 3 ("metal thing"). Regardless of the number of strokes, each stroke either depicts the scraping action of the dog or molds the bent shape of the bottle holder. Yet, in reduplications, the meaning of the whole repetitive sequence is not just the mere repetition of the meaning of the individual sub-strokes. Rather, the whole sequence of strokes creates a new, complex gestural meaning , in which the meaning of the whole repetitive sequence is not identical to the meaning of its parts. Based on the meaning of individual strokes, a new and complex meaning arises. In the constructions documented in the present corpus, this complex sign schema either expresses the lexical basis of a grammatical concept or expresses a grammatical notion. For an overview of the results, see Figure 22.

The presented results thereby clearly demonstrated that the gestural modes of representation "open a systematic access to the study of the creation of bodily signs and gestural meaning constitution." (Müller, 2010b, p. 179 translation JB) They reconstruct the practices of gestural mimesis and provide a first step towards the embodied basis of gestural meaning and such are vital both for the producing and perceiving gestures. Although gestures, as motivated form Gestalt, express schematic meaning independent of the verbal utterance, the chapter has also illustrated that speech is needed to determine and specify the gestural meaning of the repetitions. Accordingly, the twofold cognitive-semantic classification of repetitions is further explicated and supported in the following two chapters. After discussing what is known about multimodal utterances and the temporal and semantic relation of speech and gesture, Chapter 4 shows that iterations and reduplications affect the semantics of the verbal utterance in particular ways.

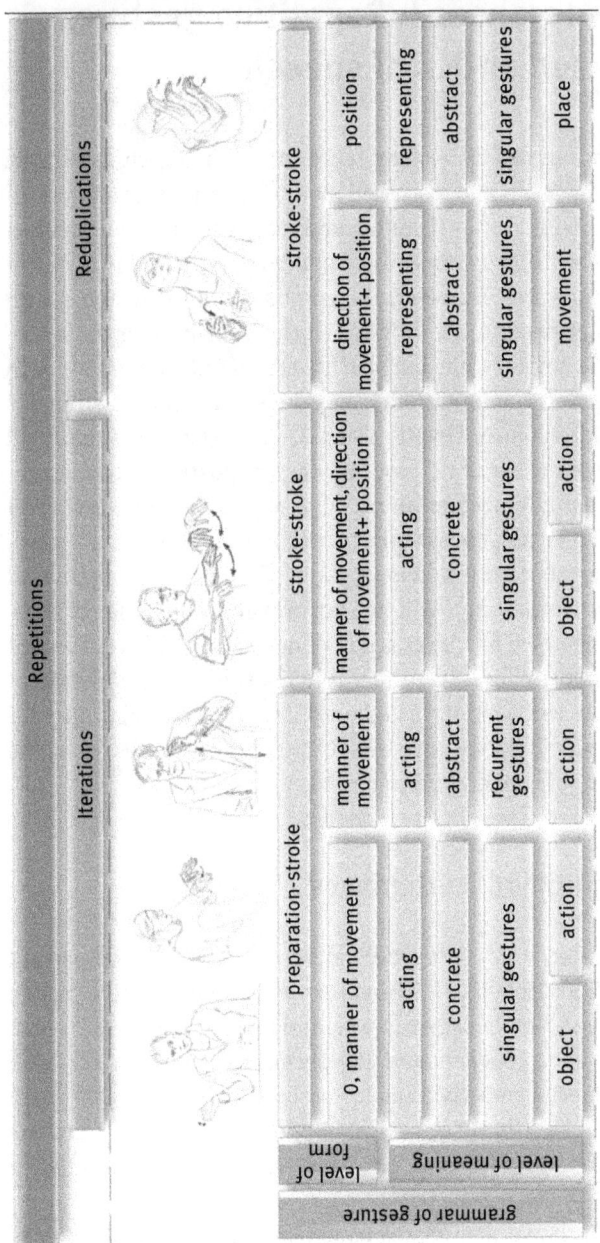

Figure 22: Overview of iterations and reduplications and their form and meaning.

4 Multimodal utterances I: Repetitive gestures affecting the semantics of speech

The previous chapter concentrated on gestural repetitions from a gesture-intrinsic perspective ('grammar' of gesture) and discussed their basic properties and principles. It demonstrated that both classes (iteration and reduplication) show distinct characteristics and thus exemplify two means of building patterns with different complexity in co-speech gestures. However, if a corpus-based study and usage-based approach aims at answering not only the question of how repetitive sequences in gestures build complex units but also how these units interrelate with spoken syntagms, a consideration of gestural repetitions in relation to speech is needed. As has been pointed out in chapter 1 and 3, gestures show a tight link with the speech on the levels of semantics, syntax, and pragmatics and are essential for creating multimodal utterance meaning. As a result, the present chapter focuses on gestural repetitions and their connection with the semantics of speech. With this, the chapter expands the previous point of view to a usage-based multimodal grammar. In particular, it will be shown that both classes of repetition achieve specific relevance for the creation of multimodal utterances and utterance meaning and as such signal different degrees of semantic integration. For this, the chapter will first discuss the notion of multimodal utterances from a cognitive-linguistic perspective and discuss how gestures affect the semantics and pragmatics of spoken utterances.

4.1 The notion of multimodal utterances

Chapter 1 has introduced the notion that speech and gesture are integral parts of language use (Kendon, 1980; McNeill, 1992) and that both modes are interrelated on several of levels. The relation between speech and gesture is thereby "reciprocal" such that the "gestural component and the spoken component *interact* with one another to create a precise and vivid understanding" (Kendon, 2004, p. 174 emphasis in original). As shortly discussed in chapter 1, speech and gesture achieve this through two main principles: temporal and semantic coordination with syntagms in speech.

Early on, research has shown that the temporal relation of gestures and body movement in general is, depending on the type of verbal unit, hierarchically organized and shows a "precise correlation between changes of body motion and the articulated patterns of speech stream." (Condon & Ogston, 1967, p. 227) As such, body movements may align with 'sub-phones', phones, syllables, words, phrases, and higher-level units. Moreover, gesture phrases, that is sequences of preparations, strokes, and holds correspond to tone units in speech. In contrast, gesture units, that is gesture phrases including retractions correspond to locutions, i.e., groupings of tone units (Kendon, 1972). Accordingly, it is assumed that "the pattern of movement that co-occurs with the speech has a hierarchic organization which appears to match that of the speech units" (Kendon, 1972, p. 190) in such a manner that the larger the speech unit, the more body parts are involved:

> sweeps of the arms or movements of the head may be sustained over larger linguistic units, such as phrases, while eye shifts, wrist and finger movements occur over smaller segments, such as syllables. (Kendon, 1972, p. 183)

Moreover, phases of gestural movement, in particular preparation phases, begin in advance to their associated verbal units and strokes are usually completed either before the nucleus of the tone unit or just at its onset (Kendon, 1980). Therefore, the speech production process is "manifested in two forms of activity simultaneously", namely in speech and gestures (Kendon, 1972, p. 205). Despite contradictory positions on the precedence of gestural segments to the verbal utterance (e.g., Butterworth, Beattie, Robin, & Philip, 1978; Butterworth & Hadar, 1989; de Ruiter, 1998; Krauss, Yihusiu, & Purnima, 1996), it is generally assumed that onsets of strokes only rarely precede co-expressive speech but rather align with the semantic nucleus of the verbal utterance: Preparations usually come before the corresponding linguistic element, strokes coincide with it, and holds ensure the temporal synchrony of speech and gesture (Kita, 1990; Kita, van Gijn, & van der Hulst, 1998).

> The nucleus of the gesture phrase, that is, the stroke and any hold that may follow it, tends to be performed in such a way that it is done at the same time, or nearly at the same time as the pronunciation of the word or word cluster that constitutes the nucleus, in a semantic sense, of the spoken phrase. This means that, by coordinating temporally the nucleus of the gesture phrase (i.e. the stroke and any post-stroke hold) with the semantic nucleus of the spoken expression, the speaker achieves a conjunction of two different modes of expression which, as we have said, also have semantic coherence one with the other. (Kendon, 2004, p. 124f)

The semantic coherence of both modalities is achieved through a common underlying conceptualization. Adam Kendon refers to this as the "idea unit", a meaning unit above the lexical meaning, underlying the multimodal utterances (Kendon, 1940, 2004a). David McNeill calls it the "growth point", the initial form of a thinking-for-speaking unit out of which a process of organization of speech and gesture emerges (McNeill, 1992, 2005). As a result, speech and gesture present more or less the same meaning, have one pragmatic reference at a time (McNeill 1992, 2005), yet while doing so never express identical aspects.

> Two core features of gestures are that they carry meaning, and that they and the synchronous speech are *co-expressive*. Co-expressive, but not redundant: gesture and speech express the same underlying idea unit but express it in their own ways – their own aspects of it, and when they express overlapping aspects so do in distinctive ways. They are also synchronous at the exact point where they are also co-expressive. Co-expressive symbols, spoken and gestured, are presented by the speaker at the same time – a single underlying idea in speech and gesture simultaneously. The synchrony is crucial, because it implies that, at the moment of speaking, the mind is doing the same thing in two ways, not two separate things [. . .].
> (Mc-Neill, 2005, p. 22f, emphasis in original)

Co-expressiveness is determined by assuming that

> both the speech segment and the visible behavior had to be interpretable as collectively referring to the same thing. [. . .] It had to be possible to specify a single conceptual category [. . .] that the spoken and visible elements collectively referred to.
> (Engle, 2000, p. 26)

This may be a single word or phrase ("lexical affiliate" [Schegloff, 1984]) deemed to correspond most closely to a gesture in meaning or a larger speech segment that may include a lexical affiliate: "It is possible that a co-expressive segment might be a lexical affiliate, but there is no necessity for it" (McNeill, 2005, p. 37) and slight temporal distance between speech and gesture is possible (De Ruiter, 2000; Sowa, 2005). The arising semantic relation between speech and gesture can thereby best be understood in terms of a "continuum of co-expressivity" (Bergmann, Aksu, & Kopp, 2011, p. 1) with speech and gesture encoding the same aspect as one end and with both modalities encoding different elements as the other end of the continuum (see Figure 23):

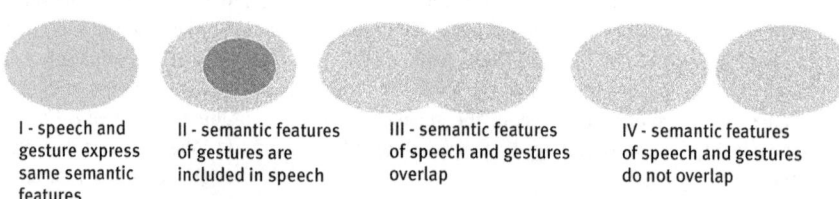

I - speech and gesture express same semantic features
II - semantic features of gestures are included in speech
III - semantic features of speech and gestures overlap
IV - semantic features of speech and gestures do not overlap

Figure 23: Continuum of co-expressivity between gestural and verbal meaning (adapted from (Gut, Looks, Thies, & Gibbon, 2002, p. 9).

I – speech and gesture express the same semantic features (redundancy): The meaning of speech and gesture may be "identical, i.e., meaning [s] = meaning [g]" (Gut et al., 2002, p. 8)

II – semantic features of gestures are included among the set of semantic features expressed in speech (redundancy): The semantic features in both

modalities differ. The co-expressive speech segment has additional semantic features not expressed in gesture. Gestural semantic features are included among the set of speech.
III – semantic features of speech and gestures overlap (complementation): Speech and gesture share semantic features yet also carry features that are not expressed by the other modality. The meaning of the gesture contributes to the verbal meaning "thus forming a subset of the meaning of the superordinate modality, namely speech" (Gut et al., 2002, p. 8).
IV – semantic features of speech and gesture do not overlap (contradiction): Both modalities carry different semantic features.[56]

Based on these semantic relations, gestures may either illustrate and emphasize what has already been uttered verbally, soften or slightly alter the verbal meaning, replace the verbal meaning, or create a discrepancy between the gestural and verbal meaning (e.g., Engle, 2000; Freedman, 1977; Fricke, 2007, 2012; Gerwing & Allison, 2009; Gut et al., 2002; Kendon, 1987, 2004a; Kipp, 2004; McNeill, 1992, 2005; Müller, 1998; Scherer, 1979). In doing so, gestures are particularly apt in transmitting information about semantic features such as entity, relative position, action, direction, path, shape, size, amount, or property (Beattie & Heather, 2001; Beattie & Shovelton, 1999, 2007; Bergmann et al., 2011; Cienki, 1998b, 2005; Cienki & Mittelberg, 2013; Engle, 2000; Holler & Beattie, 2003; Kok, Bergmann, Cienki, & Kopp, 2016; Lascarides & Stone, 2006; Lücking, 2013; Mittelberg, 2010, 2014; Müller, 1998, 2009, 2010; Sowa, 2005). In this process, gestures "are not limited to primarily depicting specific situations or individuals" but "can be used to depict types or kinds of things, like prototypes" (Engle, 2000, p. 39) and may single out exemplar interpretations by picking out a specific individual from a collection mentioned in speech (Engle, 2000). Gestures can thus refer to a meaning or concept associated with a word: a prototype or an intended object of reference. Because such gestures are not always and only tied to the representation of referents in the real world but are also capable of seemingly contradicting the intended object of reference (Fricke, 2007, 2012, 2014).[57] In addition to specifying objects, gestures very frequently differentiate actions. The gestural depiction is thereby often not only a

---

56 For similar distinctions see Bergmann et al. (2011), Bressem, Ladewig, & Müller (2013), Freedman (1977), Kendon (2004a), Scherer (1979).
57 De Ruiter (2000) assumes a similar function when stating that iconic gestures are related to the mental concept.

> kinesic equivalent of the lexical verb but is an enactment which displays a specific form of action often, also, displaying something of the manner of the action. In such cases the gesture adds referential information for it makes the utterance have a much more specific meaning. [. . .].
>
> (Kendon, 2004a, p. 185)

Gestures thus seem to be well suited for the depiction of actions, the representation of forms and sizes but less for representing colors (Fricke, 2007; Kendon, 2004a; McNeill, 1992; Müller, 1998). Accordingly, while working towards a joint utterance meaning, gesture and speech refer to and represent such aspects which are most suitably expressed in the respective modality. As a result, gestures embody elements of the verbal meaning, mark salient information, and highlight and foreground information in the flow of discourse (Alibali & Kita, 2010; Andrén, 2010; Goodwin, 2000; Ladewig, 2020; Müller & Tag, 2010).[58]

This tight structural, semantic, and functional link of both modalities also results in the ability of speech and gesture to adapt their performance to meet the necessities of articulating both modalities at the same time. The adaptation of speech and gesture may lead a) to a repetition or revision of the whole gesture-speech ensemble, b) a change of the gestural performance to meet the structure of the spoken discourse, c) an adjustment of the speech performance to the requirements of the gestural expression, or d) an addition or change of the gestural component to adapt to speech (Kendon, 1983, 2004a). This mutual adaption of both modalities underlines that speech and gesture build a functional unit that is achieved by the speakers:

> In creating an utterance that uses both modes of expression, the speaker creates an *ensemble* in which gesture and speech are employed together as *partners* in a single rhetoric enterprise. [. . .] This is why we prefer to say that the semantically coherent speech-gesture *ensemble* is a speaker *achievement*. The relationship between the gestural component and the speech component in the utterance does not seem well understood as a simple causal relationship, where the one is dependent upon the other in some kind of unchanging way.
>
> (Kendon, 2004a, p. 127, emphasis in original)

---

58 A recent study by Ladewig (2014c, 2020) has shown that these semantic functions are not specific to gestures in temporal overlap with speech but also for gestures used in substitutive function. Gestures occurring in syntactic gaps, first and foremost, substitute nouns and verbs and function either as objects or predicates of multimodal noun and verb phrases. As a result, gestures either foreground semantic information about a) objects or b) actions (see also chapter 4). This substitutive function of gestures is thereby not a particular characteristic of emblems, as so far generally assumed (Efron, 1972; Ekman, 1976; Ekman & Friesen, 1972), but rather a function that can and is fulfilled by a range of gestures types but in particular by singular gestures. "According to these findings, not gestures that exhibit a word-like status and a stable form-meaning relationship like emblems are deployed to fill in syn-tactic gaps but gestures that gain their full meaning only through the simultaneous occurrence of speech." (Ladewig, 2020).

Thus, it can be concluded that gestures are a dynamic resource in the meaning-making process. Moreover,

> gestures coming along with speech do not constitute a separate and closed sign system, as they are often created spontaneously and they are always a matter of language use. In this sense, they are part of the dynamic flow of attention in communication.
>
> (Müller, Bressem, & Ladewig, 2013, p. 711)

Following Enfield (2009), speech and gesture can thus be considered "composite signals" and elements of "composite utterances" that "are interpreted through the recognition and bringing together of these multiple signs under a pragmatic unity heuristic or co-relevance principle, i.e. an interpreter's steadfast presumption of pragmatic unity despite semiotic complexity." (Enfield, 2009, p. 15)

4.2 Repeating gestures: Emphasizing and altering speech

In chapter 3, a cognitive-semantic classification of gestural repetitions was introduced. It was highlighted that both classes of repetitions achieve particular relevance for the creation of multimodal utterances and utterance meaning and as such signal different degrees of semantic integration. The following section of the chapter will zoom in on this in more detail and address the semantic relation of both classes of repetitions with speech. Moreover, the reasons for why both classes show different depths of semantic integration will be discussed. For this, the temporal and semantic relation of speech and gestures will be investigated. The section above has highlighted that two main principles are essential for creating multimodal utterance meaning (temporal and semantic coordination with speech). As a result, the chapter begins with discussing the temporal relation of iterations and reduplication with the semantically corresponding spoken part. The goal is to see whether the different types of repetitions occur before, with, or after the co-expressive speech. Afterward, their semantic relation is taken up and the different degrees of co-expressivity are discussed (see Figure 23).[59] For this, the chapter

---

[59] In order to capture the semantic properties of gestural repetitions and speech, each gestural repetition and the co-occurring verbal utterance was characterized in their semantic potential using the following semantic features that are based on Beattie & Shovelton (1999, 2001, 2007) and Bergmann et al. (2011): 1) ACTION determines actual actions (e.g., the scraping action of a dog in the example "Arko"), 2) MANNER describes particular characteristics of actions (e.g., performing a writing action while depicting the holding of a pen), 3) POSITION determines spatial information (e.g., example "single steps", in which the hands are successively placed in different regions of the gesture space), 4) ENTITY determines concrete objects (e.g.,

concentrates on those types of repetitions that affect the semantics of speech or stand in close relation with it. Accordingly, iterations depicting actions and objects (Figure 15 example 2, Figure 16 example 3) as well as both types of reduplications (Figure 17 example 4, Figure 18 example 5) will be discussed. Gestural iterations with abstract meaning (Figure 14 example 1) are excluded because they do not affect the lexical-semantics of the multimodal utterance.[60]

In summary, the study does not bring to light surprising results concerning the temporal relation of gestures with the spoken component but rather confirms what is already known: The large majority of gestural repetitions, irrespective of the type, are produced in parallel, that is, simultaneous, with the semantically-related part of speech and thus temporarily align with the co-expressive parts of the verbal utterance (72%). 19% of gestural repetitions occur before the spoken counterpart. Post-positioning of gestures, that is, gestures being executed after the semantically corresponding speech is rare and only accounted for 6% of cases (see Table 14). All of the examples discussed in chapter 3 illustrate the most frequent pattern: iterations and reduplications being produced in parallel with the corresponding speech segment (see Table 15).

A closer look at particular types of iterations and reduplications does not reveal a complete deviation from the general pattern. Still, it shows an interesting distribution: Although pre-positioning, that is repetitions occurring before

---

handles, rain drops) as well as abstract concepts (e.g., single steps in making a decision), 5) SHAPE determines the shape of an entity (e.g., example "metal thing" and the gestural depiction of the bent shape of a metal object), 6) PROPERTY determines colors or materials of entities, 7) SIZE determines the size of entities, 8) MULTITUDE describes the number of entities involved (e.g., different steps in the example "single steps"), 9) MOVEMENT determines the movement of entities (e.g., objects being sent back and forth in the example "send back and forth"), 10) DIRECTION determines the direction of movement (e.g., example "send back and forth"). Using the semantic features listed above, it was possible to compare the semantic information contained in speech and gesture and determine the semantic relation of the gestural repetitions to the verbal utterance.

60 As discussed in chapter 3, this type of iteration expresses abstract meaning. By taking over "parsing" function (Kendon, 2004a, p. 159ff), these gestures contribute to the marking of various aspects of the structure of spoken discourse and provide visible anchor points for connecting or separating parts of discourse (see also McNeill, 1992). Accordingly, Kendon has discussed pragmatic gestures with discursive function as "discourse unit markers", highlighting the fact that gestures may be able to "mark discourse units differentially as *topic* in contrast to *comment*" and may serve to "mark discourse units which are 'focal' to the theme or argument of what is being said" (Kendon, 1995, p. 248 emphasis in original). In doing so, gestures with pragmatic functions may have the same functions as discourse markers or rising intonation in spoken language (Bavelas Beavin, Chovil, Lawrie, & Wade, 1992). For recent studies on this topic see Bressem, Stein, & Wegener (2015), Lempert (2011), Wehling (2018).

4.2 Repeating gestures: Emphasizing and altering speech — 95

Table 14: Temporal positioning of gestural repetitions with the co-expressive speech.

Type of Repetition	Level of Syntactics – Gesture and Speech	
	Gesture Phases	Temporal positioning
Iteration	prep-stroke	487	parallel
		(53%)	(81%)
			pre-positioned
			(15%)
	stroke-stroke	322	parallel
		(35%)	(58%)
			pre-positioned
			(28%)
Reduplication A	stroke-stroke	65	parallel
		(7%)	(94%)
Reduplication B	stroke-stroke	47	parallel
		(5%)	(94%)
	n= 921 (100%)		

the co-expressive speech, is documented for all types of repetitions, it is only frequent for iterations. 15% of preparation-stroke sequences and 27% of stroke-stroke sequences are produced before speech. Let us consider the following three examples as exemplary cases for the pre-positioning of iterations. In all of the examples, speakers anticipate the meaning of the semantic nucleus in advance to the corresponding speech segment when depicting concrete actions and objects.

In the first example, a woman tries to explain a particular type of handle that is used in bathtubs to facilitate getting out of a bathtub (*jetzt erinnere mich in den Hotels dass du in den Badewannen diese Griffe hast, die dir sozusagen helfen, wenn du dein Bad genommen hast wieder aus der Wanne rauszukommen* ['now I remember in hotels you have those handles in the bathtub that kind of help you to get out the tub after you took a bath']). While saying *dass du in den Badewannen diese Griffe hast* ('that you have those handles in the bathtub'), speaker BS produces two iterations made up of three strokes each, which represent the handle of the bathtub by using a hand shape with fingers bent and palm upwards which is moved up and down successively (see Figure 30). The first iteration is produced in temporal synchrony to *in den Badewannen* ('in the bathtubs'), thus pre-positioned to the corresponding speech segment 'handle'. Only the second iteration, by spanning the phrase *diese Griffe hast* ('have these

Table 15: Temporal relation of speech and gestures in examples 1–5.

Type of Repetition	Gesture Phases	Temporal positioning	Example	Temporal relation of speech and gesture – parallel / Example						
Iteration	prep-stroke	parallel	Example "weapons of mass destruction"	wenn sie	d	ˈA	s	–	-ER	Nst	meinen,
				if you	t	h	is	–	ser	iously	take
				stroke				stroke			
			Example "Arko"	rennt	er in	flur	kr	A	A	tzt	–
				runs	into the	hall	scr	a	a	pes	–
				stroke				stroke			
	stroke-stroke	parallel	Example "Metal thing"	wo die	flasche w	da in	metAllding	drinne is,			
				where the	bottle wine	in such a	metal thing	is			
					ˈEIN som						
					stroke	stroke	stroke				

4.2 Repeating gestures: Emphasizing and altering speech

Reduplication	parallel	Example					
stroke-stroke	parallel	Example "send back and forth"	dinge immer	zwischen zwei ÄM	mtern hin und	hErschi	ickt; send;
			always things	between two off	ices back	and forth	send;
				stroke	stroke	stroke	
stroke-stroke	parallel	Example "single steps"	kannste dir ja immer die	Einzel schritte	nen d'U		URCHlesen,
			you can always the	single	steps read		through
				stroke	stroke	stroke	

handles'), occurs in parallel with the lexical affiliate of the gesture, namely "handles" (see Table 4.3.). Therefore, the gestural repetition starts before the actual semantic nucleus of the gesture-speech ensemble and thus anticipates the spoken meaning in advance (see chapter 6 for a detailed discussion of this example and its relevance for a multimodal nature of attention and salience). The second example illustrates a similar pattern. Here, a woman talks about a special behavior of her dog with a particular family member.[61] While describing the successive actions of the dog to get the grandmother to fulfill a particular action, speaker MO utters *und geht von hinten mit die Schnauze immer an die Beene stubsen* ('and from behind he always pokes her legs with his snout') and produces a series of three strokes which depict the poking action of a dog. The three strokes co-occur with *von hinten mit die Schnauze immer an die* ('from behind always with the snout on the') and well before the semantic nucleus, namely the verb "poke" (see Table 4.3.). More importantly, however, the verb "poke" is uttered after executing the gestural repetition, namely when the hands already returned to the rest position. Similarly, as in the example "handles", the gestural repetition spans a rather large portion of the preceding verbal utterance and its relevance for the repetition only becomes visible after it has ended and the corresponding verb "poke" has been uttered. The iteration therefore clearly anticipates the semantic nucleus of the gesture-speech ensemble in advance. Example 3 also illustrates this gesture-speech pattern: Speaker MK produces an iteration of four strokes during which he produces a circling movement with a stretched index finger and the palm of the hand oriented towards the body while uttering *sie nicht durchdrehen im Winter* ('they [car wheels] don't spin during winter'). The first two strokes precede the verb "spin", the lexical affiliate of the gesture. Only the two following strokes are produced in parallel with semantic nucleus of the verbo-gestural utterance.

In all of the examples, the gestural repetition starts in advance to the co-expressive speech segment. Yet, at one point, speech and gesture coincide with the syntactical unit of the verbal utterance which most closely relates to the gestural meaning expressed (verbs "spin" and "poke", noun "handle"). (See chapter 5 for a detailed discussion of gestures with the syntax of speech.) In cases of post-positioning, it is the other way around. Here, gestural repetitions start with the semantically closest syntactical unit and end later. For instance, when speaker MB explains that when dogs have mites or fleas, they often scratch their ear, he produces a longer iteration depicting the scraping action of dogs (*und dann kratzen die sich permanent am Ohr* ['and then they permanently scratch their ear']).

---

[61] This example occurs right before example 1 "Arko" described in chapter 3 but is produced by a different speaker.

The sequence includes 13 strokes that start with *und dann* ('and then') ending with *Ohr* ('ear'). 7 of the 13 strokes are executed after the verb "scratch" is uttered and are thus produced in post-positioning to co-expressive speech segment.

The results presented for the temporal positioning of gestural repetitions confirm existing results for the temporal relation of speech and gesture: strokes tend to occur with the co-expressive speech segment. Yet, the documented differences in the temporal positioning raise interesting questions on the correlation of speech and gesture in the different types of repetitions. The low number of pre-or post-positioning in reduplications (6%) suggests that reduplications have a stronger temporal connection with their lexical affiliate. Iterations, however, seem to vary in this respect as they occur simultaneously but also frequently appear before the semantically corresponding part of the verbal utterance, thus anticipating the semantic nucleus of the verbo-gestural utterance. These differences may be an indication for a different semantic and syntactic integration of the gestures into speech. Moreover, based on these results, we can assume that repetitions either emphasize the verbal utterance by expressing similar semantic features or by modifying the semantics of the spoken utterance by adding new semantic information. These aspects will be discussed in the following sections of this chapter and in chapter 5. Based on the temporal relation of speech and gesture, the remaining chapter discusses the type of semantic integration. It examines whether and what kinds of semantic functions iterations and reduplications assume for the verbal utterance and in creating a multimodal utterance meaning.

Similar to the temporal relation, a rather clear-cut picture is revealed for the semantic relation: Gestural repetitions either emphasize the semantics of speech by expressing redundant semantic features or they complement the verbal utterance by adding semantic features. Furthermore, this functional distinction is reflected in the different types of repetitions: Iterations predominantly modify the verbal utterance. Reduplications, however, mostly express redundant meaning (see Table 17). Whereas reduplications thus take over an emphasizing function by expressing redundant semantic information, iterations contribute fundamentally to the creation of a multimodal utterance meaning by carrying semantic information not present in speech. The semantics of the utterance is thus not only reinforced by the gestural repetition but, in fact, considerably complemented so that the gestures are semantically more important for the creation of the multimodal utterance meaning. The different types of repetitions thus take over distinct roles in the creation of a multimodal utterance meaning. The reasons why repetitions fulfill such different functions and roles in the multimodal meaning will be discussed shortly. Let us first consider the semantic potential of iterations and reduplications in more detail.

Table 16: Examples of gestural repetitions occurring before the co-expressive speech.

Type of Repetition	Gesture Phases	Temporal positioning		Example						
				Temporal relation of speech and gesture – pre-positioning						
Iteration	preparation-stroke	pre-postitioned	Example "snout"	und geht	von	hinten	mit die	schnau	ze	an die beene stubsen
				and	from	behind	with the	snou	t	always pokes her
							stroke		stroke	
			Example "handles"	aber dass	du in	den	ba	a dewannen	d	diese griffe hast
				that	you in	those	ba	a thtubs	t	these handles have
							stroke	stroke	stroke	stroke
	stroke-stroke	pre-positioned	Example "spin"	damit	sie nicht	dURch	drehn	im Winter		
				that	they don't	spin		during winter;		
						stroke	stroke			
						stroke	stroke			

Table 17: Semantic relation of most frequent gestural repetitions.

Type of Repetition	Gesture Phases	Gestural Meaning	Gesture Type	Example	Semantic Relation of Speech and Gesture					
					Speech		Gesture		Semantic Relation
					Utterance	Semantic Features	Form	Semantic Features	
Iterations	preparation-stroke	concrete-action	concrete referential	"put it in"	*ein Fuchspel (-) pelz den sich Ladendiebinnen umlegen um da die Sachen reinzustecken (–)* ("a fox fur that shoplifters put on to put in the things")	object, action	1–5 bent, pltb, movement to the left, upper center	action, **manner**, **position**	complementary
		concrete-object	concrete referential	"handles"	*dass du in den Badewannen diese Griffe hast die dir sozusagen helfen, wenn du dein Bad genommen hast, wieder aus der Badewanne rauszukommen* ("that you have those handles in the bathtubs that help you to get out of the bathtub after you have taken a bath")	object, position	1–5 bent, pu, small accented straight movements down, periphery	object, **shape**, **property**	complementary

(continued)

Table 17 (continued)

Type of Repetition	Gesture Phases	Gestural Meaning	Gesture Type	Example	Semantic Relation of Speech and Gesture					Semantic Relation
					Speech			Gesture		
					Utterance	Semantic Features	Form	Semantic Features		
stroke-stroke	concrete-action	concrete referential	"wing"	*holen die einfach den Schlauch raus und machen oben auf die Tragfläche drauf* ("they just get the pipe and put it on top of the wing")	object, action, position	fist, pltc, straight movement left to right, upper center	action, **manner**, position	complementary		
	concrete-object	concrete referential	"metal thing"	*ich glaube dass es ja so beim Italiener, wo die Flasche Wein da in som Metallding drinne is* ("I think that in an Italian restaurant where the bottle wine is in such a metal thing")	object, position, property	lax flat hand, pd arced movements inwards and outwards, center	object, **shape**	complementary		

Reduplication A	stroke-stroke	abstract-movement	abstract referential	"send back and forth"	wo man eben immer in den den dies diesn zu beschriftenden Umschlägen Dinge immer zwischen zwei Ämtern hin und herschickt ("where you just always in these labeled envelopes send things back and forth between two offices")	object, action, movement, direction	1 stretched, pltc, arced movement away and towards body, center	movement, direction	redundant
Reduplication B	stroke-stroke	abstract-place	abstract referential	"single steps" Figure	kannste dir ja immer die einzelnen schritte durchlesen da sind ja die frisuren beschrieben ("you can always read trough the single stepts")	entity, multitude action	2–5 flapped down, pd, arced movement down, periphery upper to center	entitiy, multidude	redundant

As was shown in chapter 3, gestural iterations with preparation-stroke sequences often depict actions. This was exemplified in the example "Arko", in which speaker SU, while saying *Rennt er in Flur. Kratzt* ('He runs into the hallway. Scrapes.'), gesturally depicts the scraping action of a dog (see Figure 15). In this example, gesture and speech express similar semantic information, namely the action of scraping which is created through the semantic features ACTION and MANNER. These features are present in the gestures' handshape, the orientation of the hand, and the movement execution. In speech, they are expressed in the verb "scrapes" as well as in the larger discursive context, in which a dog is the protagonist of the story. Speech and gesture therefore express and transmit the same semantic features.

However, contrary to the example "Arko", most gestural iterations documented in the corpus give further and particular information not present in the verbal utterance. Usually, gestural iterations complement the verbal utterance by expressing additional semantic features, which specify particular characteristics of the manner of actions not expressed in speech. Let us consider an example in which speaker HF talks about shoplifters and what kinds of tricks they may use to hide the stolen goods (*ein Fuchspel (-) pelz den sich Ladendiebinnen umlegen um da die Sachen reinzustecken* ['a fox fur that shoplifters put on to put in the things there']). In parallel to the prepositional phrase *um da die Sachen reinzustecken* ('to put in the things there') and using a handshape with the fingers 1–5 bent, a palm lateral towards body orientation, and an arced movement to the left located in the upper center of the gesture space, HF produces a gestural iteration consisting of two strokes. Due to its position in gesture space, the orientation of the palm of the hand, and the movement, the speaker can express and transmit a particular idea of "putting something in", namely the action of putting something into a jacket. Contrary to the verbal utterance, which remains sketchy by solely characterizing the action as *reinstecken* ('put something in'), the gesture specifies the particular type of action and its manner and therefore complements the semantics of the verb *reinstecken*.

A further example of a gestural iteration specifying the manner of an action is given when a speaker describes how liquid is being spread over a surface (*holen die einfach den Schlauch raus und machen oben auf die Tragfläche drauf* ['they just get the pipe and put it on top of the wing']). While *saying machen oben auf die Tragfläche drauf* ('put it on top of the wing') speaker GK gesturally depicts the holding of a pipe with one hand, which is then successively moved to the left and right in the periphery upper of the gesture space. The verb *machen* ('put')[62] of the verbal utterance is specified through gesturally depicting the object with which the action is executed. Whereas the verbal utterance carries the semantic features OBJECT, ACTION, and POSITION, the co-occurring gestural iteration conveys the semantic features ACTION, MANNER, and POSITION, thus adding complementary semantic features while also sharing features with the verbal utterance. The multimodal meaning of the phrase *machen oben auf die Tragfläche drauf* ('put it on top of the wing') then comes to mean something like "spray it on top of the wing" in which the manner of the action is specified.

In the examples mentioned above, the gestures' semantic information refers to the verb of the verbal utterance, specifies its manner, and thus defines it more closely. In all cases of gestural iterations depicting actions and expressing complementary semantic features, the gestures carry at least the feature MANNER which is not expressed in speech. Depending on the type of action, other additional semantic features may be found that are not expressed through the verbal utterance (e.g., example "put it in" which also carries the semantic feature POSITION). In all of the discussed examples, the gestural iteration expresses complementary semantic information necessary to understand the multimodal utterance meaning. The semantic features of speech and gestures do not completely match and the meaning of the gestures contributes to the meaning of the spoken utterance by forming a subset of the verbal meaning. In addition to the complementary semantic features, gestural repetitions also express redundant semantic features, thus creating a semantic overlap.

The use of gestural iterations for the specification of instrumental actions is one of the main uses documented in the present corpus. It is characteristic for iterations with preparation-stroke sequences and also for stroke-stroke sequences. This overwhelming use of gestural iterations for the depiction of actions is not surprising if one considers the nature of the depicted actions: they are either durative and/ or iterative. In cases of durativity and iterativity, repetitions are needed to express the durativity of the action[63] (e.g., "fill in by hand", "pushing", "put it in") or the iterativity of actions (e.g., "scraping", "pounding", "stamping"). The predominance of gestural repetitions for the depiction of actions, therefore, rests upon the nature of the depicted referents itself: The actions themselves call for a gestural representation through repetition.

Yet, as was shown in chapter 3, gestural iterations are not only used for the depiction of actions but also very frequently for the depiction of objects. In

---

[62] Literally "do" or "make".
[63] While the depiction of preparation-stroke sequences predominantly expresses complementary semantic information, stroke-stroke sequences are characterized by an almost even distribution of redundant and complementary semantic information.

cases of depicting objects by characterizing their properties of size and shape or through handling them, gestural repetitions also take over a complementary function. Here again, gestural iterations add particular semantic features not expressed in the verbal utterance but yet needed to fully understand the multimodal utterance.

An example in which the gestural iteration provides complimentary semantic information about an object was discussed in the example "handles" (see Figure 30). Here speaker BS, using the mimetic mode "acting with specified object" and while uttering *dass du in den Badewannen diese Griffe hast* ('that you have those handles in the bathtubs'), visually represents handles in bathtubs by handling them. Using the hand shape 1–5 bent and an orientation of the palm upwards, speaker BS moves her right hand down up and down in small, accented straight movements in parallel to the preposition and article *in den* ('in the'), the noun *Badewanne* ('bathtub'), demonstrative pronoun *diese* ('this'), and the noun *Griffe* ('handles') producing two separate iterations. In both iterations, speaker BS depicts the handles in bathtubs by exemplifying their use. It specifies how to hold on to the handles, namely by touching them from below (see chapter 6 for a more detailed discussion of the example). The gestures carry the semantic features SHAPE and PROPERTY not expressed in speech.

In another example, a speaker gesturally depicts a characteristic button for German hospitals with which patients may call a nurse. While saying *ist dann einfach dieser Knopf wo die Schwester kommt* ('it is just this button and then the nurse comes'), speaker BH produces two strokes, imitating the pushing of a button by holding a vertically orientated object in one hand. Using a handshape in which the fingers 1–5 are curled in and the palm is oriented towards the center, BH moves his thumb up and down twice, imitating a pushing action on the upper side of the vertically oriented object. The object *Knopf* ('button') is thus exemplified by its use, namely how to hold and push it. Due to this gestural representation, the gestures express the complementary semantic features ACTION and MANNER not present in the verbal utterance. The meaning of the multimodal phrase then comes to mean something like "it is just this button, which you can hold in your hand and push it on top". Gestural iterations which depict objects by handling them thus add an action component along with characteristics of manner to the meaning expressed in the verbal utterance. By adding particular information about the nature of the depicted object, namely characteristics of its use, the gestural iterations specify and, more importantly, restrict the possible reference object.

This function is also characteristic of gestural iterations depicting objects by specifying their shape. Consider once again the example "metal thing", in which speaker MB describes a holder for wine bottles by depicting its shape. While saying *wo die Flasche Wein da in som Metallding drinne is* ('where the bottle wine is in such a metal thing') (see Figure 16), MB produces an iteration consisting of three strokes with which he models the shape of holders for wine bottles. Through the threefold execution of strokes with arced movements going inwards and outwards, along with the bent hands facing downwards a three-dimensional bent object, namely a bottle holder emerges. Therefore, the gestural iteration carries the semantic features OBJECT and SHAPE, whereas the co-occurring verbal utterance contains the features OBJECT, POSITION, and PROPERTY. Accordingly, the gestural iteration adds complementary semantic information not present in the verbal utterance. By providing information about the shape of the bottle holder, namely its concavity, the multimodal utterance comes to mean something like "where the bottle wine is in such bent a metal thing". Thus, the gestural iteration fulfills the function of a gestural attribute, limiting the extension of the reference object of the noun (Fricke 2007, 2012) (see chapter 5 for a more detailed discussion of the example).

In all cases of gestural iterations documented in the corpus, which specify objects in their form characteristics, the gestures carry the semantic features SHAPE and/or POSITION, therefore providing at least one semantic feature not contained in the verbal utterance. At the same time, similar to iterations depicting actions, the gestures create a semantic overlap with the verbal utterance. Both speech and gesture carry the feature OBJECT. This semantic overlap is a necessary prerequisite for the complementary function of iterations, as it sets the ground needed for the specification of particular characteristics of the objects in question. Only based on a common semantic set, gestures have the capability to specify the object illustrated in the verbal utterance.

The preceding section has shown that gestural iterations may complement the semantics of the verbal utterance by adding semantic information. Reduplications on the other hand, which represent or refer to abstract states, events or facts, exhibit a different semantic relation with the verbal utterance: They express redundant semantic information and as such do not affect the semantics of the utterance in the same way as gestural iterations do.

Let us first consider reduplications of type A, that is gestural repetitions embodying the spatial and temporal basis of Aktionsarten as illustrated in the example "send back and forth" (see Figure 17). Here, speaker BS produces a series of three strokes co-occurring with the phrase *zwischen zwei Ämtern hin und herschickt* ('send back and forth between two offices'). Using a stretched index finger and an arced movement away from and towards the body, BS gesturally represents the iterativity of the movement event expressed in the verb phrase *hin und her schicken* ('send back and forth'). Other examples in which speakers gesturally represent the concept of iterativity are instances in which speakers place their hands in different regions of the gesture space, thereby executing an arced movement going back and forth between different regions in gesture space. This is illustrated in the following examples: *Man fährt von zu Hause in sein Ferienhause und wieder zurück* ('you drive from home to your vacation house and back') or *fahren die Leute von zu Hause zur Arbeit und wieder zurück* ('people drive from home to work and back'. The gestural iterations carry the semantic features of MOVEMENT and DIRECTION, and maybe POSITION if the hands are placed in different regions of the gesture space. The verbal utterance co-occurring with the repetition can generally be characterized in terms of the semantic features OBJECT, ACTION, MOVEMENT, and DIRECTION. The gestural iteration thus expresses a subset of the semantic features expressed in the verbal utterance (see Table 4.4.) Accordingly, both speech and gesture transmit the idea of motion and path and therefore conceptualize iterativity. Due to this redundancy of the gestures' semantic features with the ones expressed in the spoken utterance, reduplications of type A do not add additional information to the meaning of the utterance. Rather, by forming a subset of the semantic features, they offer insight into the embodied basis of lexical concepts by making iterativity visible as movement between two endpoints in space (Becker et al., 2011; Müller, 2000). As such, these reduplications give insight into the nature of embodied cognition, namely the rootedness of cognitive and conceptual knowledge in bodily experiences with and in the world, and the embodied roots of language and thought (Gibbs, 2006). Accordingly, reduplications do not directly affect the propositional content of speech. Yet, they nevertheless contribute to creating a multimodal utterance meaning by underlining the embodied basis of lexical concepts and thus expressing a different conceptualization of the concept of iterativity.

A similar semantic function can be ascribed to reduplications expressing the grammatical notion of plurality (see Figure 18). In example 5, "single steps", it was illustrated that the positioning of the hands in different regions of the gesture space might be used for expressing the grammatical notion of plurality. In this example, speaker ME explains to her interlocutor that haircuts and their compositions are explained in textbooks for hairdressers. While saying *kannste dir ja immer die einzelnen Schritte durchlesen* ('well you can read through the single steps'), ME executes three strokes with an arced movement away from the body. The hands thereby successively move from a position in the upper periphery to periphery to center upper. Yet, the position in gesture space does not have a concrete meaning: it is not used to represent perceived spatial relations between objects in the world. Rather, it is an instance of "non-mimetic use of gesture space", in which the gesture space is used for creating structural relations between gestures (Müller, Bressem & Ladewig, 2013). The single strokes mark individual spaces around the speaker's body representing the single steps. Taken together, all strokes mark a sequence of individual spaces around the speaker's body, which, as a result, create a sequence of strokes representing the entirety of steps necessary for the creation of a haircut. Because the strokes are produced in spatial and temporal proximity and are marked as belonging together through constant form features, the impression of a sequence of similar yet different points in space arises. In combination with the co-expressive verbal utterance, the meaning of the gestural form is enriched (Enfield, 2009, p. 15) such that the notion of plurality emerges.

Another instance of marking plurality is given when speaker MA discusses safety keys of apartment buildings in Germany. While uttering *jede Wohnung hat dann einen wo er nicht passt* ('each apartment has one [key] where it does not fit'), speaker MA produces a series of three strokes. By successively moving his right flat hand with a palm lateral orientation and an arced movement from the center to the right periphery, speaker MA gesturally depicts different points in gesture space representing the different apartments he talks about, highlighting the notion of plurality. A similar use is documented when a speaker produces a succession of three strokes by moving a flat hand, with the palm oriented downwards from the center to the right periphery co-occurring with the phrase *nicht der einzelnen Kabinen* ('not the individual cabins') or when a speaker produces a series of three strokes while saying und *da war das gleiche Schema nochmal* ('and then it was the same schema again'). A flat hand with a palm downwards is moved from the left to the right periphery of the gestures space in small arced movements, once again indicating different yet similar points in gesture space.

All of the sequences of strokes in the examples given above are produced in spatial and temporal proximity and are marked as belonging together through constant form features (see chapter 3). Accordingly, the impression of a sequence of similar yet different points in space arises. Grounded in the gestural form features of position, movement, and handshape, gestural reduplications of type B carry the semantic features MULTITUDE and ENTITY (see Table 4.4.). In all documented instances, speakers verbally refer to multiple instances of the same aspect ("single steps", "each apartment has its own", "not the individual cabins", "the same schema once more"). Accordingly, speech always carries the semantic features MULTITUDE and ENTITY, but may also carry further features such as in the example "single steps" in which speech also expresses the feature ACTION. Accordingly, in reduplications of type B, speech and gesture are characterized by a semantic overlap: the semantic features present in the verbal and gestural modality match. As a result, reduplications of type B do not modify the semantics of the spoken utterance but rather depict the semantic nucleus of the multimodal utterance (something is present more than once) in another modality. Again, the meaning of the gestures does not affect the proposition of the utterance but, similar to reduplications of type A, exemplifies the embodied nature of language.

Gestural reduplications thus differ immensely from iterations in their semantic relation to the verbal utterance as well as in their function in creating a multimodal utterance meaning. By expressing the abstract notions of iterativity and plurality, gestural reduplications do not add complementary semantic information but create and underline the common idea unit (Kendon, 2004a) in conjunction with speech and based on redundant semantic features. Reduplications thus exemplify a fundamental characteristic of gestures in general, namely their capability for expressing and visualizing conceptualization. Consequently, they give insights into the embodied basis of thought and language. The different semantic relations detected for the individual types of repetitions (complementary vs. redundant) also result in different functions (complementation vs. emphasis). Whereas iterations are an essential aspect for the creation of multimodal meaning by adding complementary semantic information needed for an understanding of the utterance, reduplications do not directly affect the semantics of speech but exemplify particular aspects of the meaning expressed verbally in another modality, thereby highlighting and showing the embodied basis of meaning.

The present study thus supports newer studies that ground the semantic relation of speech and gesture in their temporal relation.

> [. . .] When both modalities redundantly express the same information, the gesture's onset is closer to that of the accompanying lexical affiliate than when gestures convey complementary information: the closer speech and gestures are related semantically, the closer is their temporal relation. (Bergmann, Aksu, and Kopp 2011: 1)

Almost 90% of iterations which are pre-positioned to the co-expressive speech segment submit complementary or even contrary semantic information and thus seem to support the assumption that the closer speech and gesture are semantically related, the closer is also their temporal relation. Whereas Bergmann, Asku & Kopp (2011) interpret their findings in relation to the speech production process and the processing of language, based on the gestural repetitions investigated in this book, it will be argued that this link between the semantics and temporal distance or proximity of speech and gesture allows insights into the nature of activation of meaning at the moment of speaking. It will be argued that pre-positioned iterations can anticipate or foreshadow the focus of attention by adding more prominence to particular parts of the verbal utterance. As a result, pre-positioned gestural repetitions take over a prominent role in creating and highlighting a multimodal salience structure for speakers and hearers (see chapter 6 for a detailed discussion).

4.3 Summary

After discussing what is known about multimodal utterances and the temporal and semantic relation of speech and gesture, the present chapter focused on gestural repetitions and their connection with the semantics of speech and discussed the role of gestural repetitions in creating a multimodal utterance meaning. Starting from the twofold classification of gestural repetitions introduced in the chapters before, it discussed the potential of iterations and reduplications in their semantic and functional relation to the verbal utterance and aimed at possible functional commonalities and differences in contributing to a verbo-gestural meaning.

Starting from the assumption that gestures can express meaning on their own and independent of the verbal utterance, the chapter investigated whether gestural repetitions occur in temporal overlap with the co-expressive speech segment or whether they are pre-or post-positioned. It was shown that the majority of iterations and reduplications occur in temporal overlap with the co-expressive speech, thus adhering to the attested temporal relation of speech and gesture. Yet, it was also shown that gestural repetitions may be pre-positioned to the co-expressive speech segment and that the pre-positioning is restricted to iterations. Accordingly, pre-positioning seems to be characteristic for gestural iterations and specifically for iterations expressing concrete meaning about action and objects.

Moreover, it was shown that iterations and reduplications may not only differ in their temporal relation with the co-expressive speech segment but also, and maybe even more importantly, in their semantic relation and function for creating a multimodal utterance meaning. Using an analytical method investigating the semantic relation of speech and gestures by examining the semantic features expressed in both modalities, the chapter has shown that gestural repetitions affect the semantics of the verbal utterance in quite different ways: Gestural reduplications of type A and type B express redundant semantic features and therefore do not have a direct impact on the meaning expressed verbally. By expressing the lexical basis of Aktionsarten or the notion of 'plurality', they gesturally depict the embodied basis of thought and language. As such, they provide substantial insights into the nature of abstract grammatical concepts. Although they also contribute to the creation of a multimodal utterance meaning, they do not add to the propositional content of speech.

Gestural iterations, however, affect the verbal utterance. When used to depict actions (e.g., scraping, hammering, beating) or objects (e.g., the shape of a bowl), iterations complement and specify the type of action expressed verbally regarding its manner and the object in terms of size and shape. By expressing complementary semantic features, they can modify the verbal utterance and the meaning expressed therein. The present chapter has shown that in cases of iterations used depicting objects, iterations add at least one complementary semantic feature to the meaning expressed in speech. At the same time, they also exhibit a semantic overlap with the features expressed in speech. Based on the semantic overlap and the complementary features, the gestural repetitions are used to specify the objects in their properties and in particular to their shape. A similar semantic relation between speech and gesture was also detected for iterations depicting actions. While sharing semantic features, gestural iterations add complementary semantic features through which the manner of the action is specified. Accordingly, based on the semantic relation of speech and gesture, it was argued that iterations expressing concrete meaning substantially alter the verbal utterance as they specify objects and actions.

As a result, iterations and reduplications not only stand in different semantic relations to the verbal utterance but also fulfill different semantic functions and as such show different degrees of semantic integration into the spoken utterance. Reasons for these differences can be found on the level of the gestural unit itself and the grounding and detachment of repetitions in and from bodily and visual experiences. Iterations are predominantly used to depict actions of the hand and concrete objects and events, conceptualize kinesthetic experience, and are thus grounded in direct bodily experiences. The gestural repetition serves as a means for creating a connected gestural unit that is being marked and perceived as coherent through similarities in form and Gestalt principles (see chapter 6 for a detailed discussion). Irrespective of the number of strokes, the individual strokes instantiate *one* and the *same meaning*. As a result, the repetition itself does not have the potential to create a complex meaning and thus does not convey a meaning independently. Accordingly, iterations are directly related to the semantics of the co-expressive speech segment as the speech and the semantics expressed therein creates the frame within which the gestural repetition can emphasize or contribute to the multimodal meaning. Reduplications, however, express abstract meaning and, as such, are detachment from concrete aspects of the actual world. Rather they trace a successive process of abstraction from visual or bodily experiences and as such allow for the foregrounding of the lexical basis of Aktionsarten (reduplication A) as well as for the expression of grammatical notions (reduplication B). Due to this abstract meaning and their detachment from concrete entities, reduplications do not affect the semantics of the verbal utterance in the same way as gestural iterations. Although in reduplications, the repetition also serves as a means for creating a connected gestural unit that is being marked and perceived as coherent through similarities in form and Gestalt principles, the type of unit that arises is different from iterations. In reduplications, the repetition is a means for creating a *complex*, *meaningful unit*, a construction that may either express iterativity or pluralization. This complex meaning is in a sense detached from the semantics of the verbal utterance as the reduplicative construction itself carries a meaning that does not entirely rely on the semantics of speech. Accordingly, it is argued that the fact of whether repetitions create a complex gestural meaning (reduplications) or not (iterations) may account for the different distribution of semantic features and relations described in this chapter.

5 Multimodal utterances II: Repetitive gestures interacting with the syntax of speech

The preceding chapter has shown that gestural repetitions are semantically integrated into verbal utterances, that the individual types of repetitions show differences in their semantic relation and function and thus have particular relevance for the creation of multimodal utterance meaning. Together with speech, gestural repetitions therefore work towards the expression of a common "idea unit" (Kendon 2004a) and, as such, are important on the cognitive semantic level. Taking the results on the semantic integration of gestural repetitions as the basis, the present chapter focuses on the gestures' relation with the syntax of speech and discusses their temporal and functional connections with spoken syntagms. The chapter aims to further disentangle gestures' role in the creation of multimodal utterance meaning. In particular, it will be shown that the different degrees of semantic integration discussed in chapter 4 also result in a particular syntactic relevance. After discussing the notion of "multimodal grammar" (Cienki, 2012b; Fricke, 2012), it is shown that the different types of repetitions interact with the spoken syntagms in specific ways. The chapter then concludes with a discussion of how these results may be explained in light of newer grammatical approaches, such as "multimodal construction grammar" (Bergs & Zima, 2018) and argues for an understanding of spoken language grammar that acknowledges "variable DEGREES to which gesture can have linguistic status" (Cienki, 2015, p. 508, emphasis in original) and, as a consequence of their linguistic status, may function as elements of a single language (Cienki, 2015; Fricke, 2012).

5.1 The notion of multimodal grammar

As discussed in chapter 3 for gestural repetitions but also for co-speech gestures in general, gestures are semantically and cognitively integrated into spoken utterances and take on special functions for the creation of utterance meaning. As such, gesture research assumes that they cannot be left out when examining spoken language use. In recent years, in addition to these semantic functions, numerous studies also focus on the connection of gestures with the syntax of speech. They convincingly show that a link between the grammar of speech and co-speech gestures exists.

One area is, for instance, locative expressions. For the use of particular verbal deictic expressions such as "so", "here" or "there" (De Ruiter, 2000; Fricke, 2007; Kita, 2003; Streeck, 2002; Stukenbrock, 2015), gestures are not only obligatory elements but may even differ in the gestural form depending on the intended reference object of the deictic expression (Fricke, 2007; Kendon, 2004). Gestures may furthermore not only express locations or movement towards locations (Müller, 1998) but rather establish the direction and location of the lexicalized topological configuration in space, as it is the case in the use of English and French preposition "on", for instance (Tutton, 2015).

Negation is a further linguistic phenomenon that is tightly linked with gestures. Gestures are connected with syntactic, morphological, or implicit negation and may even express negation without it being explicitly expressed in speech (Beaupoil-Hourdel, Boutet, & Morgenstern, 2015; Bressem & Müller, 2017; Calbris, 2003, 2011; Harrison, 2009, 2018; Kendon, 2003; Lapaire, 2006; Streeck, 2009). As such, it can be assumed that "they are specific bindings of grammatical and gestural form that occur when speakers use particular types of linguistic negations or perform certain negative speech acts." (Harrison, 2018, p. 45)

Besides, the relation of speech and gestures in expressing motion events is dependent on the linguistic encoding of a particular language: differences in grammatical aspects are reflected in the gestural forms, the timing of gestures relative to the verbal utterance, and in the information distributed across the modalities (Cienki & Iriskhanova, 2018; Duncan, 2005; Gullberg, 2011; Kita, 2000; Kita & Özyürek, 2003; McNeill & Duncan, 2000; Müller, 1998). Accordingly, gestural representations of the same motion event may differ across languages depending on whether they are verb or satellite-framed. Speakers of English, for instance, might express the notion of a ball rolling down a hill in one clause and one gesture which represents the motion and the direction at the same time. Japanese or Turkish speakers, however, express the same notion in two verbal clauses accompanied by two distinct gestures, one expressing the motion and the other the direction or manner of motion. Thus, if the meaning is distributed over two spoken clauses that same meaning is likely to be expressed in two gestures, each expressing similar meaning as the spoken clause (Kita & Özyürek, 2003; Kita et al., 2007). Therefore,

> gestures reflect information considered relevant for expression (what to say) as well as its linguistic encoding (how to say it), with cross-linguistic consequences. Gestures thus reflect linguistic conceptualization and cross-linguistic differences in such conceptualizations. (Gullberg, 2011, p. 148)

Yet, connections between gestural representations and grammatical forms are not only relevant cross-linguistically but can also show effects within a single language, so that distinct attention on the selection of subjects in utterances result in differences in the motion-event components appearing in gesture (Parrill, 2008).

Furthermore, studies show links of gestures with syntactic units of different sizes. In relation to single words, for instance, gestures often accompany nouns, verbs, and adjectives. For phrases, such as *ein langer Zylinder* ('a long cylinder') oder *ein Zylinder, der länger ist* ('a cylinder which is longer'), predominantly noun phrases, and in particular adjective phrases plus nouns and determiner plus noun combinations occur (Sowa, 2005, p. 106) (see also Hadar & Krauss, 1999; Morrel-Samuels & Krauss, 1992). In a more recent study investigating the relation of speech and gestures in the SAGA corpus, a video corpus of route descriptions by German speakers, Kok identified "gesture attracting" and "gesture repelling" words: Whereas pronominal adverbs, nouns, determiners, prepositions, and adverbs are often accompanied by gestures, adjectives, verbs, interjections, and particles are not (Kok, 2016b, p. 245). These results are partially in conflict with what is known from other studies. Schoonjans (2014), for instance, documented a frequent correlation of modal particles in German, such as *halt* ('well') or *ja* 'alright' with particular gestures and head movements. Also, Sowa (2005) documented a different relation with syntactic units (see above). However, the study also puts forward further empirical evidence underlining that particular determiners in German (*dies* 'this', *son* 'such a') as well as the qualitative adverb *so* 'such' is frequently accompanied by gestures (see also above). Fricke, for instance, argues, that

> *son* within a noun phrase instantiates an additional turning point, namely, between linguistic monomodality and linguistic multimodality. *Son* is the syntactic integration point on the level of the linguistic system for gestures accompanying speech in noun phrases. Gestures structurally integrated to such an extent can also be integrated functionally as attributes in verbal noun phrases. Thus, because *son* in the noun phrase requires a qualitative description, which can be gesturally instantiated as well, it is shown that iconic gestures in noun phrases constitute autonomous syntactic units detached from the nuclear noun. Furthermore, they can establish syntactic relations with the nuclear noun.
> (Fricke, 2013, p. 749)

As such, iconic gestures can be integrated into the constituent structure of spoken utterances and function as attributes, limiting the extension of the reference object of a nucleus noun in noun phrases (Fricke, 2012, p. 250ff) (see below for a more detailed discussion). Under the notion of "mixed syntax" (Slama-Cazacu, 1976), "composite signal" (Clark, 1996), "language-slotted gestures"/"speech-linked gestures" (McNeill, 2005) or "gestural realization of syntactic slots" (Ladewig, 2020), studies have also discussed the integration of gestures in other syntactic slots and gaps. Ladewig (2020), for instance, shows that gestures achieve particular relevance in syntactic gaps: The syntactic position of interrupted utterances in speech foregrounds particular semantic aspects of the gesture: "Noun positions foreground either the information of objects or of an object involved in an action; verb positions foreground the semantic information of action." (Ladewig, 2014, p. 1672)

These different foci are reflected in gestural forms, such as handshape or movement through which gestures may either become part of a multimodal noun phrase or a multimodally construed analytic verb form or verb phrase.

With this ever-growing body of evidence for a relation between gestures and the grammar of speech, awareness in gesture research has risen that methods, concepts, and theoretical models need to be adapted to account for these empirical facts. Accordingly, over the course of the last years, a range of different proposals have been put forward to include gestures and, even more generally, the notion of multimodality in grammatical models and theories (Bergs & Zima, 2018; Cienki, 2012a; Fricke, 2012; Harrison, 2018; Kok, 2016b; Kok & Cienki, 2016; Ladewig, 2020; Lücking, 2013; Muntigl, 2004; Wilcox & Xavier, 2013). Regardless of their theoretical foci, all proposals revolve around one question: Are gestures part of the language system or does their relevance reside on the level of language use?

Fricke (2012, 2013, 2014a, 2014b, 2014c), for instance, argues for a multimodal grammar of German. The proposal rests upon the basic assumption that the same structural principles take effect in speech and gesture, allowing a structural integration of both modalities on the level of the language system. Fricke argues for a) typification and semantization of gestures as potential syntactic constituents, b) a syntactic function of gestures as attributes in spoken noun phrases, and c) the display of recursivity based on gestures' linear and sequential complexity. Besides, two fundamental principles that not only take effect in gesture-speech relations but are also applicable to other semiotic sign systems, such as text-image relations, are proposed: a) two linguistic media are structurally and functionally integrated into one and the same code (code-integration) or b) one code manifests itself simultaneously in two different media (code-manifestation) (Fricke, 2012, 2014d). Based on these different types, multimodality in the narrow sense and broader sense are set apart.

> Multimodality in the narrow sense occurs when the media involved in an expression belong to different sense modalities and are structurally or functionally integrated in the same code or, alternatively, manifest the same code, e.g., "gesture-speech ensembles" (Kendon 2004). In the broad sense of multimediality, the media involved belong to the same sense modality, e.g., "language-image ensembles. It is worth pointing out that both kinds of multimodal ensembles differ with respect to their specific potential for establishing and instantiating grammatical structures and functions. (Fricke, 2013, p. 751)

As proposed by Fricke, structural and functional integration is thereby to be understood as integration in structures and function of the syntactic surface showing different "degrees of integrability" (ibid., 2012, p. 11). Gestures may be positionally integrated into the verbal utterance by a syntactic or temporal overlap. They may furthermore be integrated cataphorically through the article *son* ('such a') determining a qualitative description. As such, a continuum of degrees of integrability ranging from a) gestures that are used without speech, b) gestures and speech are used simultaneously, to c) gesture and speech are used in linear succession (see Figure 24). Gestures standing alone and between two utterances show the lowest degree of integrability. In contrast, the highest degree is achieved when speech is absent and gestures are integrated into syntactic gaps, as they then "constitute the semantic centre of a complex constituent [. . . and] provide necessary information to interpret and make sense of an utterance." (Ladewig, 2012, p. 184) (For a more detailed discussion see Ladewig, 2020).

With this perspective, Fricke propagates an approach to the multimodality of grammar which "contributes to a description of language in all its structural, functional as well as medial and cognitive particularities" (Fricke, 2013, p. 751) and aims at a theoretical and methodological framework that allows for a unified description of linguistic multimodality. The task of a multimodal grammar is to identify on which linguistic levels areas of manifestation and integration of speech and gesture can be identified (Fricke, 2012, p. 2). This implies that gestures integrate not only on the level of language use, which is widely accepted among scholars of gestures but also on the level of the language system.

A notion of multimodality that is, first of all, restricted to spoken language usage events and kinesic expressions is formulated by Cienki (2012a, 2013, 2015a, b). Taking a cognitive-linguistic perspective, Cienki argues that gestures achieve a particular relevance for the grammar of a single language: "the degree to which gesture is part of language varies, both when we consider language as a system and with regard to the use of any language in real time" (Cienki, 2012a, p. 154). Language, on the level of use and system, is thus not categorically multimodal. Instead, multimodality of language needs to be understood in terms of a prototype structure in which we find prototypical instances of multimodal language, such as when speech and gesture form rather conventional units (e.g., negation and deixis).[64] Moreover, the degree and ways to which gestures may achieve linguistic status differs. "Thus while we might not be able to support a broad claim that grammar is multimodal, the evidence suggests that a flexible model of grammar is in order (Cienki 2012)." (Cienki, 2013, p. 681). Kinesic expressions that

---

[64] Drawing on Systemic Functional Grammar, Muntigl (2004) also argues that semiotic systems must be seen along a continuum between language and proto-language and that multiple semiotic systems, such as speech and gestures, may be functionally interrelated through elaboration, extension, and enhancement, for instance. Accordingly, by adding textural, interpersonal, and ideational meanings to speech, gestures are functionally integrated into speech and as such need to be considered part of the grammar of language (see also Kok, 2016a for a further proposal integrating gestures into Functional Grammar).

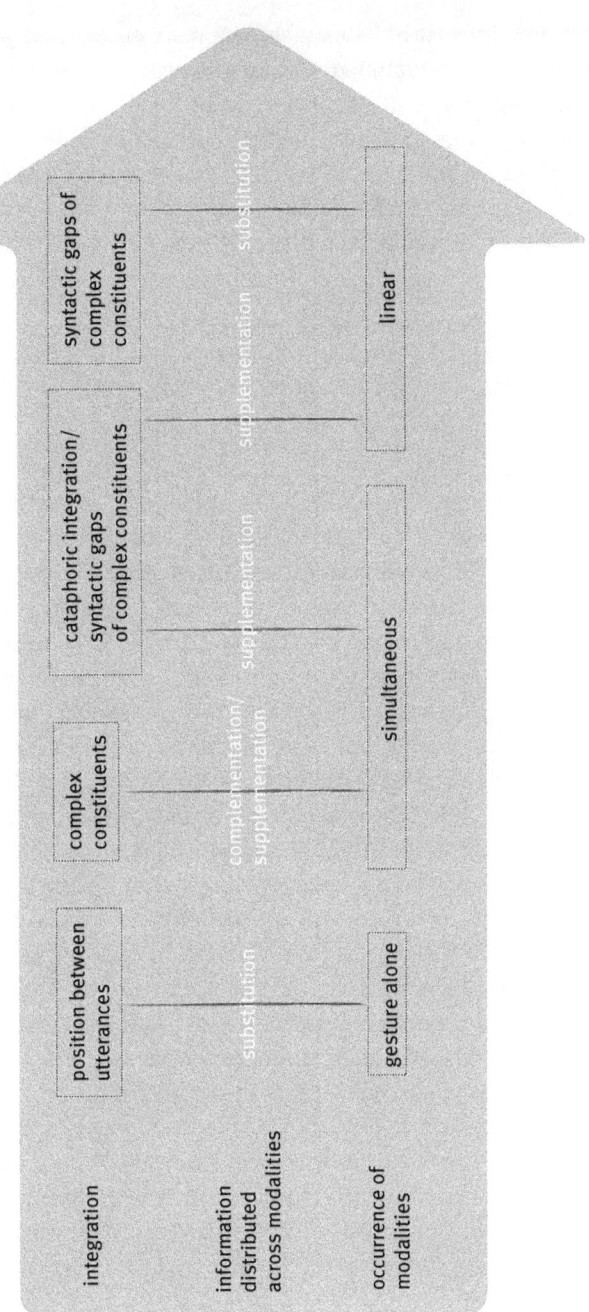

Figure 24: Continuum of integrability of speech and gesture (adapted from Ladewig, 2012, p. 184).

frequently co-occur with linguist units may become more entrenched signs and move towards the center of the grammar. Such a grammar-gesture link that is a frequent correlation of gestures with particular syntactic phenomena in speech, may be grounded in, according to Cienki, the "imagistic formalisms of cognitive grammar" (Cienki, 2015a, p. 210) and the symbolic status of both linguistic and gestural units: Conceptualization is shaped for the purpose of verbo-gestural communication and "thinking for speaking and gesturing" (Cienki & Müller, 2008).

> It is interesting to think of this in relation to gestures that occur with some regularity with certain semantic/grammatical notions, such as negation and the progressive aspect. It suggests that there is some level of imagistic thought connected with these concepts, which, though schematic in nature, appears in forms which recur across speakers of several languages. (Cienki, 2013, p. 681)

A similar position is advocated by other studies, integrating gestures into the ramework of Cognitive Grammar (Langacker, 2008). Taking up Langacker's (1999) idea that gestures, along with other types of expressive behavior, can become subject to symbolization and function as integral parts of usage events, proposals assume that "all of the theoretical and analytic framework of Cognitive Grammar can be recruited to study gesture." (Wilcox & Xavier, 2013, p. 92).[65] Accordingly, these approaches conceive of gestures as symbolic units, assume to show conceptual archetypes of spoken language, and gestures reflect meaning construal by making use of schematization, reification, and scanning as a means for symbolization (Kok & Cienki, 2016; Ladewig, 2012, 2014c, 2020). Similarly, as postulated by Fricke (2012) and Cienki (2012), the goal is to determine the applicability of the theoretical and methodological means for Cognitive Grammar as a theoretical framework for gesture-speech relation along with determining the relevance for gestures on the level of the language system and use. Here, proposals differ concerning their scope. Harrison (2018, p. 4), for instance, by focusing on the phenomenon of negation, postulates the notion of a grammar-gesture nexus, that is "a systematic binding of grammatical and gestural form". Based on this systematic binding of gestures with grammatical affiliates expressing negation in speech, "gestures associated with negation ought to be seriously considered on the level of the language system." (Harrison, 2018, p. 191) This grammar-gesture nexus constitutes a "mechanism for regularity in spontaneous gesturing" (Harrison, 2018, p. 33). In the case of negation, this results in an ordering principle organizing the temporal coordination of gestures with negation in English grammar (Harrison, 2018, p. 71ff).

---

[65] Wilcox and Xavier (2013) do not restrict themselves to a discussion of language and gesture but also include signs in their proposal.

5.2 Repeating gestures: Emphasizing or modifying the syntax of speech?

Against the background of the theoretical positions on the multimodality of grammar discussed above, the following section addresses the relation of gestural repetitions with the grammar of speech. Starting from the assumption that gestural repetitions show different degrees of integration into the semantics of speech, as shown in chapter 4, the question arises whether gestural repetitions are also integrated into the grammar of speech and if so, if different degrees of integration can be identified. The overall question addressed in this section is: Are gestures "merely" relevant on the level of language use, semantics and conceptualization, or are speech and gestures also interrelated on the level of the language system? To discuss this question for this book's object of research, first, possible relations of gestural repetitions with the grammar of speech are examined. If these can be identified, their distribution across the different types of repetitions is addressed. In the end, the question stands whether not only a semantic integration for gestural repetitions can be attested but also a more substantial syntactic relevance.

In particular, the section focuses on the most frequent repetitions occurring in temporal overlap with the co-expressive speech segment. The relation of gestural repetitions with the syntactic category of the verbal utterance will be discussed a) with respect to the individual strokes of the repetition and b) the whole gestural repetition, including the preparation phase at its beginning. This twofold investigation is chosen to allow for the detection of repetitions with verbal units of various sizes (e.g., phones, syllables, words, and sentences). Moreover, as repetitions create different types of meaning and build units of different sizes, it is assumed that they might show differences in their occurrence with particular categories.[66]

When considering the individual strokes, gestural repetitions most often accompany three syntactical categories: nouns, verbs, and adverbs. In general, it is found that 38% of all repetitions investigated in this study correlate with nouns, 20% with verbs, and 16% with adverbs. Adjectives are accompanied in 7% and prepositions in 6% of all cases. Accordingly, semantically speaking, gestural repetitions mainly accompany entities or things, processes as well as units that situate entities locally, temporally, or modally (see Table 18). An exception to the afore-mentioned results is reduplications of type A. Here, the strokes equally often accompany verbs (25%) and prepositional phrases (25%)

---

[66] The syntactical relation is only determined for the individual strokes.

Table 18: Three most common syntactical categories and relations correlating with iterations and reduplications.

Type of Repetition	Level of Syntax – Gesture and Speech						
	Gesture Phases		Temporal positioning	Syntactical category		Syntactical relation	Example
				stroke	all phases of repetition	stroke	
Iteration	prep-stroke	487 (53%)	parallel (81%)	N (46%)	S (60%)	object (43%)	Example "weapons of mass destruction"
				V (21%)	NGr (17%)	predicate (22%)	Example "Arko"
				Adv (18%)	VGr (12%)	subject (11%)	
	stroke-stroke	322 (33%)	parallel (58%)	N (34%)	NGr (36%)	object (40%)	Example "metal thing"
				V (20%)	VGr (20%)	predicate (20%)	
				Adv (15%)	S (17%)	subject (13%)	
Reduplication A	stroke-stroke	65 (7%)	parallel (94%)	V (25%)	VGr (88%)	predicate (63%)	Example "send back and forth"
				PrGr (25%)	S (12%)	object (25%)	
				Adv (19%)			
Reduplication B	stroke-stroke	47 (5%)	parallel (94%)	N (40%)	S (38%)	object (63%)	Example "single steps"
				V (8%)	NGr (29%)	subject (13%)	
				Adv (11%)	VGr (9%)	predicate (11%)	
	n= 921 (100%)						

and in third place go along with adverbs (19%). Because reduplications of type A are repetitions that go along with motion verbs (see Figure 17 for the example "back and forth" for instance), this distribution is not surprising. As discussed in chapter 3, reduplications of type A embody the spatial and temporal basis of Aktionsarten, in particular, iterativity, and thus highlight the motion and path of repeated events. The correlation with prepositions such as *von* 'from' or *zwischen* 'between' as well as adverbs such as *rein* 'into', *rauf* 'up', or *runter* 'down' thus underlines the highlighting of iterativity as gestural movement between two endpoints in space (see chapter 3 for a more detailed discussion).

The special status of type A reduplications is also maintained when examining the correlation of the whole gestural repetition with the verbal utterance, that is, all stroke phases and the preparation phase at the beginning of the sequence. In this case, reduplications of type A most frequently and almost exclusively accompany verb phrases (88%). All other types of repetitions, however, predominantly accompany either sentences or noun phrases. Iterations with preparation-stroke sequences mostly correlate with whole sentences (60%). Noun phrases (17%) and verb phrases (12%) are accompanied less frequently. On the other hand, in iterations with stroke-stroke sequences sentences only make up 17% of all cases, whereas noun phrases (36%) are accompanied most often followed by verb phrases (20%). In reduplications of type B, this distribution is yet reversed, as they show a predominant correlation with sentences (67%), whereas verb phrases (13%) and noun phrases (11%) are used less often.

The distribution of the syntactic categories across the whole repetition thus documents commonalities but also, and maybe more importantly, differences between the different types of repetitions: Whereas all repetitions, except for reduplications A, seemed to show agreement in the types of syntactic categories with which the individual strokes correlated, an examination across the whole repetition has shown interesting internal shifts and emphases. Iterations with preparation-stroke sequences and reduplications B preferably span larger units of the verbal utterance. Iterations with stroke-stroke sequences and reduplications of type A predominantly correlate with smaller units of the spoken utterance.

Taking the analysis now a step further, the syntactic functions of the spoken constituents accompanied by gestural repetitions will be discussed. The results in Table 18 document that except for reduplication A, all other types of repetitions show a similar distribution: They most often accompany units that function as the object (42%), followed by predicates (22%), subjects (12%), and adverbial determinations (11%). Only reduplications of type A go along with syntactical units that function primarily as predicates (63%) and only in the second position as objects (25%).

The different relations are illustrated in the examples introduced in chapter 3. In the example "metal thing" (see Figure 16), we see an illustration of a gestural repetition going along with the object of the sentence *wo die Flasche Wein da in som Metallding* ('where the bottle wine is in such a metal thing'). In the example "single steps" (see Figure 18), the reduplication also accompanies the object of the spoken utterance, namely *die einzelnen Schritte* 'the single steps'. Example "send back and forth" (see Figure 17), which is produced simultaneously with the sentence *wo man eben in diesen zu beschriftenden Umschlägen immer Dinge zwischen zwei Ämtern hin und herschickt* ('where you just always in these labeled envelops always things send back and forth between two offices'), illustrates the correlation with the predicate of the sentence (*hin und herschickt* 'send back and forth'). And also, the example "Arko", in which a speaker describes the scraping action of a dog *Rennt er in Flur. Katzt,* ('he runs into the hallway, scrapes') (see Figure 15), documents this relation. Here, the gestural repetition is produced in parallel with the verb *kratzt* ('scrapes') functioning as the predicate of the sentence.[67]

Summarizing, it can thus be stated that contrary to the syntactical categories, in which the individual types of repetitions showed variations in the units which they accompanied, they show an overwhelming consistency in their correlation with syntactical relations of the verbal utterance. Apart from reduplications of type A, all repetitions go along with similar relations (see Figure 5.2. for an overview of the results). The empirical results of the study thus, first of all, document a frequent correlation and then secondly also differences in the particular types of repetitions and their relation with syntactic units of speech.

Yet, the above-presented results reveal another interesting characteristic of gestural repetitions and of gestures in general. As discussed in chapter 4 (section 4.2.), iterations with stroke-stroke sequences are predominantly produced by using the acting mode, thereby creating concrete gestural meanings either corresponding to actions or objects. The analysis of the syntactical categories and relations has revealed that iterations using the acting mode for the depiction of actions accompany verb phrases and thus the predicate of the sentence,

---

[67] An example from the corpus documenting the relation with the subject of the spoken utterance is given, when a speaker talks about the construction of small sailing boats inside bottles. The speaker utters *diese großn Segelschiffe, die meistens größer sind als die Flasche* ('these big sailing boats that are usually bigger than the bottle') and produces two separate reduplications B: One is produced in parallel with the nominal phrase *diese großn Segelschiffe* ('these big sailing boats') functioning as the subject of the spoken utterance and the second reduplication accompanies the relative clause *die meistens größer sind* ('that are usually bigger') specifiying the reference object.

whereas iterations depicting objects accompany noun phrases and, therefore, the object of sentence.[68] Movement is thus either used to depict processes (actions) or as a means to an end, namely for the depiction of objects through movement. In the first case, movement depicts movement, while it is a means for depiction in the latter.

The twofold distinction of the gestural modes of representation into acting and representing and the seeming preference of the two for the depiction of actions (acting mode) and objects (representing mode) has led to the assumption that both types of mimetic modes may correlate with the grammatical categories of nouns and verbs in spoken languages. However, Ladewig (2012, 2014c, 2020) showed that such a clear allocation is impossible. Examining the potential of gestures to fill in syntactic gaps exposed in the verbal utterance, Ladewig showed that, whereas gestures first and foremost occupy the syntactic positions of nouns and verbs, for both positions the acting mode was preferred. Picking up on the notion of semantic phonology (Armstrong, Stokoe, & Wilcox, 1995; Stokoe, 1991/2001), Ladewig argues that gestures show a simultaneously-construed syntactic structure consisting of nouns referring to agents and/or patients as well as verbs referring to actions. Accordingly, "gestures are capable of depicting basic categories relying on experiences made with entities in (inter)action in the world, namely agent, patient or instruments being engaged in an (inter)action." (Ladewig, 2011, p. 119) Syntactic gaps of the verbal utterance then foreground different aspects of the internal structure of a gestural sign and trigger one of the mimed aspects of both: Noun positions foreground the aspect of objects. In contrast, the action is foregrounded in verb positions. The results documented for iterations with stroke-stroke sequences underpin Ladewig's assumption that gestures produced in the acting mode may correspond to verbs or nouns and show that a clear allocation of acting gestures with verbs and representing gestures with nouns is not maintainable. Rather, acting gestures can refer to both, whereas one aspect is made salient and foregrounded depending on the particular syntactic structure of the utterance.

Summarizing, it can be stated that iterations and reduplications frequently correlate with particular syntactical categories and relations. Depending on the type of repetition, they furthermore show specific correlations with the syntax of the verbal utterance. Picking up the question raised in chapter 3 and at the beginning of this chapter, namely whether gestures are "solely" relevant for the level of semantics and language use, the question now arises whether gestural repetitions may also achieve a functional relevance on the level of syntax. The following section will, therefore, address this question by focusing on one specific type of

---

[68] I thank Silva Ladewig for suggesting to investigate this aspect more closely.

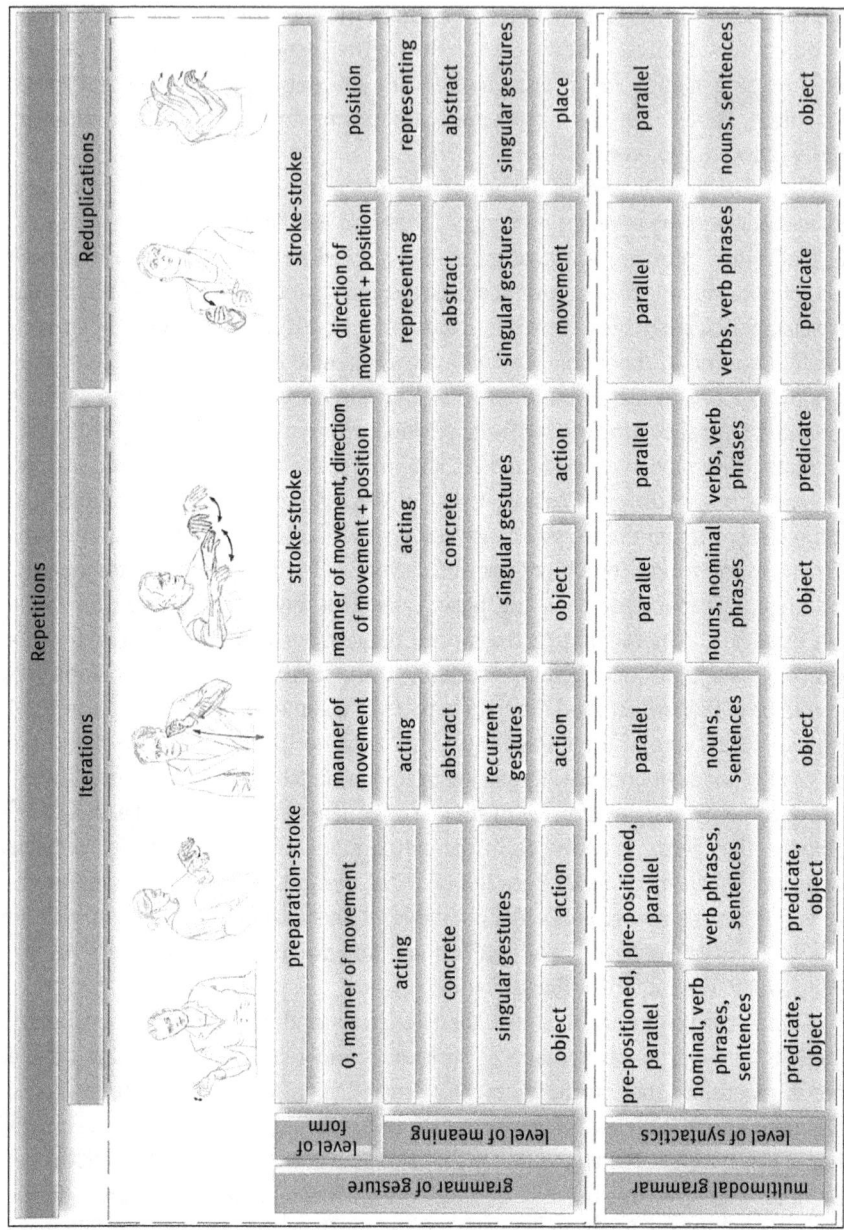

Figure 25: Overview of iterations and reduplications and their temporal and syntactical relation with speech.

5.2 Repeating gestures: Emphasizing or modifying the syntax of speech? — 127

repetitions, namely iterations expressing concrete meaning (e.g., examples "Arko" Figure 15, "metal thing" Figure 16).[69] Reasons for concentrating on this type are: second most frequent type, clearest alignment with specific syntactical units of the verbal utterance, adding semantic features to speech, modifying the semantics of the spoken utterance, existing research on the relevance of gestures in nominal and verbal phrases (Fricke, 2012; Kok, 2016b; Lücking, 2013; Müller, 1998; Streeck, 1990).

Picking up existing work on the integration of gestures into the syntax of speech, it can be assumed that gestures may be integrated into the verbal utterance by temporal overlap, syntactic gaps, or cataphorically via specific linguistic means such as deictic expressions like "so", "here", "there" or "like this" (Auer, 2000, 2005; De Ruiter, 2000; Fricke, 2007, 2012; Kita, 2003; Müller, 2008; Streeck, 1988, 1990, 2002, 2009; Stukenbrock, 2015). Considering these three possibilities of linking gestures with speech, the results of the present study reveal that the majority of gestural repetitions are positionally integrated by being executed in temporal overlap with the co-occurring speech segment (72 %).[70] This aspect will be discussed in more detail later on.

First, the chapter will zoom in on the cataphoric integration, which is the integration of by particular linguistic means. It is assumed that this type shows a higher degree of integration into speech than temporal overlap (see section 5.1.). Out of the 70 documented iterations with preparation-stroke sequences expressing concrete meaning, eight iterations are integrated through the use of the deicticon *so* ('such'), the adverb *hier* ('here'), or the pronoun *diese* ('this'). Concerning iterations with stroke-stroke sequences, 19 iterations out of 74 are cataphorically integrated into the verbal utterance. Several examples will illustrate this link between speech and gestures in the following section.

In the example "big rain drops" (see chapter 6, Figure 29 for more information on the example), speaker DA explains to her interlocutor that when it rains during summer and the rain drops are rather big, the rain will not last long (*man*

---

[69] Iterations conveying abstract meaning and reduplications or type A and B are therefore left aside. As these repetitions align with a range of different grammatical units and may even encompass whole sentences, it is assumed that their bond with the syntactic structure of the utterance is less strong and that, based on the study documented here, they achieve the greatest relevance on the level of semantics. Although reduplications of type A differ in that they show a clear alignment with verbs and verb phrase, they are excluded for the time being as they do not modify the semantics of the spoken utterance.

[70] 19 % of all repetitions occur in temporal pre-positioning to the co-expressive speech segment. 6% are post-positioned. Only 2% of the gestural repetitions occurred without speech and, more importantly, in speech pauses. Gestures in syntactic gaps were not documented in the study.

sacht wenn so große Tropfen runterkommen dann gibt's nich so viel Regen ['one says when such big rain drops are falling then there will not be much rain']). While uttering the nominal phrase *große Tropfen* ('big rain drops'), speaker DA produces a gestural iteration consisting of two strokes co-occurring with the adjective *große* ('big') and the noun *Tropfen* ('rain drops'). The strokes are cataphorically integrated into the verbal utterance through the deicticon "such" occurring right before the nominal phrase *große Tropfen* ('big rain drops') and demanding a qualitative description that can be instantiated gesturally. A similar pattern is shown in the example "metal thing" (see Figure 16.), in which the iteration produced by speaker MB, while saying *wo die Flasche Wein da in som Metallding drinne is* ('where the bottle wine is in such a metal thing'), is cataphorically integrated into the utterance through the deictic expression "such a". Another example is given when a speaker, while uttering *mit so großen Schläuchen gepumpt bekommen* ('have it pumped with such big pipes'), produces three strokes aligning with *so großen Schläuchen gepumpt* ('have it pumped with such big pipes').[71]

This functional integration of gestures is also illustrated in the next example ("Bummsinchen").[72] Not knowing the object referred to in the question, speaker MK begins to speculate and comes up with the idea that "Bummsinchen" refers to large round balls on a specific type of hat of a traditional costume used in the Black Forest. While saying *diese roten Bummsinchen oben aufm Hut* ('these red Bummsinchen on top of the hat'), MK produces a gestural iteration consisting of 7 strokes. Using a handshape 1–5 spread, with the palm orientated vertically towards the center of the gesture space, positioned above the head, MK moves both hands in small accented movement up and down while saying *diese roten Bummsinchen* ('these red Bummsinchen'). Through the gestural iteration, the nominal nucleus *Bummsinchen* is modified and gesturally specified concerning its shape, namely its roundness. Like the adjective "red" in the verbal utterance, the gesture qualifies the reference object with respect to its property. It can thus be assumed that the iteration also takes over the function of an attribute. By providing a qualitative description of the object specified by the noun, the gestural repetition modifies the nominal nucleus of the co-expressive speech segment. "This shows that the attributive function of modifying the nuclear noun in a noun phrase can also be instantiated solely by gesture."

---

[71] See chapter 6 for a further example illustrating this link of gestures with speech (example "handle", Figure 6.2.)
[72] This video example is also taken from the TV show "Genial Daneben". In this example, the comedians have to come up with an answer to the question "What is a Bummsinchen?". A "Bummsinchen" is a white roundish object, which can be attached to walls, for instance, to keep doors, cabinet doors etc. from hitting the wall.

(Fricke, 2014, p. 747). The examples discussed above are exemplarily cases of iterations that are cataphorically integrated into the verbal utterance. In the majority of all cases, they are used for the depiction of objects and add complementary semantic information by specifying the shape of the object. As such, they instantiate the function of an attribute in nominal phrases.

However, although cataphoric integration is documented for iterations in the study, most repetitions investigated are integrated into the verbal utterance by temporal overlap. Accordingly, in the majority of cases, the positional integration of the gestures is not achieved by specific linguistic meanings, particularly linking the repetition into the syntactic structure of the verbal utterance but solely by being executed at the same time with the co-expressive speech segment. Two examples will illustrate this link between speech and gestures. In the first example, speaker HS talks about and gesturally depicts neck collars for dogs. Right after one of the interlocutors uttered *dann kratzen die [Hunde] sich permanent am Ohr* ('then they [dogs] permanently scratch their ears'), speaker HS says *dann müssen die die Trichter tragen* ('then they have to wear to these collars'). In alignment with the noun "collars" and the verb "wear", HS produces an iteration consisting of three strokes. Using a flat hand positioned at both sides of the neck with a palm oriented vertically towards the center of the gesture space, she moves her hands in a diagonal movement upwards, downwards, and upwards. Whereas the verbal utterance carries the semantic features ACTION and ENTITY, the gesture carries the features ENTITY, SHAPE (triangular form), and POSITION (neck) and adds specifics about the reference object. Although two strokes of the iterations are executed in temporal overlap with the verb "wear" and the iteration thus encompasses the whole verb phrase *die Trichter tragen* ('wear those collars'), it is assumed that the repetition provides a qualitative description of the noun "collar". By starting in temporal overlap with the noun "collar" and due to the semantic feature expressed, the iteration adds complementary semantic information on the characteristics of the collars mentioned verbally. In combination with the verbal utterance and the utterance of the preceding speaker, the gestural depiction is capable of evoking the image of a specific type of collar: a pointy collar that is worn around the neck. Accordingly, similar to the cases of cataphoric integration, the repetition qualifies and restricts the reference object with respect to its property.

The same function can be observed in the example "draft beer", in which speaker BH, while uttering *ob es sich um ein Fassbier mit einem Bügel handelt* ('whether it is a draft beer with a handle'), produces a gestural iteration in which he depicts the action of pulling on a handle by moving the right fist with the palm oriented towards the center downwards with a bent movement. As a result, the gestural iteration can convey the idea of a particular type of draft beer. The verbally explicated draft beer with a handle is supplemented with the information of a specific type of handle that is gesturally depicted by showing its use. In doing so, the gestural iteration modifies the nominal phrase *ein Bügel* ('a handle') of the prepositional phrase *mit einem Bügel* ('with a handle'). It restricts the reference object with respect to its property: The handle is now a handle that is pulled down. This verbo-gestural prepositional phrase then modifies the preceding nominal phrase *ein Fassbier* ('a draft beer') of the verbal utterance. In the verbal utterance, the prepositional phrase *mit einem Bügel* ('with a handle') functions as an attribute to the aforementioned nominal phrase because it modifies the nominal nucleus. In conjunction with the gestural iteration, the nominal nucleus of the sentence *ein Fassbier* ('a draft beer') is now restricted to a draft beer with a handle that is pulled down and not, as one would typically assume, a draft beer with a tap. This attributive function of the verbo-gestural prepositional phase is underlined because the gestural repetition starts in overlap with the noun "draft beer". The temporal extension of the gestural iteration over the nominal phrase and the prepositional phrases establishes both of them as the items of reference of the iteration as a whole, thereby creating a complex multimodal utterance structure in which speech and gesture are linked in a particular way on the syntactic level.

Both examples illustrated that, even though the repetitions were not linked with speech via particular linguistic means but solely through temporal overlap, the gestures' relevance for the syntax of spoken utterance is comparable: They add complementary semantic information and specify the entity that is signified by the nominal nucleus. They instantiate the function of attributes as they constrain and modify the noun of a nominal phrase by depicting forms, sizes, and shapes of referents in the real world. This frequent co-occurrence of gestural iterations with particular syntactical categories of the verbal utterance indicates a particularly strong link between the syntax of speech and co-speech gestures.[73] This aspect will be discussed in more detail in the following section. First, iterations depicting actions will be addressed.

When discussing the semantic relation of iterations with the spoken utterance in chapter 4, it was highlighted that many iterations are used for the depiction of actions and, in particular, specify actions expressed verbally regarding its manner. Moreover, iterations depicting actions most frequently go along with verbs or verb

---

[73] This argument might even be applicable to examples, in which iterations express redundant semantic information. Even in those cases, they instantiate attribute function. Although the gestures express the same semantic information as the adjectives in speech, the gestural iterations frequently align with adjectives, nouns, or the whole nominal phrase thus specifying the nominal nucleus by expressing qualitative characteristics. Accordingly, if the verbal adjective would not have been uttered, the gestures could easily take over the function of modifying the nominal nucleus of the verbal utterance.

phrases (see Table 5.1.) and are integrated into the verbal utterance via temporal overlap. The study only documented one instance in which an iteration depicting an action was cataphorically integrated into the utterance. In this example, speaker HvS produces an iteration consisting of three strokes while saying *der andere ist schon so runtergetreten* ('the other one is already such stepped down'). Using a flat hand with the palm turned downwards, she moves both hands in straight and accented movements downwards. By encompassing both parts of the verb, namely *ist* ('is') and *runtergetreten* ('stepped down') and expressing the semantic features of ACTION, MANNER, and DIRECTION, the gestural iteration emphasizes and visualizes the idea of slippers which are stepped down. The gestural iteration is thus related to the predicate of the sentence and expresses semantic information that needs to be brought into relation with the action expressed verbally. Furthermore, the gestural iteration is integrated into the utterance through the deicticon *so* ('such') demanding for a qualitative description.[74]

An example that indicates a similar semantic and functional relation with the predicate of the sentence, yet without using a particular linguistic item linking the gesture more specifically to the verbal utterance, is given when a speaker gesturally depicts the action of stamping. While saying *es wird etwas gestanzt* ('something is being stamped'), the speaker moves her flat hand with a palm downwards twice with an accented movement. The strokes of the repetition thereby temporarily align with the auxiliary verb *wird* ('is being') and the verb *gestanzt* ('stamped'). Due to this temporal overlap and with the semantic features expressed by the iteration (ACTION and MANNER), the gestural repetition evokes the image of an action that is comparable to punching holes in a piece of paper. In doing so, the iteration specifies the manner of the action and restricts the meaning of the verb "stamping" to a specific type, namely one that is executed by pushing down a movable object with the palm of the hand. Other types of stamping, with an object that needs to pressed down by both hands, for instance, are excluded. Two further examples illustrating this modifying function concerning actions have already been discussed in more detail in chapter 4.2 but will be discussed again briefly (example "put it

---

[74] Interestingly, only the last stroke of the iteration occurs after the deicticon 'such'. The majority is produced ahead of the transition point. This structural succession has been observed in a variety of cataphorically integrated iterations documented in the corpus (see for instance example "metal thing"). In cases of gestural repetitions, it can thus be observed that the deiction *so* assumes not only a cataphoric function in looking ahead to the following stroke and the qualitative description contained therein. Rather, it also takes over anaphoric function by retrospectively highlighting the preceding strokes of the gestural repetition and the qualitative description expressed therein. See Kok (2016) and Streeck (2002) for similar examples and argument that *so* can be preceding or following.

in" and "pipe"). In the example "put it in", speaker HF explains that shoplifters might hide the stolen goods inside a fox fur.[75] In parallel to the phrase *um da die Sachen reinzustecken* ('to put in the things'), HF produces a gestural iteration consisting of three strokes. Using a handshape with the fingers 1–5 bent, a palm lateral towards body orientation, and an arced movement to the left located in the upper center of the gesture space, the speaker expresses and transmits a particular idea of "putting something in", namely the action of putting something into a jacket.[76] By occurring in alignment with the verb *reinstecken* ('to put it in') and the semantic feature present in the gestures (ACTION, MANNER, and POSITION), the iteration can modify the semantics of the verb concerning its manner. The verbal utterance itself only carries the features ACTION so that the gestural iterations adds complementary semantic features to the one expressed in speech and thus restricts the meaning of the verb *reinstecken* ('put it in').

The same semantic relation has also been shown for the example "pipe", in which a speaker depicts how the liquid is being spread over a surface. While saying *und machen oben auf die Tragfläche drauf* ('and put it on top of the wing'), speaker GC gesturally depicts the holding of a pipe with one hand, which is then successively moved to the left and right. The verb *machen* ('put') of the verbal utterance is thus modified and specified through gesturally depicting the object with which the action is executed. Although the iteration depicts an action with an object, the gestural iteration functions in relation to the predicate of the sentence. By adding the feature MANNER, which is based on the hand's successive movement from left to right, the verb *machen* ('put') is specified to mean "spray". The multimodal meaning of the phrase *und machen oben auf die Tragfläche drauf* ('put it on top of the wing') then comes to mean something like 'spray it on top of the wing', in which the afore unspecified action is now specified and restricted.

Based on the examples discussed above, it is proposed that iterations depicting actions and specifying the manner of the action expressed verbally seem to fulfill a function comparable to adverbial determinations and, in particular, to adverbial adjectives. Adverbial adjectives stand in semantic relation to the action expressed in the verb. They specify the described action and thus modify the verb (Eisenberg, 1999/2001b). Adverbial adjectives do no express a constant property of the object or the subject of the sentence but rather, by being related to the verb, qualify a temporarily restricted property of the verb itself (Helbig & Buscha,

---

75 The speaker tries to find an explanation for the concept of a fox fur.
76 This idea is thereby emphasized by the other hand, which holds open the jacket speaker HF is wearing.

1998). Relating this to the discussed examples of iterations depicting actions, it seems reasonable to assume that their function is akin to adverbial determinations. As the iterations do not relate to the sentence as a whole but only to the action and the action expressed therein, they are always related to the verb and therefore qualify to be functioning similarly to adverbial adjectives in speech. This assumption is underlined because iterations depicting actions frequently align with the verb of the sentence or encompass those syntactic constituents that include the predicate of the sentence. Moreover, most cases documented in the present study, the end of the gestural repetition coincides with the syntactic reference group of the repetition, the verb of the sentence. Instances in which iterations surpass the verb of the sentence are rare.[77] Based on their syntactic alignment with the predicate of the verbal utterance and the expression of complementary semantic features, the iterations might be semantically and functionally relevant for the creation of the multimodal utterance.

The section and the results presented above indicate that gestural repetitions are structurally integrated via temporal coordination and accompany particular syntactic units and functions. Furthermore, the results suggest that this relation of the gestures with speech is not random but instead follows a specific pattern depending on the type of repetition, underlining the semantic difference documented in chapter 4. Moreover, taking a specific group of gestural iterations as a starting point, the study also noted a specific functional relation with speech on the level of syntax. Gestural iterations may instantiate attributive and adverbial function when going along with nominal and verbal phrases. These rather close links of gestures with the syntax of speech indicate that their relevance may go beyond the level of semantics, meaning that gestures not solely serve a purpose on the cognitive level but may also have relevance for the syntax of spoken utterances. The following section will thus concentrate on how this rather tight link might be accounted for.

5.3 Explaining the link: Multimodal constructions?

One theoretical framework gaining more and more attention among gesture research for explaining possible recurrent links between speech and gestures is Construction Grammar. Construction Grammar covers a range of different approaches developed since the 1980s that share basic assumptions yet may differ quite

---

[77] The same structural characteristic holds for iterations depicting objects. Here, iterations are rarely executed after the reference group (noun or nominal phrase) has been uttered.

radically in their understanding (Bergen & Chang, 2013; Croft, 2001; Fillmore, Kay, & O'Connor, 1988; Goldberg, 1995; Lakoff, 1987). (For a detailed account and discussion of the particular lines see Ziem & Lasch, 2013.) All approaches are based on cognitive-linguistic assumptions and the view that the ability for language is grounded in general cognitive skills. Constructionist approaches aim to describe the grammar of a single language using one cognitive-linguistic unit, the "construction". Language is understood as a mental and social phenomenon that is manifested and entrenched in language use. The grammar of a single language is made up of a structured inventory of constructions, stored in the mental lexicon ("constructicon") in which grammatical, semantic, and pragmatic information is collected alongside. Constructions are form-meaning pairings, in which the form includes syntactic, phonological, and prosodic information, and the meaning side combines semantic and pragmatic information. Constructions comprise units of varying degrees of abstractness and complexity and are not per se restricted in their size. They include derivational morphemes (e.g., -er), lexical units (e.g., *banana*), idioms (e.g., *Going great guns*) and grammatical constructions such as ditransitives (e.g., *He baked her a muffin*) or passives (e.g., *The armadillo was hit by a car*)[78] (Goldberg, 2013, p. 17). Constructions "are in general holistic, that is, the meaning of the whole construction is motivated by the meaning of the parts, but is not computable from them" (Lakoff, 1987, p. 465). The meaning can be made explicit by using "Idealized Cognitive Models" (Lakoff, 1987), underlining the fact that constructional meaning is prototypically organized.

Until today, the majority of Construction Grammar approaches are directed towards an analysis of speech (written or spoken), neglecting the multimodality of spoken language. However, Langacker explicitly states that

> besides manual gestures, [. . .] facial expression, actions performed more globally (e.g. a shrug), and even factors like posture and body language [. . .] may all be closely bound up with linguistic expressions, in which case they can hardly be excluded from "language" on an a priori basis. (Langacker, 2009, p. 280)

Similarly, Chang notes the possibility that the form of a construction may also "extend to any kind of signifier, including manual and facial gestures" (Chang, 2008, p. 64).

The possibility of including other modalities besides speech into the conception of constructions and thus grammatical analyses, shortcomings of other

---

[78] Approaches differ with respect to their notion of constructions. Langacker (2009), for instance, includes inflected words in his understanding of symbolic units (constructions) but excludes morphemes and lexemes.

grammatical theories to account for spoken language use,⁷⁹ and the grounding of Construction Grammar in cognitive-linguistic principles and its usage-based perspective, has led to a range of studies exploring the link between speech and gestures aiming to account for the empirical fact that particular linguistic constructions are frequently accompanied by gestures or head movements.

Based on an analysis of the German modal particle *einfach* ('simply', 'just') used in TV news reports, Schoonjans, Brône and Feyaerts (2015), for instance, document that in 43% of the investigated cases, the modal particle co-occurs with a pragmatic headshake when used as an assertion. As both the particle and the headshake, mark intensification, an evaluation, a non-existing exception, or the existence of only one option, their frequent use is not surprising to the authors (Schoonjans et al., 2015, p. 300). More interestingly, however, they note that although the head shake is used often in temporal overlap with the modal particle, it also frequently occurs before or after and may even be executed over the whole turn. The authors furthermore discuss that the particle *einfach* is also used without the headshake and vice versa and that the headshake may occur with other particles or lexical elements, such as *halt* ('simply'), *wirklich* ('really'), *natürlich* ('of course'), *einfach* ('simply', 'just'). Based on the observed co-occurrence of the modal particle *einfach* with the headshake and because of the existing semantic and functional analogy, the authors propose two types of constructions: 1) semi-multimodal constructions, in which both the modal particle *einfach* and the headshake function as autonomous and different constructions and 2) multimodal constructions, in which the modal particle *einfach* and the headshake as a whole constitute the construction. The multimodal construction [headshake + einfach] is characterized by a prototypical structure and can thus be realized monomodally (verbally or gestural) or multimodally (verbally and gestural). Both types of constructions rest on the redundancy, that is, similarities in meaning of the headshake and the modal particle (Schoonjans et al., 2015, p. 301ff).

Based on a study investigating parent-child interactions of Swedish children between 18 and 30 months, Andrén (2010, 2014) shows that children frequently used head gestures (head shake and nodding) in combination with particular words or multi-word units and other gestures, in particular, deictic gestures. For instance, the headshake occurs in 85% with spoken elements (e.g., a response morpheme *no*) and in 94% with a deictic gesture. Moreover, Andrén found a gradual change over time in the type of lexical or grammatical unit correlating

---

79 Deppermann (2006, p. 44) highlights three main reasons for other grammatical theories to fall short of explaining spoken language: 1) sentence assumption, 2) formality assumption, and 3) compositionality assumption.

with the head shake: From a 100% correlation with a response particle at 18–20 months to only a third of the gestures being accompanied by a response particle at 27–30 months (Andrén, 2014, p. 150). He concludes that the progression observable in the children can be understood as a

> progression from a more fixed kind of use of these gestures only together with a very restricted set of words (one or a few response morphemes) to a more flexible use of these gestures in combination with all sorts of units of speech, such as words and clauses.
> (Andrén, 2010, p. 270)

As a result, Andrén proposes a continuum of multimodal constructions that is not only applicable to the use of the conventionalized gestures in the children investigated but which can be assumed to describe instead a general characteristics of multimodal language use. Multimodal constructions are understood as "conventionalized constructions that span across modalities" (Andrén, 2014, p. 147) and fall between two types: a) Item-based constructions, in which the combination of speech and gestures is more robust and fixed and only occurs with a relatively limited set of verbal elements and, b) flexible multimodal constructions, in which the gesture is used more flexible with a range of different verbal elements. Whereas in the first case, the combined units are rather a kind of "holophrase", in the latter case, the units are "creatively or at least productively combined." (Andrén, 2010, p. 270) Going along with this liberation of the gesture from a restricted use with particular spoken elements is a fading of the semantic redundancy of both modalities. Whereas a semantic doubling characterizes item-based constructions, flexible constructions show a stronger semantic separation of both modes, so that speech and gesture can transmit different contents. However, in both cases, gestures are integral elements of multimodal constructions, although they might instead be understood as optional rather than obligatory elements (see Schoonjans, et al., 2015; Zima, 2014).

A similar range between a more fixed use of gestures with particular units of speech and a more flexible use was observed by Bressem and Müller (2017) in their study on a conventionalized gesture of German speakers. Based on a corpus of 34 hours of video data of different discourse types ranging from naturalstic conversations to TV-discussions, political debates, and experimental settings, the authors identify 75 uses of the Throwing Away gesture. The Throwing Away gesture is a partly conventionalized gesture with a stable semantic core that is specified in particular contexts-of-use and as such can be regarded as polysemous because of the thematically related functions (Ladewig, 2011). The Throwing Away gesture is a culturally-shared gesture among German speakers and takes over pragmatic functions (modal, performative) (Bressem & Müller, 2014a, b). The gesture is based on a shared embodied motivation: manual actions that remove unwanted and annoying objects from which the gesture derives its particular meaning: When used in relation with speech, Throwing Away gestures enact these actions and metaphorically throw away, remove, and dismiss annoying objects. The metaphoric clearing of the body space goes along with a qualification of the rejected objects as annoying, e.g., a topic of talk is negatively assessed. Bressem and Müller (2017) show that the gesture has a particular distribution with lexical elements in speech: It is used without speech (14%), with interjections (8%), with modal particles (30%), with verbal negation (17%), and with a range of different open class elements, such as nouns, verbs, and adverbs (31%). In all of the different uses, the gesture expresses the semantic value of getting rid of topics of talk by throwing it away from the speaker's body, and it carries the pragmatic value of negative assessment. However, the gesture also carries specific, pragmatic values depending on the grammatical or lexical element it is used with: When replacing speech, the gesture predominantly fulfills performative function. When used with interjections or modals, the gesture adds a modal or affective qualification to the propositional content expressed. When used with verbal negation and different word classes, the gesture negatively assesses the referent expressed in the proposition. Based on this tight and recurrent relation with the syntax, semantics, and pragmatics of speech, the authors propose that speech and gesture form a verbo-kinesic construction, the "Negative-Assessment-Construction" [Throwing Away gesture + PRT/ADV/V/N]. The verbo-kinesic construction is grounded in an embodied frame of experience in the sense of Fillmore (1982), a schematized scene of mundane actions, namely the "Away Action scheme" (Bressem & Müller, 2014a). Moreover, based on Goldberg (1995, p. 39ff) and the assumption that "constructions which correspond to basic sentence types encode as their central senses event types that are basic to human experience", Bressem and Müller (2017) assume that the proposed construction is grounded in scenes with abstract participant roles and argument relations.[80] More importantly, however, they put forward the argument that only through the interplay of speech and gesture a scene, according to Goldberg, is evoked.

The above-discussed studies address the use of (partly) conventionalized gestures with speech. Another strand of research focuses on iconic gestures with abstract lexical and syntactical categories. With her study, Zima (2014) also addresses the question of multimodal constructions by starting from speech. Based on video data taken from

---

[80] A similar argumentation is put forward by Mittelberg (2017) for existential constructions in German. Picking up on Goldberg (1985) and Fillmore (1982), the author argues that "basic manual actions of giving and holding and the corresponding schematic scenes may not only feed into ditransitive and transitive constructions involving some sort of transfer or object manipulation but also motivate multimodal instantiations of existential constructions in German discourse."

the corpus of the Red Hen Lab (Jo, Steen & Turner, 2017), Zima investigates the use of co-verbal gestures in conjunction with two English motion constructions ([V(motion) *in circles*] and [*all the way from* X PREP Y]) and shows that both constructions are frequently used with co-verbal gestures (61% and 81%). Zima focuses her analysis on gestures that are semantically associated with the motion event and thus concentrates on gestures depicting literal motions and abstract motion. For both constructions, the results emphasize that the gestures highlight aspects of the motion events encoded in the verbal utterance (path or manner of motion). Despite these commonalities, the motion constructions differ concerning the gestures that are used. Whereas all gestures used in overlap with the [V(motion) *in circles*] construction are characterized by a multiple circular motion, the [*all the way from* X PREP Y] construction is accompanied by a range of different gestural forms (index finger, lax flat hands combined with varying patterns of motion, orientations, and positions in gesture space). For the [V(motion) *in circles*] construction, Zima identifies a tendency for it to be used more frequently with gestures describing literal physical motion than abstract motion. The [*all the way from* X PREP Y] construction shows a relatively frequent deictic use and habit for the gestural depiction of fictive motion (Talmy, 2000, p. 99ff). Concluding, Zima argues that for both cases the co-occurring gestures comply with the recurrence requirement for constructions. Moreover, together with the verbal component, they build a meaning unit. Hence, the constructions are multimodal. Zima's understanding of the multimodal construction is comparable to the one by Schoonjans, Brône, and Feyaerts (2015). Highly frequent gestures can but do not need to be part of a multimodal construction as speakers "orientate themselves on conventionalized and mentally anchored constructions in actual language use" and thus have at hand a "multimodal schema as part of their linguistic and communicational inventory" (Zima, 2014, p. 41, translation JB).

Wu (2018) addresses transitive, intransitive, and copular constructions in English. Also based on a corpus of video data of American TV talks shows retrieved from the RedHen Database, the study documents that iconic gestures are sensitive to the type of construction and distribute across the constructions differently (frequent with high-transitive and intransitive constructions, less frequent with low-transitive and copular constructions). Moreover, speakers chose particular gestural depictions for the different constructions: Miming actions are preferred for high-transitive constructions. Tracing outlines or paths is more frequent for intransitive constructions. And for low-transitive and copular constructions, a dominant use of molding gestures is documented. Moreover, for constructions encoding events with an externally caused change of state or location, the study documents a different use of gestures for path properties of events but not for transitivity: More iconic gestures occurred with events with the Agent's path and/or the Figure's path than with those without such a path. Accordingly, the author concludes that "gestures are related in different ways to different kinds of event construal and various properties of events associated with various grammatical constructions [. . .] and that the gestures are co-expressive with the constructions to varying degrees." (Wu, 2018, p. 226).

Also, using naturalistic interactional data from the Red Hen archive, Hinnell (2018) investigates five aspect-marking periphrastic constructions in North American English (continue, keep, start, stop, quit). Taking a quantitative perspective, the author documents a different expression of the construction in the accompanying co-speech gestures, and, moreover the fact that aspectual construal is iconically visible in a range of gesture parameters:

> Open aspect auxiliaries (CONTINUE and KEEP) reliably correlate with longer onset timing and a greater mean number of action phases per stroke, while phase aspect (START, STOP and QUIT) are correlated with more synchronous onset of gesture and fewer stroke segmentations. [. . .] Correlations were also seen for certain auxiliaries and particular movement directions and movement types. These were shown to parallel semantic distinctions in both aspectual and force-dynamic characteristics of the event construal.
> (Hinnell, 2018, p. 31)

Based on these results, Hinnell argues that although gestures are not an obligatory part of the spoken constructions, "when they are gestured, they certainly exhibit conventionalized forms" (Hinnell, 2018, p. 31) and as such allow for a tentative conclusion of a tight link between gestures and speech in the form of multimodal constructions. This argument is supported by the fact that gestures are a frequent element of all auxiliary constructions examined in the study (59% were co-expressed with a gesture) and that they mark aspectual information through gesture timing, the structure of stroke, and movement type.

The above-discussed studies clearly indicate a tight relation between co-speech gestures and speech on different levels (words, phrases, lexical, and syntactical categories) for particular linguistic constructions. Proposals thereby underline that the verbal construction investigated is entrenched and/or the gesture is itself a recurrent and frequent pattern (head shake, deictic gesture, recurrent gesture). Furthermore, the paring of speech and gesture is based on a recurrent and frequent use visible in a high amount of the occurrences.[81] These aspects address a central question: Is it possible to conceive of these recurrent verbo-gestural patterns as candidates for constructions, and how do these patterns meet prerequisites of constructions, that is, recurrence, entrenchment, and non-compositionality?

All authors agree that for the notion of construction to be applied to multimodal language use, recurrence, entrenchment, and non-compositionality provide

---

[81] An overview of current state of studies can be found in Bergs and Zima (2018).

essential requirements.[82] The position that is taken, however, differs. Picking up on Goldberg's (2006) definition of a construction, Zima und Bergs (2017) point out that

> there are two forms of evidence for multimodal constructions: (1) a gesture or some non-verbal feature is recurrently used with a given verbal structure and its meaning contribution to the multimodal instantiations is 'not strictly predictable'. This corresponds to the 'strong definition of constructions'; (2) in addition, a pairing of a given gesture (or facial expression etc.) with a given verbal construction could also be stored as a unit if they co-occur with 'sufficient frequency'.[83]

Lanwer (2017), for instance, argues that it may not be possible to formulate a frequency threshold, as constructions are inherently schematic to various degrees, so that the difference between mono- or multimodal constructions is also a matter of schematicity.

> Following insights from research on embodied cognition (e. g. Clark 2011) as well as from embodied construction grammar (e. g. Bergen and Chang 2005), meaning itself can in many parts be seen as being inherently characterized by cross-modal neural connections and thus seems to be inherently multimodal, too. (Lanwer, 2017 p. 2)

Zima (2017a) even argues that it may not be necessary to define a threshold at the moment, as more empirical case studies on a wide range of topics are needed to first gain a better understanding. Instead, it might be best to assume a

> continuum from constructions which are only infrequently and loosely connected to co-speech gesture use to constructions which are frequently and systematically co-instantiated with a given gesture.[84]

---

[82] Here, it seems, is multimodal research under even stronger constraints than verbal analyses. As other authors (Schoonjans et al., 2015, p. 301; Zima, 2014, p. 41) point out, the question of recurrence and entrenchment is not asked as explicitly in monomodal studies although it is of the same importance.

[83] Ningelen & Auer (2017) and Ziem (2017) align with the strong definition. From this perspective, Ziem (2017), for instance proposes four claims for multimodal constructions: "1) A multimodal construction is a conventionalized pairing of a complex form that consists, at least, of a verbal element combined with a kinetic element. 2) Multimodal constructions manifest themselves either as inherently multimodal units or as entrenched cooccurrences of a verbal and a kinetic element (as opposed to constructions solely realized in a multimodal way). 3) Multimodal constructions are in principle distinguished from both multimodal instantiations of constructions and linguistic constructions elaborated by way of gestures (and non-verbal behavior in general). 4) Multimodal constructions are part of the constructicon, that is, the system of constructions in a given language, and, as such, they co-constitute a language user's U-relevant knowledge."

[84] See also Lanwer (2017) and Schoonjans (2017).

Similarly, Cienki (2017) proposes that constructions are rooted at the level of utterances, which is, in its general structure, modality-independent so that constructions can be divided into more and less prototypical constructions with the elements of the constructions having different status and the given knowledge of a speaker of these constructions may vary.

How can the framework of Construction Grammar now be used to explain the tight link of gestural repetitions with nominal and verbal phrases documented in the present study? Before addressing this question, first, an understanding and conception of multimodal constructions are proposed that will guide the discussion of the empirical results of the study.

When trying to tackle the question of constructions in language use, one is naturally confronted with the question of what is (not) considered a construction. Following Schneider (2015), we define a construction as a complex sign schema, which "as a whole exhibits an independent meaning or discourse function [. . .] that is describable as a 'potential for semiosis' (Bücker 2012, p. 60) also independently of particular contexts of utterances" (Schneider, 2015, p. 133, translation JB). Accordingly, constructions are entrenched complex patterns that have a specific constructional meaning. Thus, we consider complex units to be examples of constructions, such as idioms or ditransitive constructions. Morphemes or simple lexemes do not fall under the notion (Langacker, 2008). As Schneider (2015) points out, the "term construction suggests that it is something composed of several parts, something that is construed, a *complex* sign. Thus, it is with good reason that simplex forms and all other single morphemes are excluded from the extension of the notion of constructions" (Schneider 2015: 132, emphasis in original). Furthermore, we assume that constructional meaning also includes pragmatic functions.

> This pragmatic bond is already guiding for language acquisition: constructions are at first used in pragmatically narrow limited contexts and forms before they are abstracted, lexically instantiated more variably and used for various purposes.[85] (Deppermann, 2006, p. 55)

As pragmatic information motivates the meaning of a construction and defines requirements for its use, it is of particular importance for the nature of constructions and, as will be made clear in the following section, even for possible constructions in multimodal language use. Furthermore, constructions are assumed to show different degrees of schematization. Verbal constructions, for instance, range from lexicalized fixed idioms (e.g., *kick the bucket*) to lexically partly specified constructions (e.g., [typically N] *typically German*) to fully schematized constructions (e.g.,

---

[85] See Ziem & Lasch (2013, p. 13ff) for a detailed discussion of the relevance of pragmatics in Construction Grammar.

[ditransitive construction] *I brought the coffee*) (see Deppermann, 2006, p. 48ff). Moreover, it is assumed that word meaning is tightly linked and grounded in mental representations of perceptual, motor, and affective experiences of the world and that constructions are grounded in the perceptual and senso-motoric system and, in particular, in image and embodied schemata (Bergen & Chang, 2013). Accordingly,

> constructions pair schematic form representations with schematic meaning representations, which are further constrained to be abstractions over perceptual and motor representations that can be simulated, or over characteristics of simulations in general.
>
> (Bergen & Chang, 2004)

Words and other constructions thus serve as pathways connecting modality-specific knowledge about forms with meaning, and "they evoke the experiential schemas (corresponding to events, actions, objects, etc.) involved in a particular utterance and specify how these are combined." (Bergen & Chang, 2013: 10). Applying this understanding of constructions to multimodal language use, the following continuum of constructions is proposed (see Figure 26).

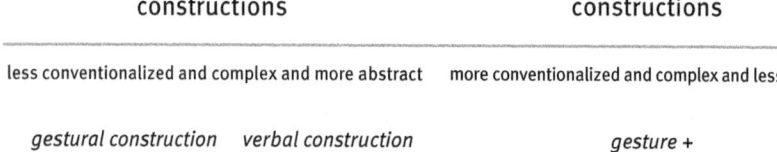

Figure 26: Continuum of constructions in multimodal language use.

It arranges recurrent patterns of speech and kinesic expressions depending on the degree of conventionalization and complexity and abstractness and distinguishes two main classes of constructions: multimodal constructions and verbo-kinesic constructions. With these two classes, the continuum sets apart a) the multimodal instantiation of gestural constructions and verbal constructions and b) instances in which speech and gesture as a whole form a complex sign schema.

The left side of the continuum includes complex sign schemas in which either gestures or speech are the "driving" force for the recurrent pairing of the modalities.

The gestural reduplicative construction expressing the notion of plurality (see chapter 3 for a detailed discussion and also Bressem [2015, submitted]) is an example in which an entrenched gestural pattern can be classified as a complex

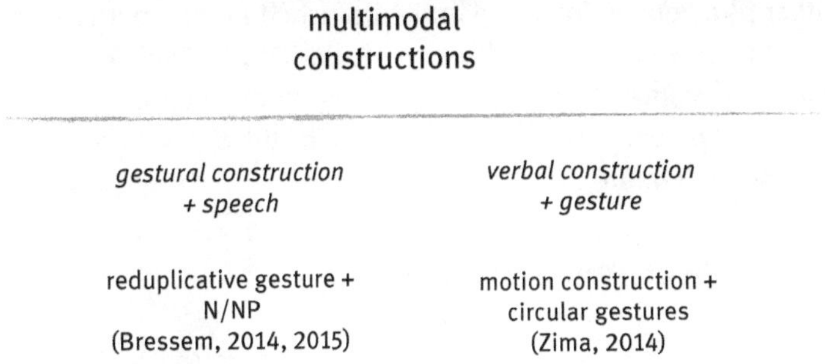

5.3 Explaining the link: Multimodal constructions?

```
                    multimodal
                   constructions
_____
   gestural construction        verbal construction
        + speech                     + gesture

   reduplicative gesture +     motion construction +
           N/NP                   circular gestures
    (Bressem, 2014, 2015)            (Zima, 2014)
```

Figure 27: Types of multimodal constructions.

sign schema on the level of the gestures themselves. Verbal motion constructions, as investigated by Zima (2014, 2017), are examples of multimodal constructions that rest upon a verbal construction. Here, entrenched complex patterns on the level of speech ([V(motion) *in circles*], [*all the way from* X PREP Y]) frequently co-occur with particular circular gestures. The abstract meaning of the verbal constructions (movement along a circular path, directionality, and extension in space) is embodied through the accompanying gestures. It thus leads to a multimodal instantiation of the verbal construction.[86]

Both types of multimodal constructions differ for the modality the construction is to be found in and in the interrelation of speech and gesture. Whereas for instantiations of verbal constructions, a gesture is optional, speech is obligatory for gestural constructions. Although the gestural construction carries an abstract meaning itself (e.g., pluralization), the meaning needs to be indexicalized by the co-occurring speech segment. Moreover, the type of gestures that are used for the particular constructions varies. In multimodal instantiations of verbal constructions, we see, as Zima (2014, 2017) for instance has shown, the frequent use of singular gestures depicting either concrete or abstract actions, objects, events, or circumstances. Furthermore, deictic gestures may be used to highlight abstract or concrete points in space. In gestural constructions, however, it is assumed that not particular types of gesture occur frequently but rather schematic gestural patterns as in the case presented by Bressem (2013, 2015).

On the right side of the continuum, we find verbo-kinesic patterns, which themselves may form a construction (see Figure 28). In these cases, the unity of speech and gesture forms a complex sign schema with a particular semantic and pragmatic meaning (Bressem & Müller, 2017). A verbo-kinesic construction

---

[86] The phenomena by Wu (2018) and Hinnell (2018) also fall under this category.

is given when either a) a conventionalized and entrenched kinesic pattern (recurrent gesture, emblem) is combined with a particular and limited set of linguistic units, or b) the syntax of speech exhibits a syntactic gap or a verbal deictic requiring a qualitative description that needs to be filled in via other modalities (e.g., *so* or *son* in German).[87]

Verbo-Kinesic constructions
gesture + speech

PRT/ADV/V/N+ throwing away gesture (Bressem & Müller, 2014a)	so + gaze + gesture + NP/VP/ ADJ/ADV (Streeck, 2016)	syntactic gap + gesture (Ladewig, 2012, 2014)
response particle + headshake (+ deictic gesture) (Andrén, 2014)	so + NP (Fricke, 2012)	
einfach + headshake (Schoonjans, Bröne and Feyaerts, 2015)		
idiom + emblematic gesture (Baur and Chlosta, 2005)		

Figure 28: Types of verbo-kinesic constructions.

Examples for the first type of verbo-kinesic construction include the Negative-Assessment-Construction (Bressem & Müller, 2014a), the headshake used with response particles in Swedish (Andrén, 2010), or the German particle *einfach* used with headshake (Schoonjans, Bröne & Feyaerts, 2015). Also, idioms, such as *to knock on wood* or *I felt this big* for which the depiction of the action is an obligatory element, are examples of verbo-kinesic constructions (Baur & Chlosta, 2005). In all cases, we see a frequent and entrenched combination of linguistic routines with recurrent kinesic expressions. Within this class of verbo-kinesic constructions, different degrees of complexity can be distinguished. Following Andrén (2010, 2014), holophrastic units of speech and gesture can be identified in which the combination of verbal and kinesic elements shows a stronger degree of fixedness. In these cases, specific linguistic elements (e.g., particles, interjections, idioms) frequently co-occur with a particular kinesic expression

---

[87] The definition given here is preliminary and might need to be adapted with growing empirical evidence. For now, such a limited understanding of verbo-kinesic constructions is meant to prevent a weakening of the notion 'construction'.

5.3 Explaining the link: Multimodal constructions? — 145

(e.g., Throwing Away gesture, headshake). However, gestures may also show a higher degree of variation in the linguistic elements with which they co-occur (e.g., words, clauses). In these cases, a more flexible use of the kinesic expression with speech can be observed, going along with a fading of the semantic redundancy that is characteristic of item-based constructions. Yet, the combination of speech and gesture in these cases is not random. The type of kinesic expression that may go along with the linguistic routine cannot be freely chosen but is rather subject to restrictions that lie within the particular semantics and pragmatics of the construction. For all of the different variants of a verbo-kinesic construction, a common constructional meaning can be identified that may differentiate into a family of different meaning variants. In the case of the Throwing Away gesture, for instance, the constructional meaning can be assumed to be a negative assessment. In the particular meaning variants, the negative assessment varies as to what is being negatively assessed (actions of others or propositional content) or whether the gesture is used to express of modal or affective qualities through which topics of talk a negatively assessed. In the case of the Throwing Away gesture, and as it may be the case with other gestures that are based on mundane instrumental actions, the semantics of the verbo-kinesic construction is grounded in an embodied frame of experience in the sense of Fillmore (1982):

> By the term 'frame' I have in mind any system of concepts related in such a way that to understand any one of them you have to understand the whole structure in which it fits; when one of the things in such a structure is introduced into a text, or into a conversation, all of the others are automatically made available. (Fillmore, 1982, p. 111)

A semantic frame evokes a schematic cognitive scene. In the example of the "commercial event" for instance, "the elements of this schematic scene include a person interested in exchanging money (the Seller), the goods which the Buyer did or could acquire (the Goods), and the money acquired (or sought) by the seller (the Money)" (Fillmore, 1982, p. 116). For verbo-kinesic constructions, this cognitive scene may be a schematized scene of mundane actions. In the case of the "Negative-Assessment-Construction", for instance, the cognitive scene is the "Away Action scheme": a shared experiential frame that is grounded in mundane actions of moving or keeping away annoying objects and which includes as the elements an unpleasant situation (starting point) in which annoying objects are in the immediate surrounding (cause). These are removed through an action of the hand (action), which then leads to the removal of the objects and a neutral situation (endpoint) (Bressem & Müller, 2014a; Teßendorf, 2016). Moreover, based on Goldberg (1995, p. 39ff) and the assumption that "constructions which correspond to basic sentence types encode as their central senses event types that are basic to human experience", verbo-kinesic constructions may also be grounded in scenes with abstract participant roles and argument relations (see Bressem & Müller, 2017 for a more detailed discussion). Furthermore, these kinds of constructions essentially rest upon pragmatic information and "interactional frames", a conceptualization of the communicative encounter including knowledge about illocutionary forces and speech event routines (Fillmore, 1982, p. 117). Through the use of modal particles, interjections, lexical, gestural, and prosodic means, the verbo-kinesic construction carries the pragmatic value of negative assessment. In particular contexts-of-use, however, a specific, pragmatic value is expressed through gestural means that effects the interpretation of the utterances.

This strong pragmatic meaning is one aspect that sets this type of verbo-kinesic construction apart from multimodal constructions. Another is the fact that in verbo-kinesic constructions speech is combined with kinesic expressions that are recurrent and entrenched patterns of use, namely either emblematic gestures (headshake), recurrent gestures (e.g., Throwing Away gesture, index finger), or instrumental actions (e.g., knock). Emblematic gestures are fully conventionalized movements of the body that have a stable pairing of form and meaning. Recurrent gestures are frequent gestural patterns used by speakers with similar form and function across different contexts. The prototypical meaning on which these standards rest arises from

> the prototypical meaning of recurrent gestures, however, emerges from a conventionalization of different types of experiential usage contexts *along with* the embodied motivation of kinesic forms in actions and movement experiences of the body. This core meaning of recurrent gestures is a conventionalized link between a gestural form motivated by embodiment and a specific selection of recurring usage-contexts.
>
> (Müller, 2017, p. 294, emphasis in original)

Furthermore, it can be assumed that the semantization and conventionalization of recurrent gestures not only rests upon their derivation from mundane actions but also on the formation of kinesthemes in language use, that is, "intersubjectively semanticized movement tokens whose similarity on the level of form correlates with a similarity on the meaning level." (Fricke 2014a, p. 1622)

In multimodal constructions, however, we do not see a similar degree of semantization and conventionalization in the kinesic expressions. Instead, the gestures occurring with the verbal construction need to be understood as singular gestures that are found in the moment of speaking and acquire a local and indexicalized meaning. This fundamental difference between multimodal constructions and verbo-kinesic constructions also explains differences in the interrelation of the modalities. In multimodal instantiations of verbal constructions, a gesture is optional. For multimodal instantiations of gestural constructions, however, speech is obligatory. The prototypical verbo-kinesic construction consists of a linguistic and a kinesic expression, yet due to semantization and conventionalization on both levels, it is possible for either of the modality to be absent.

This is different in the second type of verbo-kinesic construction in which the syntax of speech, due to a syntactic gap or a deictic element, opens up a slot that needs to be filled, for instance, through a kinesic expression. When gestures are used in syntactic gaps, a verbal unit is replaced by a kinesic expression meaning that verbal information is not supplemented but is substituted by a kinesic expression (Ladewig, 2012, 2014a; McNeill, 2005; Slama-Cazacu, 1976). In these cases, the "syntactic gaps serve as anchor points for gestures to join in interrupted utterances", while the gestures "constitute the semantic centers of complex constituents [and] provide necessary information to interpret and make sense of an utterance" (Ladewig, 2014, p. 1671ff). Without the kinesic expression, the utterances would not be comprehensible. In these syntactic gaps, a variety of kinesic expressions may be used, yet fully conventionalized gestures (emblems) are less frequent than singular and recurrent gestures (Ladewig, 2012, 2014c). A similar picture arises when deictic elements in speech open up a slot that needs to be filled. In these cases, gestures may be cataphorically integrated into the verbal utterance: Through the use of *son* or *solch* ('such a'), gestures modify the nucleus noun of the nominal phrase by specifying and restricting it, thus expanding verbal noun phrases and taking over attribute function (Fricke 2012). In these cases, also frequent use of gaze towards the hands of the speaker can be observed. Accordingly, Streeck (2016) argues that the "so-construction" is characterized by the deictic element followed by a gaze and a respective gesture.[88] In cases of syntactic gaps and "so-constructions", the construction equally rests upon both modalities, and both speech and gestures are obligatory and need to be present for the constructional meaning to arise. As such, these types of verbo-constructions form the far right of the continuum as they are characterized by the highest degree of conventionalization and complexity of how speech and gesture may form a complex multimodal sign.

This section has put forward a classification of constructions in language use based on the following characteristics: a) modality, in which the constructions is expressed, b) type of kinesic expression used, c) characteristics and functions of kinesic expression, and d) semantic, pragmatic and temporal relation of speech and kinesic expression (cf Table 19). Each of the characteristics affects the type of

---

88 In addition to the construction grammar perspective, Streeck (2016) proposes a praxeological view on 'so-constructions' and suggests that these cases may also be understood as practices of gesture use, as a "method for the coordinated, dynamic, situated realization of different resources" (2016, p. 68ff).

pattern building that is observable when kinesic expressions and speech form complex multimodal signs. As a result, two different types of constructions were distinguished (multimodal constructions vs. verbo-kinesic constructions), which may be arranged along a continuum reflecting differences in the degree of conventionalization, complexity, and abstractness of constructions.

Table 19: Characteristics of multimodal and verbo-kinesic constructions.

	multimodal constructions		verbo-kinesic construction	
modality expressing construction	gesture	speech	speech + gesture	
type of kinesic expression	schematic gestural patterns	singular, deictic gestures	conventionalized/ entrenched kinesic pattern	singular gestures, recurrent gestures, conventionalized/ entrenched kinesic pattern
function of kinesic expression	semantic	semantic	pragmatic	semantic, pragmatic, syntactic
relation of modalities	speech obligatory	gesture optional	both optional	both obligatory

Against the background of this classification, it is argued that in cases of iterations expressing concrete meaning and co-occurring with nominal or verbal phrases, two different types of constructions can be identified, that reflect different degrees of integration. First, verbo-kinesic constructions, in which the iterations are cataphorically integrated into the verbal utterance via specific linguistic means. Secondly, multimodal constructions in which the iterations are functionally integrated into the verbal utterance via temporal overlap. Following the discussion of accounts on Multimodal Construction Grammar, in cataphorically integrated iterations, gestures are an obligatory part of the construction, and the connection between speech and gestures on the syntactic level is more robust.[89] In iterations that are positionally integrated via temporal overlap, the gesture mostly achieves a semantic function for the spoken utterance yet does not affect the syntactic structure of the utterance

---

[89] For an even stronger position, arguing that without the gesture, the meaning of the construction is not the same and the construction becomes uninterpretable without the gesture see Ningelen & Auer (2017) and Ziem 2017).

in the same way as in cases in which it is cataphorically integrated. Both cases of constructions thus show a continuum of how gestural repetitions may be integrated into the syntactic structure of an utterance. Following the argumentation put forward by Cienki (2017), Lanwer (2017), Schoonjans (2017), and Zima (2017), it can be underlined that constructions are stored with different degrees of schematicity, allowing for a continuum in which gestures are more or less tightly linked with the syntax of speech and thus more or less frequently and systematically instantiated along with speech.

What is particularly interesting, however, considering the frequency of the iterations in the present corpus, is that cases of cataphoric integration are much less frequent (27 out of 144 instances). So, gestures that are integrated into the verbal utterance via temporal overlap much more frequently accompany noun and verb phrases. These results thus clearly show a variable relevance of gestural repetitions for the syntax of speech. Yet at the same time, it emphasizes the semantic and cognitive relevance of the gestures, pointing out that

> both perceptual and motor experiences underlie our cognitive ability to delineate the implied visual properties of objects or the appropriate motor properties of events described in utterances, and that such mental representations are driven by the tight link between linguistic knowledge and associated experiences in everyday life (Barsalou 1999, 2008; MacWhinney 1999; Zwaan 2004; Zwaan and Radvansky 1998). Syntactic and semantic representations, then, are processed incrementally (Sato & Bergen, 2013, p. 347)

Frequent occurrences of gestures with syntactic units in speech, in the present case with nominal or verbal phrases, thus "serve to evoke and bind embodied semantic structures, allowing language understanding to depend on both specifically linguistic knowledge and general conceptual structures." (Bergen & Chang 2005, p. 185)[90] Whereas the verbal part assumes the binding on the linguistic

---

[90] Considering the capability of gestures, based on the gestural modes of representation (Müller, 1998, 2010b, 2013) to depict either actions or objects, it becomes clear that gestures may either refer to things or processes in the sense of Cognitive Grammar. Using the notion of semantic phonology (Stokoe 1991/2001; Armstrong and Wilcox 2009), Ladewig argues for a conception of gestures in terms of a "simultaneously-construed syntactic pattern", an internal structure resembling the structure of spoken language (see Figure 5.11.) Accordingly, "gestures are capable of depicting basic categories relying on experiences made with entities in (inter) action with the world, namely agent, patient or instrument being engaged in an (inter)action." (Ladewig, 2011, p. 119) Due to this characteristic, gestures are able to substitute nouns or verbs and function as objects or predicates cases of syntactic gaps (Ladewig 2011, 2020). From the perspective of Cognitive Grammar, gestures thus have a similar capability as speech. Moreover, the fact that gestures can either be perceived as things or processes enables their potential to function as parts of a reference predication relationship (Croft, 1990, 1991, 2001). In cases of profiling things, gestures have the capability to profile non-processual relationships and as

knowledge,[91] the gestural part takes over the grounding in aspects of embodied and conceptual knowledge. As a result, speech and gesture contribute particular semantic aspects to the unit as a whole. This sets the grounds for how component and composite structures fit together in a coherent assembly (as opposed to being a collection of unrelated elements). Semantic correspondences

> specify the conceptual overlap between component structures, thus providing the basis for their integration. They also specify how each component structure overlaps with the composite structure, thereby indicating what it contributes to the unified conception that emerges. (Langacker, 2008, p. 183)

Each element of the construction thus adds certain information so that often one is schematic, whereas the other one is more specific (see chapter 6). Due to the semantic correspondence of both elements, gestural iterations, for instance, may take over attributive as well as adverbial functions. Yet, in doing so, the gestures are dependent on speech (see Wilcox, Rossini & Pizzuto, 2010). Gestures' attributive functions, for instance, cannot be described independently of the nominal phrase of the verbal utterance. "A dependent structure refers schematically to an autonomous, supporting structure as an intrinsic aspect of its own characterization." (Langacker, 2008, p. 199)

Based on the concept of constructions, it can thus be argued that the frequent correlation of gestural repetitions with particular syntactic categories and functions is by no means random but dependent on the grammatical and semantic structure of the multimodal utterance. In particular, it shows that

> while we might not be able to support a broad claim that grammar is multimodal, the evidence suggests that a flexible model of grammar is in order (Cienki 2012). We can say that the kinds of usage events (Langacker 2000: 99; 2008: 457–459) of spoken language in which gestural forms of expression are more likely to occur in a conventional way are more prototypically multimodal. (Cienki 2013, p. 681)

---

such may take over the function of modifying a noun. In cases of profiling events, gestures are capable of modifying processual relationships creating prominence to the event itself

91 A similar idea is proposed by Ladewig (2011), who assumes that the syntactic structure of the utterance triggers a particular aspect of the gestures. If an interruption by the speaker exposes a syntactic gap of a noun the aspect of object is triggered that functions or forms part of an object. If a verb is exposed by a syntactic gap then the aspect of action is triggered forming part or functioning as predicate. A syntactic gap exposing both noun and verb triggers both object and action. (Ladewig, 2011, p. 130)

5.4 Summary

Based on the results from chapter 4, discussing the semantic integration of gestural repetitions into speech, the present chapter concentrated on gestures' relation with the syntax of speech. After discussing the notion of "multimodal grammar" (Cienki, 2012b; Fricke, 2012), it was shown that gestural repetitions interact with the spoken syntagms in specific ways. The corpus study revealed that the majority of repetitions most often accompany three syntactical categories: nouns, verbs, and adverbs. Only reduplications of type A equally often accompany verbs and prepositional phrases and in third place go along with adverbs. Accordingly, semantically speaking, gestural repetitions mainly accompany entities or things, processes as well as units that situate entities locally, temporally, or modally (see Table 5.1.). Regarding the relation of the whole repetitive sequence with the syntactical structure of the utterance, the study showed that whereas reduplications of type A most frequently and almost exclusively accompany verb phrases, all other types of repetitions accompany either sentences, noun phrases, or verb phrases. Furthermore, the study demonstrated that iterations and reduplications of type B predominantly accompany syntactical units functioning as object, predicate, subject, and adverbial determination. Only type A reduplications go along with syntactical units that function primarily as predicates and only in the second position as an object.

Based on this frequent correlation of repetitions with the syntax of speech, it was questioned whether gestural repetitions might also achieve a functional relevance on the level of syntax. Focusing on one specific type of repetitions, namely iterations expressing concrete meaning (e.g., examples "Arko" Figure 15, "metal thing" Figure 16), the chapter pointed out that gestural repetitions may achieve different functional relevance for the syntax of speech. Picking up on current work on the integration of gestures (e.g., Fricke, 2007, 2012), the results of the present study revealed that the majority of gestural repetitions is positionally integrated by being executed in temporal overlap with the co-occurring speech segment. Accordingly, in the majority of cases, the positional integration of the gestures is not achieved by specific linguistic meanings, particularly linking the repetition into the syntactic structure of the verbal utterance but solely by being executed at the same time with the co-expressive speech segment. For iterations depicting objects and adding complementary semantic information by specifying the shape of the object, it was shown that in both cases (cataphoric or temporal integration), they instantiate the function of an attribute in nominal phrases (see Fricke, 2012). For iterations depicting actions and specifying the manner of the action expressed verbally, it was suggested that they fulfill a function comparable to adverbial determinations and, in particular, to adverbial adjectives.

In order to account for this tight relation with the syntax of speech, the chapter then discussed these results in light of newer grammatical approaches, such as Multimodal Construction Grammar (Bergs & Zima, 2018). Based on a definition of constructions as entrenched complex patterns that have a particular constructional meaning including pragmatic functions, a continuum of constructions in multimodal language use was proposed that arranges recurrent patterns of speech and kinesic expressions depending on the degree of conventionalization and complexity as well as abstractness and distinguishes two main classes of constructions: multimodal constructions and verbo-kinesic constructions. With these two classes, the continuum sets apart a) the multimodal instantiation of gestural constructions and verbal constructions and b) instances in which speech and gesture as a whole form a complex sign schema. Against the background of this classification, it was then argued that two different types of constructions could be identified for iterations depicting objects and events that reflect different degrees of integration: First, verbo-kinesic constructions, in which the iterations are cataphorically integrated into the verbal utterance via specific linguistic means. Secondly, multimodal constructions in which the iterations are functionally integrated into the verbal utterance via temporal overlap. Based on this concept of constructions and the results presented in this chapter, it was concluded that in spoken language grammar, "variable DEGREES to which gesture can have linguistic status" (Cienki 2015a, p. 508, emphasis in original) exist and, as a consequence of this different linguistic status, gestures may function differently as elements of a single language. Moreover, it can be assumed that whether or not semantic and/or grammatical notions are

> expressed gesturally or not seems to depend on factors such as the placement of that notion within the information flow of the utterance, and the degree of emphasis ascribed to it by the speaker – how much the speaker chooses to foreground a particular idea. (Müller and Tag 2010) (Cienki 2013, p. 681ff.)

6 Cognitive functions of repetitive sequences: Attention and salience

The preceding chapter examined gestural repetitions and their relation with the syntax of speech. It was argued that the different degrees of semantic integration discussed in chapter 4 also result in a particular syntactic relevance. Focusing on one specific type of repetitions, namely iterations expressing concrete meaning and by falling back on existing work on the integration of gestures into speech (e.g., Fricke 2007, 2012), the chapter pointed out that iterations depicting objects or actions instantiate the function of an attribute or an adverbial determination. As a result, it was concluded that iterations and reduplications fulfill different functions in creating a multimodal utterance meaning, both on the level of semantics and syntax.

The semantic and syntactic perspectives presented in chapters 4 and 5 are now rounded up by examining repetitive sequences and their relevance for processes of attention and salience in language use. After discussing the concept of attention in Cognitive Linguistics and gesture studies (e.g., Croft & Cruse, 2004; Müller & Tag, 2010; Oakley, 2009), the idea of a multimodal nature of attention is introduced. The concept is based on the relevance of gestural repetitions for establishing salience in discourse and the possibility of gestural repetitions to detach themselves from Figure-Ground structures expressed in speech. The chapter will highlight that gestural repetitions provide insight into specific aspects of attention, such as scope, focus, and scale of attention, and that both types achieve particular importance: Whereas reduplications mark the focus of attention, iterations provide further information on specific aspects of the process of attention and display what is accessible in the periphery of attention, give a fine-grained view on specific scenes, events, and objects, and, therefore, contribute aspects missing in speech. Hence, gestural repetitions provide "anchors" for the listener on what to focus on in particular. Also, they are a strategy for speakers and interactants to mark and keep track of the flow of attention when speaking (Chafe, 1994). They are a central means for the multimodal creation of salience and the coordination of interaction between speakers, assuring understanding and alignment in interaction.

6.1 Attention in Cognitive Linguistics and gesture studies

"Our minds contain very large amounts of knowledge or information." Yet "only a very small amount of this information can be focused on, or be 'active,' at any one time." (Chafe 1987, p. 22) The mind possesses a psychological ability to attend to only parts of our experience and knowledge that are relevant for the moment being: Attention (Croft & Cruse, 2004; Oakley, 2009; Pike, 1971) or the focus of the consciousness (Chafe, 1994) is the active process of the mind to selectively focus on parts in the surrounding while suppressing others. As such, it is a necessary interface between the conscious being and the world.

> Attention [. . .] adds a directional component to behavior, modulating responses to the environment by focusing the mind on specific objects, locations, persons while suppressing or attenuating surrounding irrelevancies, particularly when the cognitive load is greatest. It is a family of effects promoting the processing of one set of items over another.
> (Oakley, 2004, p. 3)

As a result, a Figure-Ground structure is created in which the most relevant information at a given moment is marked as salient by selecting it from other information. At the same time, less critical aspects are backgrounded remaining in the area of peripheral consciousness (Talmy, 1983, 2000). The foregrounded, salient information then guides the flow of attention of the speakers and hearers.

> Metaphorically, it is as if we are "looking at" the world through a window, or *viewing frame*. The *immediate scope* of our conception at any one moment is limited to what appears in this frame, and the *focus* of attention-what an expression *profiles* (i.e. designates)-is included in that scope. (Langacker, 2001, p. 145, emphasis in the original)

The process of attention is characterized by a variety of properties, among which the property of selection, that is, the active selection of particular aspects, is probably the most relevant factor (Chafe, 1994; Croft & Cruse, 2004; Oakley, 2009; Pike, 1971; Talmy, 2000). Usually referred to as the focus of attention, selection brings into foreground certain aspects of our experience or knowledge particularly relevant for the moment being. Imagine asking someone for directions on the streets in an unknown city. While looking around for a possible person to ask, you will actively focus on the people on the sidewalk, thereby ignoring the cafes, shops, and newsstands in the immediate surrounding of the people you see. Your focus of attention is only centered on the people on the street and the possible helper amongst them. Yet, although you selectively focus only on the people on the sidewalk, the cafes and shops in the surrounding remain in your scope of attention (Oakley, 2009) or area of peripheral consciousness (Chafe, 1994). Hence, selected aspects are always surrounded by a periphery of consciousness, where entities are accessible to attention but not in the foreground.

A further constant property of attention is the ability of scalar adjustment (Croft & Cruse, 2004; Talmy, 2000), that is, the conceptualization of and view taken on a particular scene by adjusting the granularity of scalar dimensions.[92] Going back to our example of asking for directions, the person giving you the direction may either tell you to "go down this street," thus providing a rather schematized or coarse-grained view (Croft & Cruse, 2004) of the scene in front of you. Yet, when telling you to "go down this street passing the newsstand on the right", the direction given offers more information and hence a more fine-grained view (Croft & Cruse, 2004) of the situation. Yet, when further explaining the way you need to go to get to the museum, for instance, the person giving you the directions may go back and forth between rather schematized and more detailed descriptions, thereby always focusing on different aspects in the surrounding. This going back and forth is intrinsically linked to another constant property of attention, its dynamics (Croft & Cruse, 2004; Oakley, 2009; Talmy, 2007): Attention can move from one aspect to another, always dependent on the moment of being and its demands.[93]

Attention is not only relevant for processes of visual perception, as illustrated above in the example of direction giving. Instead, it is rather a common cognitive process finding its expression in a range of modalities, such as vision, perception, and language. Even more so, "language and attention are inextricably related and the components of awareness and attention influence language structure and use in the same way they influence perception and sensation." (Oakley, 2009, p. 125) Language has an extensive system to assign different degrees of salience to parts of an utterance. Linguistic means setting the strength of attention and salience are, for instance, phonological, morphological, syntactical as well as semantic devices. Open class categories are more salient than closed class categories, free morphemes achieve greater attention than bound morphemes, and the semantic components in morphemes have different attentional weighing so that more attention is on the direct than on the associated concepts (Talmy, 2007, p. 269ff). Moreover, lexical categories exhibit a salience hierarchy, with prototypes achieving more attention than less frequent concepts. And a hierarchy from greater to lesser prominence also tends to be "associated with nominals in accordance with their grammatical relation in a sentence as follows: subject > direct object > oblique" (Talmy, 2007, p. 273). Accordingly, the Figure, that is the concept that needs anchoring expressed in the "subject(-like)

---

92 See also Langacker (2008) for the concept of schematization and Pike (1971) for the concept of deep and shallow focus.
93 In addition to these constant properties of attention, Chafe (1994, p. 39) distinguishes five variable properties: 1) source of experience, 2) relation of the experience to the immediate surrounding, 3) evaluation of the experience as fact or fiction, 4) nature of the experience, and 5) verbality and non-verbality of the experience.

constituent", is usually of greater relevance than the Ground, the concept that does the anchoring expressed in the "object(-like) constituent" (Talmy, 2000, p. 321). Other mechanisms indicating the object of attention are physical stress, pauses, and stretches, which single out particular linguistic expressions from the utterance.

Generally, prosody is considered an essential factor in determining the focus of attention as stress, and changes in pitch contribute fundamentally to the expression of information structure and add acoustic salience to parts of the utterance (Ladd, 1996; Välimaa-Blum, 2005). Oakley (2009, p. 178) even assumes vocal deceleration, sing-song pronunciation, intonation peaks, stop-clipped terminals, and creaky voice to make up a "prosody of attention" as they alert, orient, direct, and harmonize the attention of the interlocutors. Similarly, Chafe states that

> as we try to develop a better understanding of the flow of consciousness and language, prosody will be found to contribute in ways that cannot be ignored for spoken language or even, perhaps surprisingly, for written. (Chafe, 1994, p. 57)

Prosodic features such as pauses, pitch, changes in duration, intensity, and voice quality, are essential for delimiting intonation units, that is, functionally relevant segments of speech in which the focus of a speaker's attention is reflected. Intonation units are functional units of mental and linguistic processing for the information being focused on at the moment of speaking. They provide clues about the type and state of information and reflect different activation states of information in the speaker's mind, namely whether information can be active, accessible, or inactive (Chafe, 1987, 1994, 1996). Each intonation unit "verbalizes a different event or state from the preceding" (Chafe, 1994, p. 69) and thus continually reflects not only the speaker's focus of attention but also its dynamic character.

Apart from language inherent factors such as prosody, grammar, and semantics, temporal proximity, the speaker's physical manifestation, and bodily movements can function as foregrounding factors (Chafe, 1994; Langacker, 2001; Pike, 1971; Talmy, 2007).

> Another mechanism for singling out the speaker's intended reference object of attention is a bodily movement of the speaker. [. . .] With such a movement, say, a pointing finger, the object of attention can be a thing or an activity (*That's my horse/a gallop*), a region of space (*My horse was over there*), or a direction *horse went that way*).
> (Talmy, 2007, p. 278, emphasis in the original)

Similarly, Langacker notes that concurrent pointing gestures cannot be considered a mere aspect of vocalization but are instead "part of the expression's conceptual content" (Langacker, 2001, p. 149). The fact that gestures, and maybe even other modalities, can focus the attention of speakers and hearers thereby resides in the nature of attentional frames itself:

> An attentional frame comprises no specific conceptual or segmental content. Its conceptual value resides in the very act of making a single attentional gesture–imposing a single window of attention for the simultaneous viewing of conceptual content.[94]
>
> (Langacker, 2001, p. 155)

Although the role of gestures and other bodily resources in the creation of attention has only been studied selectively (e.g., Cooperrider, 2017; Ladewig, 2011; Müller 2007, 2008; Müller & Tag, 2010), research has shown that not only deictic gestures are a means of focusing attention but rather that gestures, in general, are a vital foregrounding strategy, which offers visual salience and guides the flow of attention. As such, gestures serve as salience markers emphasizing the accompanied utterance as more prominent (Müller & Tag, 2010), creating a multimodal Figure-Ground structure, in which verbo-gestural parts of the utterance stand out against solely verbal parts of utterance (Kendon, 2004a). Moreover, gestures can provide insights into the focus of attention at a moment of speaking, otherwise lost when ignoring this modality. For instance, gestures give new insights into the nature of intonation units and the information expressed therein. Intonation units, defined as fragmentary or truncated based on the verbal channel alone, need to be redefined as complete and substantive when examined with the accompanying gestures (Ladewig, 2012).

Accordingly, research in gesture studies addressing the process of attention from the perspective of Cognitive Linguistics underlines that gestures are not just another channel visualizing the focus of attention. Instead, they need to be understood as an additional modality, in which the focus of attention becomes visible and observable and thus needs to be considered as a fundamental component in the expression of attention.[95]

---

[94] The term "attentional gesture" used here, not only refers to the concept of 'gestures' as used in this book, but subsumes prosody, gesture, speech management, and information structure. Langacker's notion of 'gesture' is a broader one, including "structures and relationships in all relevant channels", which help to establish attentional framing (Langacker, 2001, p. 154).

[95] Gestures studies within the frame of Cognitive Linguistics thereby stand in contrast to analyses discussing gestures and their relation to attention under the view of working memory or they aid for speech production processes (e.g., de Ruiter, 1998; Goldin-Meadow, 2001, 2003). The main position taken here is that "certain cognitive tasks can be offloaded into physical means of information storage such as gesture" (Park-Doob, 2010, p. 111).

Attention emerges [. . .] as a major cognitive process orchestrating and imprinting language as it used in spoken discourse. [. . .] But there is more to the dynamic flow of multimodal utterances than attention as a purely cognitive perceptual phenomenon. The very fact that a speaker *embodies* part of his utterance transforms this utterance into a sensory experience for both the speaker and the addressee. This sensory experience entails conceptualizations, points of view but also affective qualities inherent to these embodiments of meaning. (Müller & Tag, 2010, p. 113ff, emphasis in the original)

6.2 Salience and gestural repetitions

The following section discusses how speech and gesture work together in marking the focus of attention in the gestural phenomenon explored in this book, namely repetitions. Judging from the range of meanings and functions discussed in the previous chapters, it is assumed that gestures, by embodying the speaker's conceptualization in a further modality, can focus on similar and/or additional aspects than speech. The chapter hence concentrates on the specific contribution of each modality. It shows that, first of all, speech and gesture work together towards creating a multimodal structure of attention and salience. Furthermore, it will be pointed out that gestural repetitions emphasize different aspects of the flow of consciousness: Repetitions can highlight a) different foci and/or scopes of attention, b) differences in the scale of attention, and c) variations in the activation cost. Moreover, it will be highlighted that gestural repetitions may even detach themselves from Figure-Ground structures expressed in speech. Using exemplary cases documented in the present corpus, the section concentrates primarily on gestural iterations expressing concrete and abstract meaning because they demonstrate specific aspects of the phenomenon of attention. Moreover, they offer a further essential puzzle stone in explaining the particular role of gestural iterations documented in this book.

Our analysis in this chapter rests upon the assumption that speakers have a range of foregrounding strategies at hand by which a multimodal salience structure is created. Foregrounding strategies "display the expressive effort of a speaker – or more generally that co-participants in an interaction – employ to mark metaphoricity as a salient object of attendance in the flow of a conversation." (Müller & Tag, 2010, p. 111) Speakers using more modalities simultaneously or in close temporal proximity mark these parts of utterances, and thus, the information contained therein as more prominent than others. This "iconicity principle" (Müller & Tag 2010) denotes the fact that more material is more meaning and that expressing meaning in more than one modality at a time results in a higher salience of the information. The "interactive principle" (Müller & Tag, 2010) allows for the highlighting of utterances by meta-comments of the speaker or hearer, by prosodic marking, by directing the gaze towards the hands, for instance, or by performing particularly large gestures. The "syntactic and semantic principle" (Müller & Tag, 2010) foregrounds gestures when they are integrated into the verbal utterance, such as in syntactic gaps (see Ladewig 2014, 2020) or speech pauses. Moreover, deictic particles and pronouns mark the gesture as an obligatory part of the verbal utterance highlighting its salience at the moment of speaking (e.g., Fricke, 2007, 2012; Streeck, 2002, see chapter 5 for a more detailed discussion). The more foregrounding strategies are used, the more activated the meaning and the concept is at the moment of speaking. Accordingly, differences in the degree of activation of a particular concept become discernible. High activation can be set in relation to being in the focus of attention, while low activation would correspond to being in the scope or the periphery of consciousness (Müller, 2008; Müller & Tag, 2010; see also Kolter et al., 2012).

In the following, we will use four exemplary cases for explaining commonalities and differences of speech and gesture in creating a multimodal structure of attention and salience (see Table 20). In discussing these examples, we will first concentrate on the particular modalities involved (speech, gesture, and gaze) and afterwards on their interplay. When focusing on speech, apart from the semantics and syntax, specific emphasis will be paid to the prosodic structure. For the gestures, we will address the type of gesture and gestural repetition, their relation with speech (semantics, syntax, intonation units), the length of the repetition, and changes in form features. All of these features, our assumption, play a significant role in marking and highlighting attention and salience in multimodal language use.

Table 20: Iterations marking aspects of attention.

Focus of attention	example 1 "big drops"
	example 2 "weapons of mass weapons"
Scale of attention	example 3 "handles"
Activation cost	example 4 "metal thing"

The first two examples are instances in which both modalities together mark the focus of attention. Yet, although the focus of attention centers on the same parts of the utterance, it will become clear that the modalities may differ in the particular aspects of the utterance that are set in focus. In example 6.1., we see that a specific type of iteration is used for marking semantic and prosodic aspects of the multimodal utterance as salient. In contrast, other iterations, like example 6.2., are used to highlight solely prosodic aspects.

In example 6.1., an iteration used to depict concrete objects, semantic, and prosodic aspects of the utterance are equally activated in the speaker's focus of attention, demonstrating that the speaker marks the content of the utterance as well as the structure of the utterance as salient. In the example "big drops", speaker DA explains to her interlocutor that when it rains during summer and the raindrops are rather big, the rain will not last long (*man sacht wenn so große Tropfen runterkommen dann gibt's nich so viel Regen* ['one says when such big raindrops are falling, then there will not be much rain']). While uttering *große Tropfen* ('big raindrops'*)*, speaker DA produces a gestural iteration consisting of two strokes co-occurring with the adjective *große* ('big') and the noun *Tropfen* ('raindrops'). Using a bent index finger and thumb and a straight accented movement away from her body, DA represents the raindrops falling (see Figure 29).

Figure 29: Example 6 iteration "big rain drops".

Through a range of foregrounding strategies , the concept of "big raindrops" expressed in the noun phrase is marked salient: The gesture is foregrounded by a gaze directed towards the hand during the first stroke executed parallel to the adjective "big".[96] Through the use of the adverb "such", the gesture is made an obligatory element of the verbal utterance and takes over modifying function by specifying the noun in its extension (Fricke, 2012). In the verbal utterance, the adjective "big" and the noun "raindrops" are marked by accents. Similarly, the gestural strokes are prosodically marked by accented movement patterns.

---

96 During the execution of the second stroke, in parallel with the noun *Tropfen*, the speaker directs her gaze toward the interlocutor as depicted in Figure 6.1.

Accordingly, the concept "big raindrops" is iconically, interactively, semantically, and syntactically foregrounded in speech and gesture.

Although this instance is an exemplary case in which speech and gestures together mark and highlight semantic and prosodic aspects, not all gestural iterations show such frequent foregrounding strategies. As discussed in chapter 5, most iterations expressing concrete meaning is integrated into the verbal utterance through temporal overlap and not cataphorically, like in example 6.1. Moreover, gazing at the gestures is characteristic for many but not for all iterations. Accordingly, the number of foregrounding strategies used in the particular iterations may vary. One principle, however, is characteristic for all repetitions, namely the principle of iconicity. As gestural repetitions always consist of at least two successive strokes, the iconicity principle "more material is more meaning" (Jakobson, 1966; Mayerthaler, 1980) always takes effect.

Apart from the identified foregrounding strategies, exemplified in example 6.1., the focus on semantic and prosodic aspects of the utterance in these gestural iterations is furthermore highlighted by additional structural aspects, such as the length of the sequences, the number of intonation units spanned, the correlation with verbal accents, and the temporal relation with the co-expressive element of speech. Regarding these aspects, gestural iterations depicting concrete objects or events documented in the present corpus have the following characteristics: They generally consist of a) shorter sequences with up to three repetitions, b) encompass not more than two intonation units, c) align with verbal accents, d) temporarily overlap with the co-expressive concept in speech, and e) only occur concrete referential gestures. Gestural iterations with concrete meaning, like example 6.1., hence have a narrow range relating to the verbal utterance. They only encompass smaller portions of the verbal utterance and are closely related to particular words or phrases of the verbal utterance (see also chapter 4 and 5). The co-expressive speech segment and the gestural repetition temporarily align so that the iterations are used in parallel to the expression of the semantic concept in speech. Moreover, assuming that "usually each intonation unit verbalizes a different state or event from the preceding" (Chafe, 1994, p. 69), iterations only relate to a limited number of ideas as they encompass only a bound number of intonation units. The concurrent prosodic focus is apparent in the tight structural coupling of speech and gesture. Gestural strokes align with the accents in speech, highlighting a coordination of gestural strokes with the prosodic structure of the verbal utterance (e.g., Loehr, 2004, 2007; McClave, 1991). Accordingly, it is assumed that semantic and prosodic aspects of the utterance are activated in both modalities.

Foregrounding semantic and prosodic aspects simultaneously is thereby characteristic for gestural iterations expressing concrete meaning. Usually, these types of iterations or, in particular, gestures with such characteristics are classified as "superimposed beats" (McCullough, 2005; McNeill, 1992, 2005) or "anaphoric beats" (Tuite, 1993). These are singular gestures combined with a repeated up and down movement that help structure the utterance, indicate contrast, and emphasis and highlight the topic-comment structure of the verbal utterance. The present study, however, classified these gestures, not as superimposed or anaphoric beats but instead assumed them to be singular gestures with prosodic marking. Rather than being a separate gesture type, it is argued that the movement characteristics considered to be typical for the gesture type "beat" needs to be understood as a function of gestures that are grounded in particular movement characteristics, namely variations of the movement quality understood to be part of a rudimentary gestural prosody. Gestural movements might be marked in their size, acceleration, and intensity. Gestural movements may, therefore, be reduced or enlarged, decelerated and accelerated, and may be accented either at the beginning of the movement or at the end (see Prieto et al., 2018; Ruth-Hirrel & Wilcox, 2018; Shattuck-Hufnagel & Ren, 2018 for a similar argumentation).

This concept of a rudimentary gestural prosody is also important for the following example, in which, different than in example 6.1., solely prosodic aspects are foregrounded in the bodily movement. Here, the semantics of the verbal utterance is less critical, while structural aspects, such as prosodic features, seem to be foregrounded. Let us consider once again example 1 (see Figure 14), in which the politician Trittin produces a gestural iteration consisting of a sequence of various recurrent gestures. Over 28 seconds, Trittin articulates his position against Germany's nuclear partaking and strongly attacks the government and their proposed constitution of a national security council. Trittin's verbal utterance is characterized by strong prosodic marking. Changes in accent, pitch, and speed in the verbal utterance help to structure the utterance, indicate contrast and emphasis, highlight the topic-comment structure, and, more generally, function as a contextualization device (Auer, 1986; Gumperz, 1982). At the same time, they express Trittin's emotional stance. This strong prosodic focus is also apparent in the gestures. While articulating his position, Trittin produces several gestural iterations using a range of recurrent gestures, such as the ring, the Palm Up Open Hand, and the index finger (see Bressem & Müller, 2014b for a repertoire of recurrent gestures in German). The 44 strokes produced in this sequence are characterized by frequent and rapid changes of their movement quality: they carry enlarged, reduced, and accented movements pattern. These changes in the movement quality fulfill prosodic functions on the gestures themselves. Also, by following the prosodic structure of the verbal utterance in almost temporal synchronicity,[97] the gestural iterations also underline and highlight the prosodic structure of the verbal utterance. Accordingly, speech and gesture work together to mark primarily prosodic aspects of the utterance such as accents (primary and secondary), stress, temporal structuring through tempo and rhythm, and different phonological units (phones, syllables, words) as salient. Both modalities thus create a multimodal prosodic structure and highlight the speaker's particular focus of attention.

However, speech and gesture differ in the importance attached to semantic aspects of the utterance. Whereas in the verbal modality, both prosody and semantics create the overall meaning of the utterance, the semantic information in the gesture is less relevant. In his bodily movement, the speaker focuses on the prosodic side of the utterance: Not the content of what is being talked about is of interest but the how in terms of prosodic structure. The speaker's gestures hence foreground a fine-grained view on prosodic aspects while back-grounding semantic information. The proposed focus on prosodic aspects is made visible as gestural iterations with abstract meaning, such as example 1, generally consist of a) longer sequences with five and more repetitions, b) encompass several intonation units, c) span even whole utterances, and d) only occur with recurrent gestures with prosodic marking. Thus, these iterations have a broader range relating to the verbal utterance and, due to their length, are less attached to particular words or phrases but rather to the verbal utterance as a whole. Moreover, following Chafe (1994) and the idea that each intonation unit introduces a new idea or aspect of an idea, it can be assumed that the iteration encompasses quite a range of different ideas expressed in the verbal utterance. Moreover, and maybe more importantly, the prosodic focus is highlighted because these gestural iterations generally consist of recurrent gestures. Comparable to modals or negatives, by which the verbal utterance is modified or specified, recurrent gestures graduate and qualify the content of an utterance, influence its interpretation, and are indicators for particular speech acts and thus affect larger portions of the utterance and even whole sentences (see chapter 3 for a detailed discussion of recurrent gestures). These characteristics argue against a strong semantic focus of the

---

[97] The gestural strokes, although occurring in close correlation with the prosodic structure of the utterance, do not adhere to the generally assumed strict correlation of strokes with accented syllables of the verbal utterance, but rather form an "isochronous patterns in which the occurrence of beats is determined by a gestural rhythm which is sensitive to stress on the tone unit nucleus and multisyllabic words but not necessarily to other stressed syllables." (McClave, 1991, p. 75) Accordingly, strokes occur on accented as well as non-accented syllables of the verbal utterance.

gestural iterations but rather underline that the gestures' focus centers on marking prosodic aspects in speech and gesture.[98]

Although examples 6.1. and 3.2. differ with respect to foregrounding aspects of the verbal utterance (semantics + prosody vs. prosody), they share a characteristic which has not been documented for any other type of repetition in the corpus, namely the marking of prosodic aspects. The foregrounding of prosodic aspects is a particular characteristic of gestural iterations. A similar relation of focusing the attention on prosodic aspects was not detectable for any other type of repetition in the corpus. Foregrounding prosodic aspects, often in addition to the verbal utterance, thus seems to be an essential cognitive aspect in the use of these gestural iterations.

In the following, we will discuss an example in which gestures differ from the verbal modality as to which aspects of the focus of attention are highlighted. More importantly, it will be shown that the frequent temporal pre-positioning of iterations observed in the present corpus can be explained by assuming different degrees of activation. In the example "handles" (see Figure 30), speaker BS tries to come up with an answer to the question "What is a Fritz handle?". In the preceding part of the interaction, one of the other participants brought up the king of Prussia, Friedrich II., as a possible source for the object "Fritz handle".[99] After stating that "the old Fritz" was old and not young and therefore might have had problems getting out of the bathtub, BS starts to give her explanation of the question. After uttering *jetzt erinnere ich mich in Hotels* ('now I remember that in hotels'), she produces two gestural iterations of altogether six strokes going along with the verbal utterance *dass du in den Badewannen diese Griffe hast die dir sozusagen helfen, wenn du dein Bad genommen hast, wieder aus der Badewanne rauszukommen* ('that you have those handles in the bathtubs that help you to get out of the bathtub after you have taken a bath'). Overlapping with *dass du in den Badewannen diese Griffe hast* ('that you have those handles in the bathtubs') and using a hand shape in which the fingers are bent and the palm is turned upwards, BS visually represents handles in bathtubs by handling them. Using the mimetic mode "acting with specified object" (Müller, 2014), BS moves her hand down up and down in small, accented straight movements once in parallel to the pronoun and article *in der* ('in the'), twice when uttering the noun *Badewanne* ('bathtub'), once with the pronoun *diese* ('this') and again twice with the noun *Griffe* ('handles'). Same

---

[98] If semantic information is foregrounded in longer sequences of iterations, changes in hand shapes occur which correspond to intonation units and syntactic phrases. These changes in form features then serve discourse-pragmatic function, by indicating the topic comment structure, highlighting noteworthy aspects as well as signaling narrative shifts on the verbal utterance (Bressem, Stein & Wegener, 2015; Loehr, 2007; McNeill, 1992; Queck et al., 2002).
[99] The nickname of Friedrich II. was "der alte Fritz" ('the old Fritz').

as in example 6.1., the strokes specify the noun "bathtub" and also the noun phrase "those handles".[100] Through a range of foregrounding strategies, the noun phrases *in den Bandewannen* ('in these bathtubs') and *diese Griffe* ('those handles') are iconically, interactively, semantically as well as syntactically foregrounded. The gesture is highlighted by gazing towards the hands before and during the first execution of the gestural stroke. With the pronoun *dieses* ('this'), the gesture is syntactically integrated into the verbal utterance. Speech and gestures are prosodically marked: Speech carries primary and secondary accents on the nouns "bathtubs" and "handles" and the gestures are marked through repeated and accented movement downwards.

Figure 30: Example 7 iteration "handles".

Besides, each gestural iteration encompasses only one intonation unit of which each intonation unit focuses on different aspects of the referents: In the first intonation unit, the reference object is uttered (bathtubs), while the second one focuses on its elaboration (handles). Similar to example 6.1., the range of foregrounding strategies work towards focusing the semantic and prosodic aspects of the utterance. Once again, the what and how of the utterance is of importance. Moreover, as both modalities show different degrees of activation regarding the concept "handles", the example illustrates the dynamic and embodied nature of conceptualization. Speaker BS produces the first gestural iteration when uttering *in den Badewannen* ('in these bathtubs') and thus in advance to

---

100 For a discussion of gestural modification, see chapter 5.

mentioning the reference object in speech. Only the following iteration co-occurs with "handles" so that the concept and its elaboration are expressed temporarily separated in speech and gesture. Thus, the activation state of the concept changes throughout two gestural repetitions. In the first repetition, the concept "handles" is expressed solely in the gestural modality without verbalizing it. Because the concept is only expressed monomodally, it remains in the background or the periphery of attention. Although the concept is emerging, it is still only minimally activated (Müller, 2008). With the execution of the second repetition produced in temporal overlap with *diese Griffe* ('these handles'), the concept moves to the foreground of attention. By being executed in more than one modality, namely in gestures and speech, the concept "handles" is now activated in the speaker's mind. Over the course of the two repetitions, the concept thus moves from being only minimally activated to the highest degree of activation at the end of the gestural repetition by being expressed both gesturally and verbally. Gestural repetitions thus resemble, in a very short period of time, a process described for the activation of metaphoricity, in which the bodily conceptualization precedes the verbal one (Kolter et al., 2012). Similar to cases of metaphoricity, in pre-positioned gestural iterations, the concept is first in the body and only later in speech.[101] The pre-positioning of iterations expressing concrete meaning can be seen as a "transfer from implicit to explicit memory" (Kolter et al. 2012, p. 203), serving as a point of reference for the conceptualization of another element (Langacker, 1999, 2008).

> We have the ability to invoke the conception of one entity in order to establish "mental contact" with another. The entity first evoked is called a **reference point**, and one accessed via a reference point is referred to as **target**.
> (Langacker, 2008, p. 83, emphasis in the original)

Reference points are fundamental to the linguistic and cognitive organization as they can be seen as the initial focus of attention.[102] As an entity, the reference

---

[101] This aspect has consequences for a further property of the phenomenon of attention, namely its activation cost. Activation cost captures the status of the expressed information at a given moment in discourse so that information can be activated, newly activated or semiactive, i.e., accessible as activated from a previously active state (Chafe, 1994). In cases of verbo-gestural utterances, the status of the information can vary in the respective modalities, such that the information status can be verbally new, gesturally however be regarded as active or vice versa (see also Müller 2008).

[102] The reference point relationship resembles in parts the Figure-Ground distinction proposed by Talmy (1983, 2000). Similar to Langacker (2000), Talmy understands the Figure-Ground relation as a cognitive function, in which one concept functions as a reference point or anchor (Ground) for another concept (Figure).

point directs the attention to a perceptually salient entity as a point of reference for its conceptualization. It allows for a process of mental scanning, providing speakers with the possibility of successively attending to various aspects of a scene.

> The first phase consists of mentally accessing the reference point, which is thereby placed in focus. Its activation creates the conditions for accessing elements of the reference point's dominion, one of which is focused as the target. As focus shifts to the target, the reference point – having served its purpose – fades into the background. Hence the reference point and target are both salient, each at a certain stage of processing.
>
> (Langacker, 2008, p. 85)

In the present example, the reference point "bathtubs" evokes and eases the conceptualization of the target "handles" so that the concept "handles" is emerging and activated after mentioning the reference point "bathtubs". Yet, as the reference point relation is closely connected with the scope or periphery of attention in which entities are available and accessible to attention, it is able to explain why the first gestural repetition already occurs in temporal overlap with the reference point: The first gestural repetition highlights that, when uttering the verbal reference point, the target has already moved into the speaker's periphery of attention. Although only minimally activated, it is nevertheless accessible to attention: The conceptual linkage of reference and target is already established gesturally in the moment of uttering the reference point verbally.

Apart from indicating the scope of attention, the first gestural iteration serves another important function: It helps to keep the reference point active even when the focus has already shifted to the target. As the gestural iterations encompass both reference and target, the gestures function as a bracket, linking both aspects for speakers and hearers. This capability to indicate the scope of attention, to foreshadow the target of a reference point relationship, and also the focus of attention, seems to be particularly characteristic of gestural iterations. As discussed in chapter 4, 19% of all repetitions documented in this corpus occur in temporal pre-positioning to the spoken counterpart (see section 4.1.). However, although pre-positioning was documented for all types of repetitions, it is only of significance for iterations with concrete referential function.[103] The foreshadowing of the target in a reference point relationship, therefore, seems to be especially relevant in conceptualizing and depicting concrete objects and actions. For the speaker, it eases the process of mental scanning and linking of related parts of the utterance. For the hearer, it facilitates understanding and keeping

---

[103] For both types of reduplications, pre-positioning is only documented for 6% of the cases (see Table 4.1.).

track of the speaker's perspective because the repetitions function as a guiding post in making visible the speakers' process of mental scanning.

Apart from giving insight into the scope of attention, the example "handles" illustrates another characteristic of not only gestural repetitions but of gestures in general: Gestures have the ability to mark differences in the conceptualization and view taken on a particular scene. In the majority of repetitions documented in the present study, speech and gesture usually differ in their granularity: the spoken utterance generally expresses a coarse-grained view, whereas the gestures indicate a fine-grained view (Croft & Cruse, 2004). In speech, the concept is viewed in light of a more encompassing category excluding particular properties (e.g., handles, metal thing). The co-occurring gestures, however, specify the referents in focus by visualizing characteristic aspects. In the conceptualization of events, objects, and actions, for instance, speech and gesture take over different roles and construct the referents at varying levels of schematization (Langacker, 2008). Although the concept "bathtub" qualifies and constrains the concept of "handles" to a certain extent, by using the superordinate noun "handles", speaker BS conceptualizes the referent in a schematic way not specifying the type of handles, thus neglecting particular aspects of the referent. The gestural iteration, however, individualizes the referent by depicting its use, namely as handles touched from underneath. A similar pattern can be observed in the example "metal thing", in which speaker MB, while saying *wo die Flasche Wein da in som Metallding drinne is* ('where the bottle wine is in such a metal thing') (see Figure 16), models the shape of holders for wine bottles. Through the threefold execution of strokes with arced movements going inwards and outwards, along with the bent hands facing downwards, the gestural object, a bent bottle holder, emerges. MB's schematic verbal characterization of the referent in focus as "such a metal thing" is gesturally specified with information about the shape of the referent (bent and longish). Accordingly, whereas the verbal utterance in both examples offers only a coarse-grained view, the co-occurring gestural iterations, by depicting particular aspects of the referent in focus, add a fine-grained view.[104] Such a division of labor between speech and gesture is, according to Fricke (2012), characteristic for gestures in nominal phrases with attributive verbal and gestural extensions. As gestures are remarkably akin to the depiction of action, forms, sizes, and shapes, they take over modifying function in a noun phrase. However, the analysis of gestural repetitions in chapter 5 has shown that such a division of labor is not only restricted to gestures functioning as attributes in nominal phrases but might be rather understood as a general characteristic of gestures.

---

104 See chapter 4 for a more detailed analysis of the semantic relation of gestural repetitions and speech.

The examples discussed so far illustrated that gestural iterations highlight and mark properties of attention in a variety of ways and thus provide additional insight into the nature of attention at the moment of speaking. Moreover, it was argued that particular characteristics and functions of iterations are explicable by taking attention into account. As a result, the frequent use of concrete referential gestures and recurrent gestures with prosodic marking as well as the frequent pre-positioning of iterations with concrete meaning is accounted for.

Now, turning back to the second type of gestural repetitions classified in this book, that is, reduplications, we see a clear difference of these repetitions for the process of focusing attention. Although gestural reduplications help to create a multimodal salience structure by expressing the conceptualization of actions and events in the visual modality, they do not a show comparable relevance for specifying and enriching the phenomenon of attention. Considering reduplications of type A (lexical basis of Aktionsarten) and reduplications of type B (grammatical notion of plurality), it can be stated that speech and gesture mark similar aspects of the flow of attention. Speech and gesture in these cases focus the attention on the same semantic aspects of the utterance and work together to express the notion of Aktionsarten and/ or plurality. Consider the example "send back and forth" given in chapter 3 for reduplications of type A (see Figure 17). Here, speaker BS, while uttering the verb phrase *zwischen zwei Ämtern hin und herschickt* ('send back and forth between two offices') produces a series of three strokes, which represent the iterativity of the movement event expressed in the verb *hin und her schicken* ('send back and forth'). Here, both speech and gesture focus on the expression of the Aktionsart, and the reduplication, although embodying its spatial and temporal basis, does not focus on different aspects. The gestures do not provide further insights into the scope or scale of attention nor its activation cost. Instead, speech and gesture in combination highlight similar aspects. The same is true for reduplications of type B, as exemplified in the example "single steps" (see Figure 18). Here, speaker ME, while saying *kannste dir ja immer die einzelnen Schritte durchlesen* ('well you can read through the single steps'), produces a series of three strokes co-occurring with *einzel* ('single'), *nen schritte* ('steps'), and *durch* ('through') in different positions of the gesture space. Same as in the verbal utterance, the gestural reduplication focuses on the expression of the notion of plurality without highlighting additional aspects. Both speech and gestures work together towards creating a multimodal understanding of plurality as multiple bounded areas in space (Bressem, submitted). This agreement of speech and gestures in gestural reduplications in the present corpus is grounded in the fact that gestural reduplications usually encompass one intonation unit, temporarily align with the co-expressive speech segment, and recurrently correlate with similar syntactical relations. In addition, gestural reduplications do not represent actions, concrete objects, or events but lexical and grammatical concepts (see chapters 3 and 4). Gestural reduplications are thus much more bound to the co-occurring verbal utterance than gestural iterations and therefore do not foreshadow information in advance to the verbal utterance, express the status of the information differently, nor adhere to particular aspects or characteristics of referents.

Concluding, it can thus be stated that gestural reduplications and gestural iterations take over different roles with respect to the phenomenon of attention. Although both help create and highlight a multimodal salience structure for speakers and hearers, gestural iterations can add substantially more prominence and assume an important role in specifying the nature of attention in multimodal language use.

6.3 Reconsidering the nature of attention: New insights from gesture studies?

The preceding section has discussed cognitive functions of gestural repetitions and examined their relevance for processes of conceptualization, attention, and salience. It was argued that repetitions highlight a) different foci and/or scopes of attention, b) differences in the scale of attention, c) variations in the activation cost, and d) that gestural iterations and reduplications contrast with respect to the phenomenon of attention. The results have underlined the dynamic and flexible nature of attention. More importantly, they show that attention is created and influenced by particular functions of gestural repetitions, such as prosodic marking, lexical, and grammatical specification. Moreover, certain aspects of attention, such as focus, scope, scale, and activation cost, cannot be determined independently of the modality in which it is conveyed. Rather, attention is expressed in particular ways, depending on the modality that is used. Speakers systematically use the advantages of the modalities available to them to articulate facets that move or are in their focus of attention. A discussion of the phenomenon of attention thus needs to consider the multimodal nature of spoken language and include other modalities to unravel the particularities of its nature.

The fact that other modalities can take over an important role in the process of attention is not entirely new. Already Langacker, in his discussion of attentional frames, has argued that the ability to build a "single window of attention for the simultaneous viewing of conceptual content" (Langacker, 2001, p. 155) is not bound to a particular modality. Rather, through a range of foregrounding strategies, attention can be highlighted and marked in a range of modalities (Ladewig, 2011; Müller, 2008; Müller & Tag, 2010; Kolter et al., 2012). Capturing

6.3 Reconsidering the nature of attention: New insights from gesture studies?

the dynamics of attention thus calls for a joint analysis of speech and gesture because gestures are a vital foregrounding strategy offering visual salience and guide the flow of attention. Gestures contribute immensely to the constitution of shared attention (Oakley, 2009) and are a central mechanism for guiding the flow of attention for speakers and hearers. Accordingly,

> it is not only the attentional system of language that triggers and guides the flow of attention, but also the specific properties of multimodal utterances and the flow of spoken discourse in a conversational interaction that plays a highly significant role in allocating attention.   (Müller & Tag, 2010, p. 113)

Apart from underlining the multimodal nature of attention and the need for multimodal analyses of the phenomenon, the results presented in this chapter challenge the existing notion of attention and foregrounding made on the basis of analyses of spoken language alone. As pointed out in the example "handles" and "metal thing", gestural repetitions indicate what resides in the periphery of attention and are thus capable of foreshadowing the target of a reference point relationship, indicating that, well in advance of verbalizing the target, it is accessible to attention. These results question the assumed implicitness of the mental scanning process. "For the most part, however, our reference point ability remains below the threshold of explicit attention; we simply use it without realizing that we are doing anything of the kind." (Langacker, 1999, p. 173) Yet, our results highlight that gestures and a range of other foregrounding strategies (e.g., eye gaze, syntactical integration) foreshadow the target in the speaker's focus of attention. The proposed implicitness of the reference point thus needs to be reconsidered when considering multimodal language use.

The results furthermore also raise interesting questions regarding the Figure-Ground distinction as proposed by Talmy (1972, 1983, 2000). The Figure-Ground distinction describes two fundamental cognitive functions apparent in language: The Figure, a concept that needs anchoring and is considered to be more salient and foregrounded, is anchored by a Ground, a concept that does the anchoring and considered to be less salient and backgrounded (see Table 21). Moreover, Talmy relates the concept of Figure and Ground to particular syntactical relations of the verbal utterance and states a "possible universal property: in their basic expression, the Figure has syntactic precedence over the Ground." (Talmy, 2000, p. 334) Accordingly, Talmy assumes that in the majority of cases, "the subject(-like) constituent functions as Figure and object(-like) constituent functions as Ground." (Talmy, 2000, p. 321)

However, the choice of the subject in a sentence is dependent on the speaker's focus of attention (Talmy, 2000; see also Parrill, 2008). Speakers may shift their attention during the production of an utterance resulting, for instance, in

Table 21: Characteristics of Figures and Grounds (based on Talmy, 2000, p. 315).

	Figure	Ground
definitional characteristics	– unknown spatial (or temporal) properties to be determined	– acts as a reference entity, known properties that can characterize the Figure's unknown
associated characteristics	– more movable – smaller – geometrically simpler – more recently on the scene/in awareness – of greater concern/relevance – less immediately perceivable – more salient, once perceived – more dependent	– more permanently located – larger – geometrically more complex – more familiar/expected – of lesser concern/relevance – more immediately perceivable – more backgrounded, once Figure is conceived – more independent

a gradual shift of focus from the subjective referent to a clause about the subject referent. This relative "freedom" of Figures and Grounds and their relations with the syntactic structure of the utterance challenges the direct link with attention and sentence structure (Engberg-Pedersen, 2011, see also Tomlin, 1997). Following Engberg-Pedersen (2011), we assume that a differentiation of the concepts of Figure and Ground is needed, which distinguishes the following three types of attentions contributing to a Figure-Ground relation:

1. The centre of attention as a result of the context, which influences the choice of subject, e.g., *The bike* in *The bike is in front of the house*.
2. The centre of attention coded in the sentence as the asserted part, i.e., *is in front of the house*.
3. The centre of attention that the sentence brings about in our under- standing of the represented situation, i.e., the view of the situation that is encoded in the sentence and that makes us conceptualise the scene with the bike as the figure and the house as the ground in the Gestalt-psycho- logical sense. (Engberg-Pedersen, 2011, p. 693, emphasis in original)

This understanding of a complex relation of attention and Figure-Ground relation is also underpinned by the results discussed above. An evaluation of the gestural repetitions with the syntactical relations of the verbal utterance has shown that gestural iterations most frequently accompany syntactical units functioning as objects (see chapter 5). Accordingly, assuming the proposed tight link of Figure and Ground with the syntactic structure of the utterance, many gestural iterations align with the Ground and not the Figure of the verbal utterance, therefore

6.3 Reconsidering the nature of attention: New insights from gesture studies? — 173

foregrounding the less salient concept of the Figure-Ground relation. This tendency for an "exceptional" alignment was shown in both of the examples discussed above ("handles", "metal thing"). Assuming the proposed link of Figures with the subject and Grounds with the objects of the spoken utterance, the gestural iteration starts in temporal overlap with the Figure of the utterance and extends until the Ground. This pattern is yet not only characteristic for those two examples but rather for the majority of pre-positioned iterations. Accordingly, gestural iterations frequently span both the Figure and the Ground, thus also align with the less salient concept of the Figure-Ground relation. Yet, based on the dynamic theory of meaning activation (Müller, 2008, Müller & Tag, 2010; Kolter et al.; 2012), using more than one modality at a time marks and highlights those parts of the utterance as more salient. Therefore, it can be assumed that in the discussed examples the Ground is marked more salient and foregrounded because it is expressed in the verbal and gestural modality. As such, the examples show an "exceptional" pattern for a Figure-Ground relation.

However, when considering the conceptualization and attentional focus of the described scene expressed in the bodily movement independent of the syntax of the spoken sentence, it is indeed possible to assume that the gestures co-occur with the Figure of the perceived scene and not the Ground. Consider the examples "handles" and "metal thing" with the assumption in mind that the gestures foreground the Figure by concentrating solely on the semantics of the verbal utterance:

Example "handles": 'that you have in the bathtubs (Ground) those handles (Figure)'.

Example "metal thing": 'At an Italian restaurant where the bottle wine (Ground) is in such a metal thing (Figure)'

Now, the gesturally depicted objects (handles and metal thing) are perceived against the background of those objects encompassed by the pre-positioned parts of the gestural repetition (bathtub, bottle wine). Here, more movable, smaller, more dependent, and more salient aspects of the scene, characteristics of a prototypical understanding of the Figure (see Table 6.2.), are gesturally depicted. This reading would also be in line with the reference-point relationship discussed above in which the concept 'handles' is accessed via 'bathtubs' and where the concept 'bottle wine' establishes the mental contact with the 'bottle holder'. Accordingly, based on the types of gestural repetitions, the proposed list of different kinds of attention by Engberg-Pedersen (2011) needs to be complemented by a further one:

4. The center of attention in the gestural utterance is a result of the conceptualization of the represented event or situation.

Summarizing, it can thus be assumed that attention and the allocation of the concepts of Figure and Ground may differ in the gestural and verbal modality. A simple correlation of Figure and Ground with the syntax of the verbal utterance alone is not sufficient. It rather needs to be established based on the particular modalities involved in forming a multimodal utterance. In particular, gestures seem to provide substantial insights into the nature of focusing attention at the moment of speaking. The ability to mark and highlight a range of properties of attention such as focus, scope, and scale, therefore not only gives insight into the cognitive functions of gestural repetitions but, more importantly, also yield further insights into the relation and interaction of speech and gesture.

6.4 Summary

The present chapter has looked at the phenomena of gestural repetitions from a cognitive perspective and discussed their relevance in creating attention and salience in spoken language. It illustrated that repetitions give insight into particular aspects of attention, such as scope, focus, and scale of attention. Moreover, it was shown that iterations and reduplications assume different importance by providing specific insights into the nature of attention in multimodal language use. Whereas reduplications mark the focus of attention, namely that part of the utterance which is gesturally accompanied, iterations provide further information on particular aspects of the process of attention. As such, gestural iterations may not only indicate the focus of attention but, more importantly, also highlight what is accessible in the periphery of attention. Furthermore, iterations provide a fine-grained view of particular scenes, events, and objects, therefore, providing a more detailed representation than the verbal utterance. Concluding, it was shown that gestural iterations call into question the proposed Figure-Ground structure (Talmy, 2000). Based on the temporal pre-positioning of gestural iterations and on recent studies questioning the syntactic alignment of Figures and Ground, a counter-argument was presented arguing for a foregrounding of the Figure. Based on the assumption that the more material is used, the more meaning is expressed (Müller & Tag, 2010), it is assumed that gestures mark those aspects of the utterance as most salient and thus highlight the Figure even if this is contrary to the proposed Figure-Ground relation as proposed by studies focusing on speech alone.

The analysis in this chapter has thereby underlined that a cognitive perspective on the phenomenon of repetition was able to reveal and explain particular characteristics of iterations and reduplications. As a result, apart from structural and functional aspects on the level of gestures alone or in relation to speech, as presented in previous chapters, an account of the phenomenon of repetitions in gestures needs to consider cognitive aspects. They offer another important piece to the puzzle in explaining the nature of gestural repetitions. With these aspects, the present chapter rounded up the corpus-based analysis of gestural repetitions and presented the last puzzle piece to a usage-based and cognitive-linguistic analysis of repetitive sequences in coverbal gestures. As such, the present chapter, along with the three preceding chapters, has discussed the more general processes of building patterns and units in language from a perspective of language as being "inherently and variably multimodal" (Cienki, 2012; Fricke, 2007, 2012; Müller, 1998, 2008a) and of grammar as being "potentially multimodal" (Cienki, 2012).

7 Closing the stage

The present book has focused on a pattern-building device and a basic systematic linguistic means on all levels of language in spoken and signed languages: repetitive sequences. By pursuing a usage-based approach grounded in a cognitive-linguistic perspective, the book expands studies on this phenomenon towards a multimodal perspective on gesture-speech relation in spoken language and posed the following questions:
- Do gestures exhibit different types of repetitive sequences?
- Do gestures build complex units based on these types, and if so, how is the pattern building to be described?
- How is the interrelation of gestural and spoken units in such complex units?
- Is it possible to identify repetitive patterns that are comparable to spoken and signed languages and/or patterns specific to the gestural modality?

Against the background of existing concepts and principles of how spoken and signed languages build patterns of different complexity (chapter 2) and based on a corpus-linguistic study, the book presented a cognitive-semantic classification of gestural repetitions: 1) Iterations, in which the repetition of gestural material results in the repeated recurrence of one and the same meaning and does not lead to the construction of a complex gestural meaning. 2) Reduplications, in which the repetition of gestural material results in a complex gestural meaning and a coherent reduplicative construction. The book grounded this classification in specific structural and semantic aspects characteristic for iterations and reduplications, which sets them apart as distinct ways of building (complex) units in the gestural modality.

For this, chapter 3 presented evidence that gestural iterations and reduplications show commonalities as well as differences on the level of form, and, in particular, in their gesture phase characteristics and length of sequences: Whereas iterations either consist of preparations-stroke sequences or stroke-stroke sequences, reduplications solely consist of stroke-stroke sequences. As a result, sequences of strokes without inserted preparation phases show a stronger degree of unity and thus a more complex gestural meaning than strokes that are separated by preparation phases. Moreover, in iterations and reduplication different, structural and functional gestural units are created: Iterations may either consist of several gesture phrases (preparation-stroke sequences) or single gesture phrases (stroke-stroke sequences). Reduplications however, solely construct single gesture phrases consisting of several strokes. In addition, both types of gestural repetitions clearly show preferences and a particular distribution on the linear level:

The majority of repetitions were composed of two-three strokes. Only iterations showed a greater range in their length of up to 9 strokes and more. Based on these results, it was concluded that the use of repetitions to create a reduplicative construction, namely a complex gestural meaning is a less frequent use of gestural repetitions.

Following the complexity on the linear level, the book discussed the simultaneous complexity and the semantics of iterations and reduplications. Firstly, it was shown that gestural repetitions, in general, do not change in more than two parameters at a time. Furthermore, iterations and reduplications differ in the number of changing parameters. Whereas in iterations, gestural forms remain constant or change in one or two parameters across the sequence, in reduplications form features always change. Depending on the type of reduplication either one or two parameters are affected. If form features change, they occur only in particular parameters, namely movement and position. These changes are thereby particularly distributed: 1) In iterations, the quality and direction of the movement as well as the position in gesture space change. 2) In reduplications of type A, only the direction of the movement and the position in gesture space change. And 3) in reduplications of type B, only the positioning of the hands in gesture space varies. Based on these results, it was concluded that the instantiation of the same features across sequences of gestures causes a connection between the gestural units (Fricke, 2012) and is thus necessary to mark the sequence of strokes as belonging to one gestural repetition (chapter 3).

Based on the assumption that gestures are motivated form Gestalts, the book also addressed basic techniques of meaning creation (gestural modes of representation) in iterations and reduplications. Here, a rather clear-cut distribution was documented: Whereas iterations predominantly use the acting mode, for reduplications, the representing mode is most frequent. As a result, in these sequences, abstract meanings prevail. For iterations, concrete meanings were most frequent, and in particular, these sequences primarily depicted a) objects through handling them, b) actions with objects, and c) actions. Accordingly, in iterations with stroke-stroke sequences, concrete meanings are most common. For reduplications, overwhelming use of representing mode and singular gestures. Based on these results, it was concluded that in iterations the same meaning is repeated. In reduplications, however, a new and complex meaning is created. In particular, it was argued that gestural reduplications either embody the spatial and temporal basis of the Aktionsart 'iterativity' and recreate the lexical basis of a grammatical concept or depict the relation of objects or states to one another by which the gestural conceptualization and construal of plurality as different areas in gesture space arises (chapter 3).

This twofold cognitive-semantic classification of repetitions was further explicated and supported in chapters 4 and 5. After discussing what is known about multimodal utterances and the temporal and semantic relation of speech and gesture, Chapter 4 showed that iterations and reduplications achieve particular relevance for the creation of multimodal utterances and utterance meaning and, as such, signal different degrees of semantic integration. This different semantic relevance is based on two aspects: temporal relation of the gestures with the co-expressive speech segment but also, and maybe even more importantly, their semantic relation and function for creating a multimodal utterance meaning. The book showed that the majority of iterations and reduplications occur in temporal overlap with the co-expressive speech and that pre-positioning is restricted to iterations. Using an analytical method investigating the semantic relation of speech and gestures by examining the semantic features expressed in both modalities, it was argued that gestural reduplications of type A and type B express redundant semantic features and therefore do not have a direct impact on the meaning expressed verbally. By expressing the lexical basis of Aktionsarten or by expressing the notion of "plurality", they gesturally depict the embodied basis of thought and language. As such, they convey verb-semantic and grammatical meaning in a further modality and, thus, need to be described as supportive in their semantic function for the construction of a multimodal utterance meaning. However, iterations not only emphasize the semantics of the utterance but also modify the verbal referent. When used to depict actions (e.g., scraping, hammering, beating) or objects (e.g., the shape of a bowl), iterations complement and specify the type of action expressed verbally regarding its manner and the object in terms of size and shape.

Accordingly, based on the semantic relation of speech and gesture, it was concluded that iterations expressing concrete meaning substantially alter the proposition of the verbal utterance. As a result, it was argued that iterations and reduplications not only stand in different semantic relations to the verbal utterance but also fulfill different semantic functions and show different degrees of semantic integration into the spoken utterance. Reasons for these differences can be found on the level of the gestural unit itself and the grounding and detachment of repetitions in and from bodily and visual experiences: Iterations are predominantly used for the depiction of actions of the hand and concrete objects and events, conceptualize kinesthetic experience, and are thus grounded in direct bodily experiences. Accordingly, iterations are directly related to the semantics of the co-expressive speech segment as the speech and the semantics expressed therein creates the frame within which the gestural repetition is able to emphasize or contribute to the multimodal meaning. Reduplications, however, express abstract meaning and as such are detached from concrete aspects of the actual world. Rather, they trace a successive process of abstraction from visual or bodily experiences and as such allow for the foregrounding of the lexical basis of Aktionsarten (reduplication A) as well as for the expression of grammatical notions (reduplication B). Due to this abstract meaning and their detachment from concrete entities, reduplications do not affect the semantics of the verbal utterance in the same way as gestural iterations. Moreover, due to the complex meaning arising from the gestural construction itself, reduplications are, to some degree, detached from the semantics of the verbal utterance as the reduplicative construction itself carries meaning that does not entirely rely on the semantics of speech. Accordingly, it was argued that the fact of whether repetitions create a complex gestural meaning (reduplications) or not (iterations) might account for the different distribution of semantic features and relations described in this chapter.

Taking the results on the semantic integration of gestural repetitions as the basis, the book then concentrated on the gestures' relation with the syntax of speech and discussed their temporal and functional relation with spoken syntagms. Chapter 5 provided a further puzzle stone to the question of how repetitive sequences in gestures relate and contribute to multimodal utterance meaning. After discussing the notion of "multimodal grammar" (Cienki, 2012b; Fricke, 2012) and by focusing on one specific type of repetitions, namely iterations expressing concrete meaning, the book discussed that gestural repetitions might achieve different functional relevance for the syntax of speech. Picking up on existing work on the integration of gestures (e.g., Fricke, 2007, 2012), the results of the present study revealed that the majority of gestural repetitions is positionally integrated by being executed in temporal overlap with the co-occurring speech segment. For iterations depicting objects and adding complementary semantic information by specifying the shape of the object, it was shown that they instantiate the function of an attribute in nominal phrases in cases of cataphoric or temporal integration (see Fricke, 2012). For iterations depicting actions and specifying the manner of the action expressed verbally, it was suggested that they fulfill a function comparable to adverbial determinations and, in particular, to adverbial adjectives.

In order to account for this tight relation with the syntax of speech, and in light of "multimodal construction grammar" (Bergs & Zima, 2018), a definition of constructions as entrenched complex patterns that have a particular constructional meaning including pragmatic functions was proposed. This definition laid the grounds for a continuum of constructions in multimodal language use that arranges recurrent patterns of speech and kinesic expressions depending on the degree of conventionalization and complexity as well as abstractness and distinguishes two main classes of constructions: multimodal constructions and verbo-kinesic constructions. With these two classes, the continuum sets apart a) the multimodal instantiation of gestural constructions and verbal constructions and b) instances in which speech and gesture as a whole form a complex sign schema. Against this classification, it was then argued that two different types of constructions could be identified for iterations depicting objects and events that reflect different degrees of integration: First, verbo-kinesic constructions, in which the iterations are cataphorically integrated into the verbal utterance via specific linguistic means. Secondly, multimodal constructions in which the iterations are functionally integrated into the verbal utterance via temporal overlap.

The semantic and syntactic perspective presented in chapters 4 and 5 was rounded up by examining repetitive sequences and their relevance for processes of attention and salience in language use in chapter 6. After discussing the concept of attention in Cognitive Linguistics and gesture studies (e.g., Croft & Cruse, 2004; Müller & Tag, 2010; Oakley, 2009), the idea of a multimodal nature of attention was introduced. The concept is based on the relevance of gestural repetitions for establishing salience in discourse and the possibility of gestural repetitions to detach themselves from Figure-Ground structures expressed in speech. The empirical findings of the study revealed that gestural repetitions provide insight into specific aspects of attention, such as scope, focus, and scale of attention, and that both types achieve particular importance. Whereas reduplications mark the focus of attention, iterations provide further information on particular aspects of the process of attention and display what is accessible in the periphery of attention, give a fine-grained view on particular scenes, events, and objects, and, therefore, contribute aspects missing in speech. With this focus, the chapter rounded up the corpus-based analysis of gestural repetitions and presented the last puzzle piece to a usage-based and cognitive-linguistic analysis of repetitive sequences in coverbal gestures.

With these results, the book contributes to two perspectives on gestures: First, it provides further insight into a "grammar" of gesture and the linguistic potential of gestures with their medial and functional properties. Secondly, it addresses the concept of a multimodal grammar and the question of whether gestures may be considered structural and functional elements of spoken utterances. More specifically, it points at how both perspectives are connected and necessary for a deeper understanding of gestural and verbo-gestural signs and the multimodal nature of language. The book thereby not only aims at setting verbal and gestural structures in relation but rather tries to identify fundamental means of signs and meaning construction crosscutting modalities.

The following section of this chapter, therefore, brings together the empirical findings of the corpus-based study with findings from repetitions in spoken and signed languages discussed in Chapter 2. In particular, it argues for the universality of repetitive sequences and postulates that repetitions are a basic principle of building linguistic patterns that need to be conceived of as independent of the articulatory modality and rather as a modality independent principle yet showing modality and mediality specific characteristics. The criteria by Gil (2005) on the distinction between iterations and reduplications in spoken languages are used to support his argument (see chapter 2). The chapter concludes by spelling out further implications of the perspective taken in the book for an analysis of multimodal language in use from a cognitive linguistic point of view and discusses further research perspectives.

7.1 Iteration as a basic principle of pattern-building in speech, sign, and gesture

Starting from a critique on the distinction between iterations and reduplications in spoken languages that are based on the unit "word", Gil (2005) expands existing classifications by proposing criteria that include further aspects of form along with semantic and functional ones (see chapter 2 Table 2.4.). Form-based criteria include not only the unit of input, contiguity, and number of copies but also the interrelation of the repetitive sequence with the intonation structure of the utterance. As a result, spoken repetitions are characterized by two or more segments that may be adjoining or separate and occur within one or more intonation groups. In spoken reduplications, however, the copied segments are always adjacent, usually consist of two and only occur within one intonation group.

All of the criteria discussed by Gil (2005) also apply to gestural iterations and reduplications: Meaningful parts (strokes) either follow each other directly or are separated via preparational phases. Whereas reduplications usually consist of sequences with no more than three strokes, iterations can be made up of sequences of up to nine strokes. The majority of repetitions enclose one intonation unit, yet iterations may accompany up to six intonation units. In addition to the form-based criteria, also the semantic and functional criteria proposed by Gil (2005) can be applied to gestural repetitions. Spoken repetitions usually do not have an independent meaning. Reduplications in speech, however, go along with meanings that are iconically or arbitrarily motivated. Accordingly, reduplication is used cross-linguistically to mark plural, aspect, intensification, or number/amount (Mattes, 2014). Repetitions, however, serve to create particular effects, changes on the connotative level or are used for stylistic, textural, or pragmatic reasons (Kotschi, 2001; Stolz, 2007a). As a result, the function of both patterns is different in spoken languages. For repetitions, the element of communicative reinforcement, that is, the use of repetition for focusing attention, is characteristic. For reduplications, this is not the case.

Similar semantic and functional characteristics can also be applied for gestural repetitions and yet in specific ways depending on the type. Whereas the meaning of gestural reduplication is iconically motivated and grounded in the principle of diagrammatic iconicity, iterations are grounded in metonymic relations with actions and objects (see Mittelberg, 2010 for metonymy in gestures).

Communicative reinforcement plays a major role in iterations. They mark focus of attention and may detach themselves from Figure-Ground relations in speech and instantiate independent foci of attention. In gestural reduplications, communicative reinforcement in this sense is not relevant.

Apart from these similarities of gestures with patterns of repetitions in spoken languages, interesting overlaps can be drawn, in particular, with reduplications in sign languages. In signs and gestures, reduplication is used to mark iterativity and plurality. Moreover, both share particular characteristics on the paradigmatic level of form parameters. In sign languages, aspect or Aktionsart is expressed via modulation of movement. The marking of plural is achieved by repeating signs along the horizontal, vertical, or sagittal axis (Klima & Beluggi, 1979; Pfau & Steinbach, 2006). In gestural reduplications, similar changes in form parameters were documented. As a result, it can be concluded that gestures use an analog structure for a comparable function. Due to the fact that gestures and signs use the same modality, these similarities are not surprising. Yet at the same time, they raise the question, whether gestural means of expression and the marking of iterativity and plurality may be the basis for grammaticalization processes in sign languages, as already documented by Wilcox (2007) for modal verbs or the marking of aspect. In relation to the phenomenon of reduplication, the argument that it is a modality independent means spoken and signed languages (Pfau & Steinbach, 2006, see chapter 2), can now be expanded to coverbal gestures based on the similarities discussed above.

But how are these commonalities in speech, signs, and gestures possible? Our argument for answering this question is the following: Due to particular structural characteristics, gestural repetitions are perceived as Gestalts following the principles of Gestalt theory. Following Stolz (2008), we furthermore assume that an abstract principle of multiple setting via copying is a semiotically basic means that lays the grounds for similar form-based and semantic structures in the verbal and the visual modality. Moreover, we assume that reduplications in speech, sign, and gesture are based on diagrammatic iconicity (Peirce, 1960) or relative motivation in Saussurean terms (1966). Before discussing these particularities for reduplications in more detail, the following section first concentrates on structural characteristics on which both types of gestural repetitions are based.

The creation of coherent gestural units, such as the argument put forward here, rests upon two structural aspects, namely the form parameters and the number of successive strokes. Based on these structural characteristics, gestural repetitions are being perceived as Gestalts following the principles of Gestalt theory (e.g., Koffka, 1962; Köhler, 1935; Wertheimer, 1925). Finally, along with the co-occurring speech segment, a distinction between the repetition of the same meaning and the creation of a complex meaning is possible (see chapter 3).

7.1 Iteration as a basic principle of pattern-building in speech, sign, and gesture — 183

Based on an analysis of gestural form features using the four parameters of sign language, the book has shown that gestural repetitions change in not more than two parameters at a time and moreover only in particular ones, namely movement and position. Furthermore, changes in form parameters are distributed across repetitions differently so that iterations show changes in the quality and direction of movement as well as position, whereas reduplications only vary in the direction of movement and position (see chapter 3). Reasons explaining the variation of those parameters have been given throughout the book, showing that the specific aspects of form contribute in particular ways to the meaning and function of repetitions. What is yet interesting regarding the process of unit formation in gestures is the fact that variations of form were not documented for handshapes or orientations. Based on the repetitions investigated in this book, it will thus be argued that the differentiation of gestural repetitions rests upon these parameters: The maintenance of the shape along with the orientation of the hand ensures the coherence of the individual strokes and marks them as belonging together. Thus, it provides the structure for the creation of a coherent gestural unit.[105]

The parameter handshape can be considered to be one of the perceptually most important ones (see chapter 3) and together with the orientation of the hand is often considered to be essential in the creation of meaning and contrast of meaning in gestures (Brookes, 2004; Calbris, 1990; Fricke, 2012; Kendon, 2004; Mittelberg, 2010b; Müller, 2004; Seyfeddinpur, 2006; Sowa, 2005; Webb, 1996). These parameters are thus essential in constituting gestural meaning. As a result, in the majority of gestures, these parameters are semantically loaded (Fricke, 2012; Müller, 2010b, 2017). The semantic loading of the parameter, therefore, hinders possible changes and assures both the maintenance of the gestural form as well as the gestural meaning. Accordingly, it is assumed that, except in cases depicting movement, the parameters handshape and orientation are a central means for the creation and marking of unit boundaries. Through their upkeep, individual strokes of the repetitive sequences are marked as belonging together as either multistrokes or complex strokes (see chapter 3). Consequently, changes in handshapes or orientations, therefore, have delimitative character and function

---

[105] This assumption is underlined when considering the process of collecting the data corpus investigated for the present book. In sifting through the data, only those instances of gesture sequences were included in the corpus which did not involve a change in the parameter handshape. Excluding these types of sequences was not intended at the outset of the analytical procedure and only became apparent in the course of the analysis. Yet, it seems to confirm the assumption that in order to be counted as a repetitive sequence in the sense of the ones investigated in the present book, a change of this parameter is excluded.

like boundary signals (Trubetzkoy, 1939).[106] Boundary signals are linguistic means for delimitation and, in particular, "specific phonological means [. . .] that signal the existence or nonexistence of a sentence, word, or morpheme boundary at a particular point in the continuous sound stream." (Trubetzkoy, 1939, p. 242; translation JB) Based on the principle of terminal devoicing,[107] the occurrence of the phonemes /b, d, g, v, z/ can be understood as a boundary signal either indicating the beginning of a word or its inner part of a word in German (Ternes 1999, 192). Boundary signals not only occur on the phonological level but also on the syntagmatic level at which they also achieve delimitative character. In cases of gestural repetitions, changes in handshapes or orientations indicate the end of the present unit and thus the beginning of a different gestural unit. Accordingly, changes in these two parameters in repetitive sequences are involved in marking the end of a gestural unit.

A similar function is assumed for the parameter movement in repetitions, in which movement is used for the depiction of movement and not as a means to an end for depiction. When depicting movement, as in reduplications indicating iterativity, changes in the type of movement may function as boundary signals indicating the end of the repetitive sequence. More importantly, they function as boundary signals, even if the parameters handshape and orientation remain the same. As such, type and direction of movement may outplay the parameters handshape and orientation in these cases.

A different functional relevance is however assumed for the quality of movement and the position of the hands in gesture space. Changes in these parameters lead to internal variation within multi-strokes or complex strokes. The performance of gestural strokes as small, large, accentuated, or decelerated only affects the individual strokes but has no implication on the process of marking the repetitive sequence as a unit, as a whole. Changes in the quality of movement only lead to variations within the sequence by marking individual strokes. As such, the individual strokes become visible as separate units within the unit. A similar function is assumed for the parameter position. Accordingly, it might be assumed that changes in the quality of movement as well as the position in space mark boundaries of the individual strokes of the repetitive sequence also function in the sense of boundary signals, yet on a different level of unit formation.

---

106 See Fricke (2012) for an adaptation of the concept to the level of gesture phases.
107 Final devoicing in German describes the fact that the voiced consonants such as [b d g v z] are realized voiceless [p t k f s] at the end of a word in German (see for instance Ternes, 1999).

7.1 Iteration as a basic principle of pattern-building in speech, sign, and gesture — 185

In addition to the form parameters, it is assumed that the number of successive strokes plays a central role in the process of gestural unit formation. The present study has shown that the majority of gestural repetitions are made up of two to three strokes, suggesting that repetitions generally consist of smaller units. As a result, in cases of gestural repetitions, it can be concluded that the process of gestural unit formation seems to favor the creation of smaller units.[108] These results suggest an interesting parallel with the mean word length in speech as well as in signed languages. Although word length might be variable, the length of a word is a function of its frequency. In many languages, the more frequent a word is, the shorter it is. Accordingly, German, for instance, shows a trend to a mean word length of two syllables (Altmann & Best, 1996; Best, 2006; Köhler, 2005). Similarly, core lexemes in signed languages show a preference for a mean length of two syllables (Brentari, 1998; Jantunen & Takkinen, 2011). Linking this back to the results of gestural repetitions investigated in this book, the preference for smaller units, in particular, in processes of word formation seems not only to be a characteristic for spoken or signed languages but may also be identified in particular cases of processes of gestural unit formation. Especially, the preference for shorter sequences seems to play an important role in creating units with complex meaning, such as in gestural reduplications. Whereas iterations varied in their length and also consisted of sequences of up to 9 and more strokes, reduplications of type A and B only were made up of sequences with up to three strokes (see chapter 3). Accordingly, in cases in which the repetition is used for the process of creating meaning and is thus comparable to a means for word-formation, gestures seem to share similar structural as well as functional properties with the words in spoken languages or signs in signed languages.

The preference for shorter sequences along with the maintenance of form parameters is a major factor in creating coherent gestural units and for sequences of gestures to be perceived as belonging together. Yet, furthermore, and maybe even more importantly, it is assumed that these processes of unit formation in gestures are grounded in preferences of visual perception. As such, it is concluded that repetitions rest upon Gestalt principles, which are the basic requirement for the creation of coherent gestural units.

As unconscious perceptual mechanisms, Gestalt principles allow us to construct wholes or Gestalts out of incomplete perceptual input (Koffka, 1935; Köhler, 1935; Wertheimer, 1925). They "represent the most basic level of constituting experience

---

[108] Iterations expressing abstract meaning are an exception. These sequences may be composed of more than three strokes (see chapter 3).

and giving it a structure or Gestalt" (Croft & Cruse, 2004, p. 63, emphasis in original) and thus provide structure to and constrain our experience.

> There are wholes, the behaviour of which is not determined by that of their individual elements, but where the part-processes are themselves determined by the intrinsic nature of the whole. (Wertheimer, [1925] 1999, p. 4)

Accordingly, the elements of a whole "are determined as parts by the intrinsic conditions of their wholes and are to be understood "as parts" relative to such wholes" (Wertheimer, [1925] 1999, p. 15). Although being perceived and conceived of as wholes, Gestalts have internal structure, and this internal structure along with its particular elements is necessary for the whole to be perceived as such. In order to account for the perception of wholes and not only its individual elements, Gestalt theory distinguishes a range of principles regarding the visual perception. The superordinate and most essential one is the "law of simplicity" or the "law of Prägnanz", which states that single elements are combined into Gestalts based on concise visual input. In combination with the following subordinate Gestalt principles, they structure and guide our visual perception leading to the emergence of structured wholes:

- Principle of Figure and Ground: Human perception essentially rests upon the tendency to separate Figures from their Ground, that is, their background by variables such as color, size, contrast, etc.
- Principle of proximity: Entities that are in close proximity will be perceived as belonging together, regardless of their characteristics.
- Principle of similarity: Entities that share characteristics, such as size, shape, or color, will be perceived as belonging together.
- Principle of closure: Effect of completing incomplete figures even if parts of the input are missing and elements are not in connection with each other.
- Principle of continuity: Tendency of human perception to perceive continuous figures and thus the tendency to continue shapes beyond their endpoints.
- Principle of smallness: Smaller entities tend to be seen as figures against a larger ground.

If we consider these principles in relation to the gestural repetitions investigated in this book, we see that a range of these principles seems to be at work in iterations and reduplications. As was already discussed in chapter 6, gestures, in general, are a vital foregrounding strategy, serving as salience markers that emphasize the accompanied utterance as more prominent (Müller & Tag, 2010). They create a multimodal Figure-Ground structure, in which verbo-gestural parts of the utterance stand out against solely verbal parts of the utterance. Accordingly, it is assumed that the principle of Figure and Ground is at work in all instances of gestural repetitions, leading to the visual salience of repetitive sequences.[109] For iterations and reduplications, however, the principles of proximity, similarity, and smallness are of particular importance leading to their perception as coherent gestural sequences.

Based on the fact that iterations and reduplications are instances of preparation-stroke or as stroke-stroke sequences and, as such, create gesture phrases, it can be assumed that the principle of proximity leads to their coherent perception. Iterations and reduplications are executed in direct temporal succession and are not delimited by retractions, which, according to Fricke (2012), function as boundary signals indicating the end of a gestural unit and moreover, create a temporal distance between the individual strokes. Missing retractions between individual strokes, therefore, result in the creation of close temporal proximity between the individual strokes. Due to the principle of similarity, which states that entities that share characteristics will be perceived as belonging together, it can be assumed that iterations and reduplications are being perceived as distinct yet similar elements of a Gestalt. Due to the consistency of form features, a strong similarity between the individual strokes is created, assuring their perception as a coherent unit. This perception is supported by yet another Gestalt principle, that is, the principle of smallness, stating that smaller entities tend to be seen as figures against a larger ground. According to this principle, individual strokes of iterations and reduplications are perceived as Figures against the Ground of the whole repetitive sequence. The Gestalt itself, i.e., the gestural repetition, makes the perception of the individual strokes possible. Hence, it is assumed that the principles of Figure and Ground, proximity, similarity, and smallness offer the perceptual framework for iterations and reduplication to be perceived as wholes, while at the same time allowing for the particular characteristics of the individual strokes within the sequences. The underlying structures and characteristics of the individual strokes provide the necessary foundation allowing for a continuous perception of the whole Gestalt. As such, Gestalt principles account for the Gestalt as a whole but also for its internal structure and may be seen as offering an explanatory background by which the perception of repetitive sequences as coherent gestural units is describable.

The proposed argument that Gestalt principles seem to offer the grounding for the perception of coherent gestural units is thereby not restricted to the types of sequences investigated in this book. In all gestural sequences in which gestures form connected units, both on the level of form and semantics, it is assumed that the process of gestural unit formation can be accounted for when assuming Gestalt principles that structure and guide the visual perception.

---

109 The principle of Figure-Ground is yet not only of relevance for highlighting the salience of verbo-gestural parts of the utterance but seems also to be at work within gestural units leading to particular patterns of parameter prominence.

Depending on the type of gestural unit, it is furthermore argued that Gestalt principles have particular relevance leading to differences in the perception of gestural units. Due to the fact that only what is considered to be temporally close is also perceived as belonging together, it is assumed that the principle of temporal proximity takes over a particular role in cases of gestural unit formation. The principle of similarity, mostly in connection with the principle of temporal proximity, also seems to be of particular importance in structuring and guiding our visual perception. In tying together similar and temporally connected units, they are a central means for creating coherence in gestures. As such, in cases of compound gestures, that is, gestures resembling the structure of compounds in speech (Müller, Bressem & Ladewig, 2013), coherence is created by maintaining a kinesic form feature e.g., spatial position, and through their temporal proximity. Other Gestalt principles, however, such as the principle of closure, that is, the effect of completing incomplete figures, seems to be of less importance in cases of gestural repetitions, whereas taking particular effect in cases of object description, for instance. Based on the principle of closure, a both handed stroke with a flat hand with a palm lateral towards center orientation followed by a both handed stroke with a flat hand with a palm down orientation comes to be perceived as representing the four sides of a box.

Accordingly, it is argued that individual Gestalt principles assume particular relevance in different types of gestural unit formation and that, depending on the type of gestural unit, a range of different principles take effect in guiding their coherent perception. Gestural repetitions thereby seem to be a particularly interesting case, as in these sequences all principles except the principle of closure come into play. Whether other types of gestural units show comparable characteristics and what particular types of Gestalt principles may give structure to the Gestalt of gestural units goes beyond the scope of the present book and awaits further empirical evidence. The presented argument for a perception of gestural units based on Gestalt principles was meant to provide first insights. More importantly, it highlights that in discussing processes of gestural unit formation, form-based aspects (gesture phases, parameters, length of sequences) offer important insights into the nature of gestural unit formation. Considering the level of perception and, in particular, preferences of visual perception is an important step in understanding the nature of the medium gesture and the process of building gestural units.[110]

---

[110] Aspects of form and visual perception offer important insights into principles of coherence and unit formation in gestures, however a final decision whether the subsequent execution of strokes results in the creation of a gestural unit in which the same meaning is repeated or whether the repetition leads to semantic change and thus the creation of a complex meaning

The nature of gestural unit formation thus rests upon aspects of form on different levels of unit formation, preferences of visual perception, the gestural meaning expressed as well as the relation to the verbal utterance. As a result, gestures have the ability to create coherent gestural units, mark boundaries of gestural units, and allow for internal variation within gestural units. These aspects then permit gestures to use the principle of iteration for two diverging functions: as a means for creating coherent gestural units (iterations) and as a means for creating complex gestural meanings and units (reduplications). The capability of gestures to use the principle of iteration for those functions then calls into question whether they could be considered as a possible universal process of pattern building. Moreover, regarding reduplication, it raises the question of which characteristics allow for its similar nature not only in two different modalities (verbal and visual) but also in two different semiotic systems (language vs. gesture).

Similarities in speech, sign, and gestures, thus our argument, rest upon a universal principle that is based on the copying of segments, their structural order, and the iconicity arising from it. Following Stolz (2008), we furthermore assume that the abstract principle of multiple settings via copying is a basic semiotic means that lays the grounds for similar structures of form and meaning in the verbal and visual modality.

According to Stolz (2008), the "naturalness" of the process of copying is the requirement for any case of reduplication and the development of different forms of reduplication. Regardless of whether reduplication results in the copying of all features (full reduplication) or the copying of some features (partial reduplication), both forms share the elementary principle of copying features from one segment to the other. "It is [this] abstract pattern of combining original and copy that has a grammatical function and none of the parts for themselves." (Stolz, 2008, p. 100) Through this process of copying, the reduplicative construction as a whole achieves grammatical or lexical function, and it is this aspect, which assures for its occurrence in different modalities and semiotic systems and allows for its use in speech, sign, and gesture. Although the nature of reduplication is conceived of differently focusing either on form-based aspect and/ or semantic aspects (see chapter 2), it is generally attested that reduplications in speech

---

and unit calls for a verbo-gestural analysis. As strokes only carry an inherent meaning which is "enriched" (Enfield, 2009) by the verbal utterance, an evaluation of processes of gestural unit formation needs to rest upon a gestural and verbal analysis. In particular, in cases in which singular gestures may be used to compose entire scenarios (Müller, Bressem & Ladewig, 2013), the verbal utterance is a necessary companion in marking the gestures as belonging together.

and signed languages make use of this abstract pattern of copying. More importantly, however, the present study has shown that also in gestures, this process of copying is observable. By repeating segments, i.e., gestural strokes and by changing form features, it is possible to create reduplicative constructions in gesture that achieve lexical function in indicating the Aktionsart "iterativity" or grammatical function in indicating plurality. Accordingly, despite modality differences that lead to form-based distinctions (see chapter 2), the pattern of copying features from one segment to another seems to be constitutive for speech, sign, and gesture. This process, which seems to cut across modalities and semiotic systems, thereby suggests an elementary ability of speakers to use this process for unit formation allowing for a similar semantics of reduplicative constructions in verbal and visual modalities.

Moreover, we assume that these similarities of reduplications in speech, sign, and gesture are based on diagrammatic iconicity (Peirce, 1960) or relative motivation in Saussurean terms (1966). Diagrammatic iconicity is a structural principle that is of relevance for a range of levels of the language system (Posner, 1980) and underpins the systematic arrangement of signs into units of larger complexity such as words, phrases, and sentences, for instance, in which the "combined signifiers mirror the relationships between the things and events referred to." (Mittelberg, 2006, p. 122) Contrary to cases of imagistic iconicity, that is, a simple type of a physical similarity relation between form and meaning of signs, the iconicity in diagrams arises from the similarities that exist in relations of successions of complex signs and the expressed complex relational conceptualization (Jakobson, 1966; Haiman, 1985; Posner, 1980; Pusch, 2001). Diagrams represent only basic relations or proportions of an object and may be understood as schema or construction. As a result, diagrams do not need to resemble the object. Their similarity only exists regarding the relation of their parts.[111] Diagrammatic iconicity is thus "not representing but *designing* similarity" (Bauer & Ernst, 2015, p. 44 italics in original; see also Stjernfelt, 2007). Because diagrams reduce the event to basic features, they provide the observer with "information about elements and structures, relations and proportions that constitute an event" (Bauer & Ernst, 2015, p. 46) and as such build the basis for further patterns and implication processes (diagrammatic reasoning Peirce, 1960). "By direct observation of it other truths concerning its object can be discovered than those which suffice to determine its construction." (Peirce, 1960 CP 2.279)

The linear sequence of signs, for instance, is used to express succession in space and time, continuity, duration, or motion (Pusch, 2001). In the famous

---

[111] For a discussion of the notion of iconicity and problematic aspects of its discussion in linguistics see for instance (Nöth, 2008).

example *veni-vidi-vici* given by Jakobson, for instance, the temporal order of the verbs mirrors the order of the narrated events and thus exhibits diagrammatic iconicity on the level of syntax. In many Indo-European languages, diagrammatic iconicity on the morphological level, as exemplified in the gradual increase in phonemes in comparisons such as *high-higher-highest*, for instance, mirrors the gradation in the signified (Jakobson, 1966, p. 27). In many spoken and signed languages, plural marking is diagrammatic iconic regarding the semantic class "more": More of the same form (quantity) leads to an increase in complexity (reduplicated word form is semantically more complex). This is illustrated by verbs, for instance, in the Austronesian language Chamorro, in which the perfective is expressed in a less complex form, whereas the imperfective is expressed in a segmentally more complex form (*mañocho* – 'have eaten' vs. *mañochoocho* – 'are eating') (Stolz, 2007a, p. 329). Accordingly,

> every reduplicated word form which expresses any kind of quantity change with respect to the meaning of the base (i.e. intensity, plurality, diminution, etc.) is an example of "iconic" reduplication, because the change of quantity in meaning corresponds to a change of quantity in form. (Mattes, 2014, p. 121)

The paradigm case for the reduplication and the notion of diagrammatic iconicity is the singular-plural distinction in nouns. Plural nouns are usually marked. They receive more morphological features and are thus more complex. The singular, however, due to less morphological material, is less complex.

Also, for repetitive sequences in gestures, comparable structures can be identified. Similar to speech and signs, gestural reduplications are iconic in relation to the aspect of quantity and complexity: More of the same form leads to a change in quantity, and, in particular, regarding the number of units (plurality) or the occurrence of events (iterativity). Moreover, also the criterion of semantic complexity applies to gestural reduplications. The meaning of the individual strokes is semantically less complex that the meaning of all strokes together. As a result, the reduplicative construction carries a more complex meaning. Both aspects, quantity and complexity, are also at work in constructions that are discussed for intensification (Müller & Tag, 2010). In these cases, comparable to cases of iterativity and plurality, the position of the hands successively changes but not in the direction of the movement or their horizontal arrangement. Rather, the hand marks different areas in front of the speaker's body by moving them vertically upwards.

Diagrammatic iconicity in reduplications is furthermore accompanied by processes of grammaticalization. Characteristic for grammaticalization is the "semantic development from a concrete to an abstract meaning of unit, that is grammaticized." (Hurch & Mattes, 2005, p. 9) Such a development can also be observed for repetitive sequences in gestures: Gestural iterations are directly associated with bodily or visual experiences, reduplications, however, trace a successive process of abstraction from these experiences. This process of abstraction does not foreground the actual movement event but the lexical basis of Aktionsarten. An even stronger process of abstraction allows for the expression of concepts such as plurality or intensification by different positioning of the hands in relation to each other. Accordingly, it can be assumed that diagrammatic iconicity is also a means for building patterns and constructions in co-speech gestures. With this argument, we follow Fricke (2012), who, based on Saussure, postulates that relative motivation is not only a matrix for grammatical constructional rules in spoken languages but also a means of typification and an indicator for rudimentary processes of grammaticalization in co-speech gestures. Moreover, our argumentation supports Jakobson (1966, p. 350f) in his view that diagrammatic iconicity may be a universal or modality independent means of sign constitution.[112]

Concluding, it can thus be assumed that the process of repetition and in particular the process of reduplication due to its basis on the abstract pattern of copying (Stolz, 2008), the principle of diagrammatic iconicity, and the type of meaning arising from the iconicity seems to have a universal basis despite of the modality or the semiotic system in which it is expressed. Accordingly, speech, sign, and gestures use the principle of iteration for similar formal and functional differentiations, thereby indicating that the adaptation of structural processes for processes of unit formation and the creation of meaning is not restricted to the verbal modality.

---

[112] A range of studies argues that diagrammatic iconicity as a semiotic means plays a significant role in gestures for processes of sign constitution, pattern building, and conceptualization. Mittelberg (2006, 2008, 2013), for instance, shows that it is a basic principle structuring the systematic arrangements of gestural sings in discourse about spoken language grammar. Müller (2004), for example, argues that the flat open hand carrying the semantic core of presenting, giving, showing may be varied depending on the particular movement pattern that is executed (e.g., up and down movement for listing arguments, circular motion for providing further arguments). A both handed execution of the flat open hand may be understood as resulting in the semantic feature of intensification. The meaning of intensification is based on diagrammatic iconicity arising between both hands. Enfield, for instance, underlines the significance of diagrammatic iconicity in visual representations of abstract kinship relations. He highlights that gestures and other bodily movements are used as "tools for diagramming thoughts on a rich three-dimensional virtual sketch space anchored in the body" (Enfield, 2009, p. 164). Others highlight its importance for the conceptualization and expression of abstract thought such as observable in mathematical thinking, talking and gesturing about physics, music or architecture as well as joint communicative activities or problem-solving (see Mittelberg & Gerner, in preparation for a collection of papers).

> Reduplication in spoken and signed languages shows some similarities in form and function [. . .]. Functionally, reduplication is used to express similar aspects of meaning in both modalities. Spoken and signed languages use reduplication, for instance, for pluralization, aspectual marking, reciprocal marking, and nominalization (Rubino 2005). Hence, reduplication of verbs and nouns seems to be a modality-independent means for expressing certain aspects of meaning. (Pfau & Steinbach, 2006, p. 153)

Based on the investigation of repetition in gestures presented in this book, the argument for reduplication as a "modality-independent means" (Pfau & Steinbach, 2006) can now be extended to include gestures thus hinting at a possible universality of the structure and meaning of the process of reduplication. Yet, although reduplication seems to have a universal nature regarding its structure and semantics, the process is expressed differently in speech, sign, and gesture. Depending on the abilities and preferences of the respective modality, the process is adapted, leading to particularities on the level of form. Whereas the form-based distinction between full and partial reduplication, that is, the copying of all or only particular features, seems to be applicable to all three types of signs, particularities in the use of form seem to differ.

> Despite this similarity to partial reduplication in spoken languages, sideward reduplication as well as backward reduplication differ crucially from all kinds of reduplication found in spoken languages, since sign languages have the unique possibility of making distinctions through the use of the signing space. (Pfau & Steinbach, 2006, p. 154)

Gestures, by using the same modality as signed languages, thereby clearly show more similarities on the level of form with signs than with speech. Accordingly, gestures and signs use the parameter "movement" to express "aspects such as onset, duration, frequency, recurrence, permanence or intensity of states or events" (Klima & Beluggi, 1979, p. 247) and the repetition of movements along the horizontal, vertical, or sagittal axis as well as by positioning the hands in different places in gesture space (Klima & Beluggi, 1979; Pfau & Steinbach, 2005) is used to indicate plurality (see chapter 2 for more details).

Despite these differences between verbal and visual modalities, it can be assumed that the process of repetition is universal to a certain degree as it shows commonalities in form and function in speech, signs, and gestures. Differences across and within modalities thereby clearly indicate the flexibility of the process to be used in different modalities and allows for the principle of iterations to be modality encompassing and not restricted to particular types of modalities. Speaking with Sapir, it can thus be concluded that

> nothing is more natural than the prevalence of reduplication, in other words, the repetition of all or part of the radical element. The process is generally employed, with self-evident symbolism, to indicate such concepts as distribution, plurality, repetition, customary activity, increase of size, added intensity, continuance. (Sapir, 1921, p. 76)

7.2 Implications for (Cognitive) Linguistics and further research perspectives

The proposition argued for in the book, namely that repetitive structures as a fundamental means of sign constitution are also a basic principle for building patterns and units of different complexity and functionality in coverbal gestures, addresses a core notion of Cognitive Linguistics: the question of universal principles crosscutting modalities. By departing from the assumption that linguistic patterns and structures rest upon general cognitive principles that are not particular for spoken or written languages but can play out in the visual modality as well, the book grounded gestural processes of pattern building in general principles of conceptualization and explained their relevance and characteristics for a multimodal understanding of language use. This assumption was further strengthened by the book's aim at identifying characteristics of repetitive sequences that cut across modalities (verbal and visual) and semiotic systems (language vs. gesture). In comparison with the phenomenon of repetition in spoken and signed languages, the book explored, on the one hand, the specifics of gestures and of multimodal spoken language use. On the other hand, it attempted to identify basic principles for building patterns irrespective of the modality on which they are based. By addressing the processes of building patterns on the level of gestures alone as well as in relation to speech, the book offered a further facet in examining how the same linguistic processes, structures, and functions may manifest themselves in speech and gesture. Moreover, by discussing the interaction and relevance of gestures for the semantics and syntax of speech, it examines possible areas of integration of speech and gesture. By taking up the notion of constructions as a framework for explaining the principles of pattern building in gestures alone and in relation with speech, the book joins in the strand of research on Construction Grammar within Cognitive Linguistics research and, in particular, the discussion of multimodal constructions (Bergs & Zima, 2018).

The present book has grounded this argumentation on one particular type of gestural repetition, namely repetitions within gesture phrases, and moreover, based on the frequency of the particular repetitive patterns in the investigated corpus, on particular types repetitive phenomena. As a result, the study has not particularly addressed the relation of gestural iteration in depicting movement,

7.2 Implications for (Cognitive) Linguistics and further research perspectives — 195

for instance. But a detailed analysis based on a larger number of occurrences pursuing a similar perspective as taken in the present book would contribute to a more comprehensive description of gestural repetitions and in particular gestural iterations. Specifically, a comparison of iterations depicting movement and gestural reduplications expressing iterativity might contribute to a deeper understanding of how gestures function as means of unit creation and means of word-formation. Similarly, diagrammatic iconicity and its relevance for gestural reduplication could be investigated based on more empirical material. The cases discussed in the present book fell into cases in which more form goes along with more meaning (iterativity and plurality). However, as Stolz (2008), for instance, pointed out, more form can also be used to expressed less content. De Jorio (1832/2000, p. lxxxiv), for instance, mentions that repetition and, in particular, the reduction of gestural movement may be used to express diminution. Studies investigating whether the iconic nature of reduplication may also be used for such cases would contribute to a deeper understanding of the nature of reduplication in gesture and moreover offer a further ground for comparison with the phenomenon in spoken or signed languages.

Regarding the two analytical strands for the description and analysis of gestural repetitions followed in the present book, namely the perspective of a grammar of gestures and a multimodal grammar, a range of further research questions can be posed. Concerning the perspective of a "grammar of gesture", the identified preference for smaller units in the creation of unit formation could be a further line of research offering substantial insights into the nature of processes of unit formation in gestures. Based on the results presented in this book, the question arises whether also in other cases of linear successions the created units consist of a rather small number of consecutive strokes and if not, what would be able to explain the differences with the repetitions discussed in this book. Further analysis of the creation of gestures in linear succession would thereby add fundamental insights into the ability of gestures to form linear structures. In doing so, another aspect touched upon only briefly in the preceding section could be discussed in more detail, namely the role of gestural form parameters and their possible functions as boundary signals in the process of meaning and unit formation. Focusing on this aspect from a simultaneous as well linear perspective would add more empirical evidence to the claims made so far that gestures have the potential for combinatorics and hierarchical structures and, as such, a potential for language (Müller, 1998). In addition to these investigations, the question of Gestalt principles touched upon with respect to gestural repetitions in the previous sections could be a valuable line of further research. It would provide further insights into the nature of how gestures, based on preferences of form and visual perception, are able to create coherent units of meaning and function. In doing so, this perspective could not only be of relevance for the study of gestures but would also provide a framework allowing for comparisons with studies trying to approach the processes of meaning based on visual input (e.g., Kappelhoff & Müller, 2011).

Concerning the perspective of a multimodal grammar, additional studies focusing on the semantic relation of speech and gesture would contribute to a better understanding of the functional relation of both modalities and tackle the question of what gestures are able to contribute to the semantics of speech and by which means they are able to do so. In doing so, more empirical evidence would be gained on how speech and gesture are semantically linked in expressing a common idea unit and how they are able to appear together as "manifestations of the same process of utterance" (Kendon, 1980, p. 208). This aspect could furthermore be supported by studies analyzing the temporal relation of speech and gesture, in particular, with respect to the syntactic structure of the utterance. Examining this in a range of gestural phenomena and range of gesture types would help to understand how the integration of speech and gesture is achieved and by which means. Possible frequent correlations of gestures with units in speech would thereby be able to confirm the tendency and arguments put forward in the present study, in which the temporal correlation was seen as an indication of a functional integration of gestures into speech. In doing so, studies would contribute to a "grammar of speech" by contributing to a "description of speaking in all its structural, functional as well as medial particularities" and a "description of the cognitive creation processes of speaking" (Fricke, 2012, p. 277).

Moving away from the type of repetitions discussed in the present book, research on repetitions in gestures could be broadened by concentrating on recurring form features in non-consecutive gestures, so-called catchments (McNeill, 1992, 2002, 2005), which offer "a kind of thread of consistent dynamic visuospatial imagery running through the discourse segment that provides a gesture-based window into discourse cohesion" (McNeill et al., 2001, p. 10). So far, only isolated and little systematic investigation has been done on this type of repetition (e.g., McNeill, 2000; McNeill, et al. 2001, 2002; Montredon, Amrani & Benoit-Barnet 2008; Parrill, 2007). More research on this topic would complement the analysis presented in this book. Contrary to iterations and reduplications, which are a means of unit and meaning creation, catchments are relevant for discourse structure. By operating on the level of thematic organization, catchments provide cohesive linkages within discourses. Investigating this type of repetition, for instance, from a text-linguistic perspective could provide insight into how non-consecutive gestural repetitions contribute to the structure of texts or discourse and how the structure of a text and its themes and rhemes are interrelated creating cohesion and coherence relations (e.g., Vater, 2001). Furthermore, it could be questioned "which features of the gestural modality do catchments tend to employ? What governs the mapping between semantic concepts and gestural features? What sorts of ideas tend to be expressed via catchments, rather than (or in addition to) spoken language?" (Eisenstein, 2008, p. 31) Analyses of gestural catchments would direct the focus to a different level of structural and functional relations between gestures and thus broaden the perspective from a description of structures and functions of gestural units in close temporal relation to units that are not temporally connected.

Apart from catchments, the phenomenon of gestural repetitions could be expanded by considering repetitions across speakers (e.g., Fornel, 1992). An interactive perspective might reveal insights into stylistic and or pragmatic purposes of gestural repetitions for creating coherence and understanding in discourse. As such, it would allow for further comparisons between speech, sign, and gestures on aspects of regulating interaction and pragmatic purposes as well as for achieving particular effects, attention, or emphasis, for instance.

Considering all the aspects discussed above, the book, along with links to other topics, addressed not only basic principles of Cognitive Linguistics, namely that "language is not an autonomous cognitive faculty, [that] grammar is conceptualization, [and that] knowledge of language emerges from language use" (Croft & Cruse, 2004, p. 1) but has also fundamental implications for the study of language: the book contributes to a discussion of the general principles of linguistic multimodality from the perspective of gesture-speech relations (Cienki, 2012; Fricke, 2007, 2012; Mittelberg, 2006; Müller, 1998, 2008) by supporting the view that language (use) is multimodal.

Appendices

A Notation conventions

Using Elan, the first step of the transcription, notation, and coding of the gestural repetitions was done (see chapter 1). In particular, the program ELAN was used for the following aspects:
- Transliteration of verbal utterance
- Segmentation of verbal utterance into intonation units following Chafe (1994)
- Transcription of speech using GAT and GAT2 (Selting, Auer, Barden, et al. 1998, Selting, Auer, Barth-Weingarten et al., 2009)
- Transcription of phonological units, utterance final intonation, and primary and secondary accents of the verbal utterance following Ladd (2008)
- Segmentation of gestural movement sequences and coding of gesture phases following Bressem & Ladewig (2011)
- Description of gestural form features following Bressem (2013).

See below for an example window.

202 — A Notation conventions

B Description of gestural form features

The description of gestural form features is based on a notation system for gestures, which, by focusing solely on gestures' physical appearance, directs the attention to the different facets of a gesture's form and focuses on its detailed characterization (Bressem, 2013). The system is grounded in a linguistic-semiotic approach to gestures, assuming a heuristic separation of form, meaning and function in the analytical process.

The notation system is characterized by the following basic attributes (see Bressem, 2013 for more details):
- The system pursues a phonetic perspective, and aims at an articulatory representation of gestural forms.
- The notation system is data driven and has been designed while working with and on the material. Later on, it has been adjusted to incorporate further phenomena, which emerged in other types of material.
- The system only provides notation guidelines for the hands and leaves out articulatory as well as anatomical descriptions of arms, other body parts and body postures (see for instance Sager, 2001; Sager & Bührig, 2005; Martell, 2005).
- A systematic characterization of gestural forms in all four parameters of sign language based on the parameters formulated in Sign Linguistics (Battison, 1974; Klima & Bellugi, 1979; Stokoe, 1960). The notation conventions thereby follow a particular logic by arranging the parameters according to their prominence (hand shape, orientation, movement, and position).
- A characterization of gestural forms independently of speech.
- Avoidance of gestural form notation including paraphrases of meaning and function.

The following figures are published in Bressem (2013).

1 Classification of parameter "hand shape"

1.1 Form clusters for hand configuration

1. "Fist"   2. "Flat hand"   3. "Single fingers"   4. "Combinations of fingers"

1.2 Numbering of fingers

1.3 Shape of digits

stretched   bent   crooked   flapped down   connected   touching

1.4 List of documented hand configurations by Bressem (2006) (see Ladewig and Bressem fc.)

1. flat hand				2. fist	3. single fingers				
Flat hand	Lax flat hand	Spread flat hand	Flat hand 1 facing forward	Fist	1 stretched	2 stretched	2 bent	3 stretched	5 stretched	1+2 stretched

3. single fingers

2+3 stretched	2+5 stretched	1+5 stretched	1–3 stretched	1–4 stretched	2–4 stretched

4. combination of fingers

1+2 connected	1+3 connected	1+2 crooked	1+2 bent	1–5 crooked	1–5 bent	1–5 spread bent
2–5 flapped down	2–5 flapped down 1 stretched	2–5 bent	1–5 touching	1–5 connected	1+2 touching	

2 Classification of parameter "orientation"

- depending on 1.) palm and 2.) gesture space
- orientation = orientation 1 + orientation 2 (e.g. palm lateral towards center (PLTC))

1. palm

- palm up   PU
- palm down   PD
- palm lateral   PL
- palm vertical   PV
- marker "diagonal" Di

2. gesture space

- towards center   TC
- away center   AW
- towards body   TB
- away body   AB

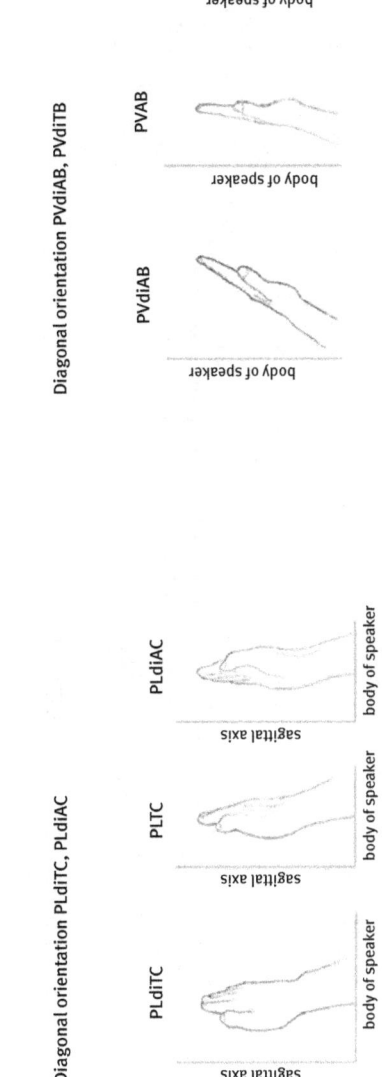

Diagonal orientation PVdiAB, PVdiTB

Diagonal orientation PLdiTC, PLdiAC

208 — B Description of gestural form features

3 Classification of parameter "position"

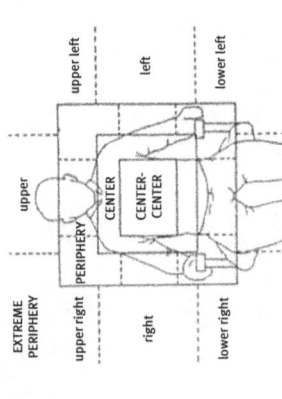

McNeill's gesture space (figure taken from McNeill 1992)

4 Classification of parameter "movement"

4.1 "Type of movement"

4.1.1 Movements of the arm, shoulder or single fingers

straight   arced   circle

zigzag   s-line   spiral

4.1.2 Movements of the wrist and single fingers

bending to puls   raising   bending to 1   bending to 5   rotation

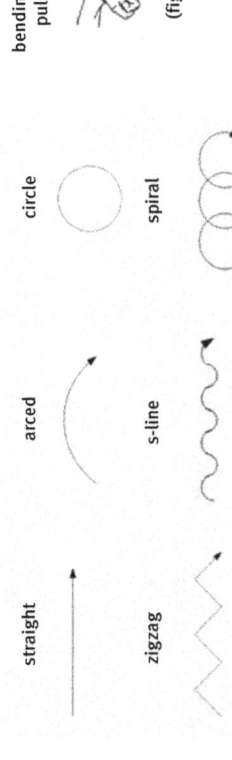

(figures taken from Prillwitz et al. 1989)

4.2 "Direction of movement"

4.2.1 Movements along the vertical and horizontal axis

vertical axis: up, down
horizontal axis: right, left

marker diagonal: diagonal right up, diagonal left up, diagonal right down, diagonal left down

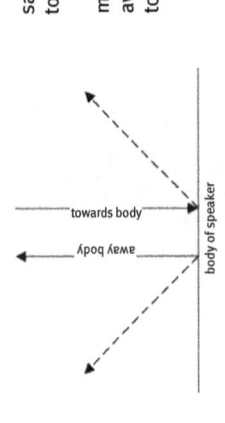

4.2.2 Movements along the saggital axis

sagittal axis: away body, towards body

marker diagonal: diagonal away body, diagonal towards body

4.3.2 Spiral and circular movements

clockwise

counter clockwise

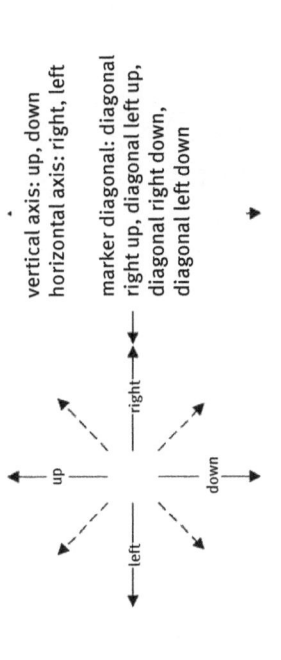

4.2.4 Movements of the wrist and single fingers

bending to puls   raising   bending to 1   bending to 5   rotation

(figures taken from Prillwitz et al. 1989)

4.3 "Quality of movement"

1. size of movment
- Reduced
- enlarged

2. speed of movtion
- decelerated
- accelerated

3. flow of movement
- accentuated ending
- accentuated beginning

C Excerpt from the excel sheet for the example "send back and forth"

The following tables are excerpts from the Excel sheet in which the second part of the analysis was carried out (see chapter 2 for more details). Using the Excel sheet, the following aspects were analyzed:
- Changes of form parameters, length of repetitions, number of strokes within and across intonation units
- Gestural modes of representation, gestural meaning, type of gesture, temporal positioning with verbal utterance, semantic features expressed in speech and gesture
- Relation with syntactic category and relations, function of the gestural repetition.

212 — C Excerpt from the excel sheet for the example "send back and forth"

example	Intonation Unit	Gesture phases-speech	Gesture phase sequence	Gesture phases	Hand shape	Orientation	Position	Movement type	Movement direction	Quality of movement	Handedness	Number of changing parameters	Type of changing parameter
send back and forth	briefumschläge hat die hauspost oder wie das heißt	dInge immer		preparation									
	dInge immer zwischen zwei Ämtern hIn und hErschickt,	zwischen zwei ÄM	stroke-stroke	stroke	2 stretched	PLTC	c	bent	away body	-	one handed	2	movement type position
		mtern hIn und	stroke-stroke	stroke	2 stretched	PLTC	c	bent	towards body	-	one handed	2	movement type position
		her schi	stroke-stroke	stroke	2 stretched	PLTC	c	bent	away body	-	one handed	2	movement type position
		ickt;		retraction									

C Excerpt from the excel sheet for the example "send back and forth" —— 213

example	Intonation Unit	Gesture phases-speech	Gesture phase sequence	Phonological unit speech	Level of form-gestures in relation to speech				
					utterance final intonation	nucleus intonation unit	number of stroke per intonation unit	length of repetition	number of intonation units encompassed by repetition
send back and forth	briefumschläge hat die hauspost oder wie das heißt								
	dinge immer zwischen zwei Ämtern hIn und hErschickt,	dInge immer							
		zwischen zwei ÄM	stroke-stroke	Words-syllable			3		
		mtern hin und	stroke-stroke	words		Nucleus	3	3	
		her schi	stroke-stroke	Words-syllable					
		ickt;			rising				1

C Excerpt from the excel sheet for the example "send back and forth"

example	Intonation Unit	Gesture phases-speech	Gesture phase sequence	temporal postion of gestues with speech	gestural mode of representation	gestural mode of representation-subtyp	action, object etc.	abstract, concrete	abstract referential etc	Level of meaning-gestures in relation to speech							semantic relation of gesture with speech
										semantic feature 1- gesture	semantic feature 2- gesture	semantic feature 1- speech	semantic feature 2- speech	semantic feature 3- speech	semantic feature 3- speech	
send back and forth	briefumschläge hat die hauspost oder wie das heißt	dinge immer														
	dinge immer zwischen zwei Ämtern hin und hErschickt,	zwischen zwei ÄM	stroke-stroke	parallel	Repr	motion and path	movement/abstract		abstract referential	movement direction	movement direction	movement	movement direction	action	object	redundant
		mtern hin und	stroke-stroke	parallel	Repr	motion and path	movement/abstract		abstract referential	movement direction	movement direction	movement	movement direction	action	object	redundant
		her schi	stroke-stroke	parallel	Repr	motion and path	movement/abstract		abstract referential	movement direction	movement direction	movement	movement direction	action	object	redundant
		ickt;														

C Excerpt from the excel sheet for the example "send back and forth"

example	Intonation Unit	Gesture phases-speech	Gesture phase sequence	syntactical category-stroke	Level of syntax-gestures in relation to speech			
					syntactical category-whole repetition	syntactical relation-whole repetition	type of integration into speech
send back and forth	briefumschläge hat die hauspost oder wie das heißt						
	dinge immer zwischen zwei Ämtern hin und hErschickt,	dInge immer					
		zwischen zwei ÄM	stroke-stroke	PrGr	VGr	S	semantic integration
		mtern hin und	stroke-stroke	V	VGr	S	semantic integration
		her schi	stroke-stroke	V	VGr	S	semantic integration
		ickt;					

D Transcript example iteration "weapons of mass destruction"

D Transcript example iteration "weapons of mass destruction"

utterance		'Ich s-A:ge ihnen 'E:Ins-				
		'ich	s-A		ge ihnen	'E:Ins
translation		i	i		te	ll you
gesture phases		i tell you one thing	preparation		stroke	stroke
"form parameter"	hand shape	1+2 touched PLTC			1+2 touched PLTC	1+2 touched PLTC
orientation						
position	cr		cr		cr	cc
"movement-type"	straight		straight		straight	straight
"movement-direction"	downwards		downwards		downwards	downwards
"movement-quality"	accentuated ending		accentuated ending	reduced	decelarated
"number of strokes per repetition"	4					

D Transcript example iteration "weapons of mass destruction"

					wenn sie d´As -ERNst meinen,	d	´A				er ´En
		wenn sie				if you take this seriously					
						if you	t	hi	s	–	
one thing	–	preparation				stroke	preparation	stroke	preparation	stroke	
stroke											
1+2 touched						1+2 touched		1+2 touched		1+2 touched	
PLTC						PD		PD		PD	
						clo	clo		clo		
							straight		straight		
							down		down		
dann müssen sie eines endlich verstehen						accentuated ending	reduced		reduced		
						4					

D Transcript example iteration "weapons of mass destruction"

Nst	meinen,	wˇA	mˈAssenvernˈIchtungswaffen und die verbrˈEItung von mˈAssenvernˈIchtungswaffen gˈE:ht nˈU:r	wAs sie in dˇˈIEsem papˈIEr	sie in	dˇˈIEse	m pa
				what you have written in this paper	what	you in	this
seriou preparation	sly stroke	take preparation			stroke	stroke	preparation
	1+2 touched PD				1+2 touched PD	1+2 touched PD	
	clo	cc			clo		clo
	straight	straight			straight		straight
	down	down			down		down
	reduced	accentuated beginning			accentuated ending		—

4

D Transcript example iteration "weapons of mass destruction" — 221

	"über den k´Ampf gegen nICHTverbreit ung			
p´IER	über	den k´Ampf	f gegen n´ICHT	verbreitung geschr
pa stroke	per stroke	about the fight against the non distribution about preparation ctd.		against the non stroke
		the fight stroke		
1+2 touched PD	1+2 touched PD	1+2 touched PD		1+2 touched PD
c		c	c	
straight		straight	straight	
up		down	down	
—		accentuated ending	accentuated ending	
	3			

D Transcript example iteration "weapons of mass destruction"

w´Enn die atOmwaffenbesitz enden lÄnder Endlich Abrüsten	dann m´Üssen	sie ´Eines	es ´Endlich	´Endlich	verst	e	hen	–
ieben haben;	–	then you have to finally understand one thing						
distribution	written		than must	you one	finally	under	finally	st
hold	stroke	preparation	stroke	stroke	preparation	stroke	preparation	and stroke
1+2 touched		1+2 touched	1+2 touched	1+2 touched		1+2 touched		1+2 touched
PD		PD	PD	PD		PD		PD
clo	c	c	c	c	c	c		
straight	straight	straight	straight	straight	straight		straight	
down	down	down	down	down	down		down	
reduced	accentuated beginning	accentuated beginning	accentuated beginning	accentuated beginning	enlarged		reduced	
5								

D Transcript example iteration "weapons of mass destruction"

	m'Assen	ver	nICHtungs	waffen und	die verbr'Eitung	von	m'Assn
	weapons of mass destruction and the distribution of weapons of mass destruction						
—							
—	preparation ctd.	weapons	of	mass	destruction and	the distribution of	
preparation		stroke	stroke	hold	preparation	stroke	stroke
		1+2 touched	1+2 touched			1+2 touched	1+2 touched
		PD	PD			PD	PD
	p	cc			c	c	
	straight	straight			straight	straight	
	down	down			down	down	
	accentuated beginning	accentuated ending			accentuated beginning	accentuated beginning	
	7						

D Transcript example iteration "weapons of mass destruction"

vern	n´Ichtungs	waffen	.h gE:	g-E:	ht n´U:r,	w´Enn	
weapons preparation	of stroke	mass hold	destruction preparation	only stroke	is possible preparation	stroke	
	1+2 touched PD			1+2 touched PLTC		1+2 touched PLTC	
clo			p		p	p	
straight			straight		straight	straight	
down			down		down	down	
accentuated ending			accentuated beginning		accentuated beginning	accentuated beginning	
						7	

D Transcript example iteration "weapons of mass destruction"

			.h Alles ʾANdere ist keine nʾIchtverbreitungspolitʾIk,			
	die atʾOmwaffen		tʾOmwaf	fn besʾItz	endn lʾÄnd	lʾÄn
if the countries who own nuclear weapons finally demobilize						
if		the nucleur		weapons	countries	
stroke		stroke		preparation	stroke	stroke
1+2 touched PD		1+2 touched PLTC		1+2 touched PLTC	1+2 touched PLTC	1+2 touched PLTC
	pu		pu	pu	pu	
	straight		straight	straight	straight	
	down		down	down	down	
	accentuated beginning		accentuated beginning	accentuated beginning	accentuated beginning	

D Transcript example iteration "weapons of mass destruction"

					"s 'Ondern die l'Egitimation für ^aufrüstung	und w'Enn	nn d'EUtschland
er 'En	'End	lich 'AB	rüs	tn,			and if Germany finally gives up the nuclear partaking
preparation	stroke	finally preparation	demo stroke	bilize stroke		preparation	and if stroke
	1+2 touched PLTC		1+2 touched PLTC	1+2 touched PLTC			1+2 touched PLTC
epu		c	cc	cc			epu
straight		straight	straight	straight		straight	straight
down		down	down	down		down	down
accentuated beginning		accentuated ending	reduced		accentuated beginning		accentuated beginning
					9		

D Transcript example iteration "weapons of mass destruction"

nd d'le: nu	die nu	kleAre	re t	teil	habe	(-) En	dlich
germany stroke	the stroke	nuclear preparation	par stroke	taking stroke	stroke	preparation	fin stroke
1+2 touched PLTC	1+2 touched PLTC		1+2 touched PLTC	1+2 touched PLTC	1+2 touched PLTC		1+2 touched PLTC
		c	c	c		pu	c
straight		straight	straight	straight		straight	straight
down	down	down	down	down		down	down
accentuated beginning	accentuated beginning	accentuated beginning	accentuated ending	reduced		accentuated beginning	accentuated ending

D Transcript example iteration "weapons of mass destruction"

´AU	fgibt,	.h All		es ´AN	ndre,	ist
ally	gives	up	everything else is not a policy of stopping distribution	everything	else	
stroke	stroke	preparation		stroke	stroke	preparation
1+2 touched	1+2 touched, 3-5 bent		1+2 touched		1+2 touched	
PLTC	PLTC		PLTC		PLTC	
cc		pu		c		pu
straight		straight		straight		straight
down		down		down		down
-		accentuated beginning	accentuated beginning	accentuated ending		accentuated beginning
		6				

D Transcript example iteration "weapons of mass destruction"

keine n´Icht	verbreitungs	poli	t´lk	s´On	dern die l´Egi	tima
is	not a policy	of	stopping	distribution	but the legimization for mobilzation elsewhere	the legit
stroke	stroke	hold	stroke	stroke		stroke
1+2 touched	1+2 touched		1+2 touched	1+2 touched		1+2 touched
PLTC	PLTC		PLTC	PLTC		PLTC
c		cc	pu	pu	cc	
straight		straight	straight	straight	straight	
down		down	up	down	down	
accentuated ending		reduced	enlarged	accentuated beginning	accentuated ending	
				3		

			rüstung anderswo;							
					for	1+2 touched				
					stroke	PLTC				
			für ˇAUF		preparation					accentuated ending
							cc	straight	down	
		tion		mation						
				hold						

E Transcript example iteration "Arko"

utterance	da kratzt = er	dann rennt = er in den flur,		rennt er in flur,		krAtzt,		oma muss die kiste, (-) vorschiebn,		und das wars	
utterance-intonation unit	da kratzt = er	dann rennt = er in den flur,	rennt	er in flur	kr	A	A	tzt,	oma	muss die kiste, (-) vorschiebn,	und das wars	
translation	then he scrapes	then he runs into the hallway	runs	into the hallway					grandma	needs to push forward the box	and that was it	
gesture phases				prep	prep	stroke	prep	stroke	retraction			
form parameter	hand shape					flat hand	flat hand	flat hand				
	orientation					PD	PD	PD				
	position					C	C	C				
	movement-type				scr	straight	straight	straight				
	movement-direction				y	down	down	down				
	movement-quality					–	–	–				
number of strokes per repetition						3						

F Transcript example iteration "metal thing"

utterance	<<pp>ich glaube dass es ja so beim>> ital'IEner, wo die flasche w'Ein da in som metAllding drinne is, wo man dann (--) äh mit dem bÜgel die flAsche inner hand hält,				
utterance-intonation unit	<<pp>ich glaube dass es ja so beim>> ital'IEner,	wo die flasche w'Ein	da in som	metAllding	drinne is,
translation	i think that in an italian restaurant	where the bottle wine	in such a	metall thing	is
gesture phases	preparation	stroke	stroke	stroke	retraction
form parameter — hand shape		1-5 bent	1-5 bent	1-5 bent	
form parameter — orientation		PD	PD	PD	
form parameter — position		C	C	C	
form parameter — movement-type		arced	arced	arced	
form parameter — movement-direction		inwards	outwards	inwards	
form parameter — movement-quality		–	–	–	
number of strokes per repetition		3			

| utterance (cont.) | wo man dann (--) äh mit dem bÜgel die flAsche inner hand hält, | where you then (--) ehm with the holder hold the bottle in the hand |

G Transcript example reduplication "send back and forth"

utterance	brIEfumschläge hat, (.) die h´AUSpost oder wie das heißt, wo man eben Immer in den=den dies diesn zu beschriftenden umschlÄ:gn, dInge immer zwischen zwei ÄMtern hin und hErschickt;						
utterance-intonation unit	brIEfumschläge hat, (.) die h´AUSpost oder wie das heißt,	wo man eben Immer in den=den dies diesn zu beschriftenden umschlÄ:gn,	dInge immer	zwischen zwei ÄM	mtern hin und	hErschi	ickt;
translation	envelopes, (.) internal mail or how you call it,	where you just always in these labeled envelopes,	always things	between two off	ices back	and fourth	send;
gesture phrases			prep	stroke	stroke	stroke	retraction
form parameter — hand shape				2 stretched	2 stretched	2 stretched	
form parameter — orientation				PLTC	PLTC	PLTC	
form parameter — position				cc	cc	cc	
form parameter — movement-type				arced	arced	arced	
form parameter — movement-direction				away body	towards body	away body	
form parameter — movement-quality				-	-	-	
number of strokes per repetition				3			

H Transcript example reduplication "single steps"

H Transcript example reduplication "single steps"

utterance	und dann fing der halt an zu texten oder steht Och steht ja in den büchern kannste jA, kannste dir ja immer die Einzelnen schritte d'URCHlesen, da sind ja die frisuren beschriebn;									
utterance intonation unit	und dann fing der halt an zu texten	oder steht Och steht ja in den büchern	kannste dir ja immer die	Einzel	nen schritte	d'U	URCHlesen,		da sind ja die frisuren beschr'IEBN;
translation	and then he started to babble	or it is written in the text books	you can always the	single	steps	read	through		well there the hair cuts are described
gesture phases			preparation	stroke	stroke	stroke	retraction		rest position
form parameter — hand shape				2–5 flapped down	2–5 flapped down	2–5 flapped down			
form parameter — orientation				PLTC	PLTC	PLTC			
form parameter — position				pu	p	cu			
form parameter — movement-type				arced	arced	arced			
form parameter — movement-direction				away body	away body	away body			
form parameter — movement-quality				–	–	–			
number of strokes per reptition					3				

References

Abbi, Anvita. 1992. Contact, conflict, and compromise: The genesis of reduplicated structures in South Asian Languages. In Edward C. Dimock, Braj B. Kachru & Bh. Krishnamurti (eds.), *Dimensions of Sociolinguistics in South Asia: Papers in memory of Gerald B. Kelley*, 131–148. New Delhi: South Asia Books.
Alibali, Martha W. & Dana C. Heath. 2000. Effects of visibility between speaker and listener on gesture production: Some gestures are meant to be seen. *Journal of Memory and Language* 44. 169–188.
Alibali, Martha W. & Sotaro Kita. 2010. Gesture highlights perceptually present information for speakers. *Gesture* 10(1). 3–28.
Altmann, Gabriel & Karl-Heinz Best. 1996. Zur Länge der Wörter in deutschen Texten. *Glottometrika* 15. 166–180.
Andrén, Mats. 2010. *Children's Gestures from 18 to 30 Months*. Lund: Lund University.
Andrén, Mats. 2014. Multimodal constructions in children: Is the headshake part of language? *Gesture* 14(2). 141–170.
Armstrong, David, William C. Stokoe & Sherman E. Wilcox. 1995. *Gesture and the Nature of Language*. Cambridge: Cambridge University Press.
Armstrong, David F. & Sherman Wilcox. 2007. *The Gestural Origin of Language*. Oxford/New York: Oxford University Press.
Auer, Peter 1986. Kontextualisierung. *Studium Linguistik* 19. 22–47.
Auer, Peter. 2000. On-line-syntax-oder: was es bedeuten könnte, die Zeitlichkeit der mündlichen Sprache ernst zu nehmen. *Sprache und Literatur* 31(1). 43–56.
Auer, Peter. 2005. Syntax als Prozess. *InLiSt (Interaction and Linguistic Structures)* 41.
Battison, Robin. 1974. Phonological deletion in American Sign Language. *Sign Language Studies* 5. 1-19.
Battison, Robin. 1978. *Lexical Borrowing in American Sign Language*. Silver Spring, MD: Linstok Press.
Bauer, Matthias & Christoph Ernst. 2015. *Diagrammatik: Einführung in ein kultur- und medienwissenschaftliches Forschungsfeld*. transcript Verlag.
Baur, Rupprecht S. & Christoph Closta. 2005. "Du hast ja 'nen Vogel!"–Phraseologie und Gesten in der Alltagssprache. *Essener Unikate* 26. 68–75.
Bavelas Beavin, Janet, Nicole Chovil, Douglas A. Lawrie & Allan Wade. 1992. Interactive Gestures. *Discourse Processes* 15. 469–489.
Beattie, Geoffrey & Shovelton Heather. 2001. An experimental investigation of the role of different types of iconic gesture in communication. A semantic feature approach. *Gesture* 1(2). 129–149.
Beattie, Geoffrey & Heather Shovelton. 1999. Do iconic hand gestures really contribute anything to the semantic information conveyed by speech? An experimental investigation. *Semiotica* 123(1/2). 1–30.
Beattie, Geoffrey & Heather Shovelton. 2007. The role of iconic gesture in semantic communication and its theoretical and practical implications. In Susan D. Duncan, Justine Cassell & Elena Tevy Levy (eds.), *Gesture and the Dynamic Dimension of Language*, 221–241. Philadelphia: John Benjamins.
Beaupoil-Hourdel, Pauline, Dominique Boutet & Aliyah Morgenstern. 2015. A child's multimodal negations from 1 to 4: The interplay between modalities. In P. Larrivée &

C. Lee (eds.), *Negation and Polarity: Experimental Perspectives, Language, Cognition, and Mind*, 95–123. Cham, Switzerland: Springer.

Becker, Raymond, Alan Cienki, Austin Bennett, Christina Cudina, Camile Debras, Zuzanna Fleischer, Michael Haaheim, Torsten Müller, Kashmiri Stec & Alessandra Zarcone. 2011. Aktionsarten, speech and gesture. *Paper presented at the 2nd Workshop on Gesture and Speech in Interaction– GESPIN, Bielefeld, Germany*.

Bergen, Benjamin, Nancy Chang & Shweta Narayan. 2004. Simulated action in an embodied construction grammar. *26th Annual Meeting of the Cognitive Science Society*. Chicago, Illinois: Citeseer.

Bergen, Benjamin & Nancy Chang. 2005. Embodied construction grammar in simulation-based language understanding. In Jan-Ola Östmann & Mirjam Fried (eds.), *Construction Grammars: Cognitive Grounding and Theoretical Extensions*, 147–190. Amsterdam: John Benjamins.

Bergen, Benjamin & Nancy Chang. 2013. Embodied Construction Grammar. In Graeme Trousdale & Thomas Hoffmann (eds.), *The Handbook of Construction Grammar*, 168–190. Oxford: Oxford University Press.

Bergman, Brita. 1982. *Verbs and Adjectives: Some Morphological Processes in Swedish Sign Language*. Stockholm: Institutionen för lingvistik, Stockholms universitet.

Bergmann, Kirsten, V. Aksu & Stefan Kopp. 2011. The relation of speech and gestures: temporal synchrony follows semantic synchrony. *2nd Workshop on Gesture and Speech in Interaction– GESPIN*. Bielefeld, Germany.

Bergs, Alexander & Elisabeth Zima. 2018. Multimodality and Constructions. *Linguistics Vanguard*.

Best, Karl-Heinz. 2006. Wortlängen im Deutschen. *Göttinger Beiträge zur Sprachwissenschaft* 13. 23–49.

Bohle, Ulrike. 2007. *Das Wort ergreifen, das Wort übergeben: Explorative Studie zur Rolle redebegleitender Gesten in der Organisation des Sprecherwechsels*. Berlin: Weidler Verlag.

Botha, Rudolf P. 1988. *Form and Meaning in Word Formation: A study of Afrikaans Reduplication*. Cambridge: Cambridge University Press.

Boutet, Dominique, Aliyah Morgenstern & Alan Cienki. 2016. Grammatical Aspect and Gesture in French: A kinesiological approach. *Russian Journal of Linguistics* 20(3). 132-151.

Brandstetter, Renward. 1917. *Die Reduplikation in den indianischen, indonesischen und indogermanischen Sprachen*. Luzern: Kantonsschule.

Brentari, Diane. 1998. *A Prosodic Model of Sign Language Phonology*. Cambridge, Mass.: MIT Press.

Bressem, Jana. 2012. *Repetitions in Gesture: Structures, Functions, and Cognitive Aspects*. Frankfurt (Oder): European University Viadrina PhD Thesis.

Bressem, Jana. 2013. A linguistic perspective on the notation of form features in gestures. In Cornelia Müller, Alan Cienki, Ellen Fricke, Silva H. Ladewig, David McNeill & Sedinha Teßendorf (eds.), *Body – Language – Communication. An International Handbook on Multimodality in Human Interaction. (Handbooks of Linguistics and Communication Science 38.1.)*, 1079–1098. Berlin/Boston: De Gruyter Mouton.

Bressem, Jana. 2015. Repetition als Mittel der Musterbildung bei redebegleitenden Gesten. In Christa Dürscheid & Jan Georg Schneider (eds.), *Satz, Äußerung, Schema* (Handbücher Sprachwissen 4), 421–441. Berlin/Boston: de Gruyter.

Bressem, Jana. submitted. Conceputalizing plurality as bounded areas in space – Reduplication and diagrammatic iconicity as semiotic forces in multimodal language use. In Irene Mittelberg & Alexander Gerner (eds.), *Body Diagrams: On the Epistemic Kinetics of Gesture*. Amsterdam: John Benjamins.

Bressem, Jana & Silva H. Ladewig. 2011. Rethinking gesture phases: articulatory features of gestural movement? *Semiotica* 184(1–4). 53–91.

Bressem, Jana, Silva H. Ladewig & Cornelia Müller. 2013. Linguistic Annotation System for Gestures (LASG). In Cornelia Müller, Alan Cienki, Ellen Fricke, Silva H. Ladewig, David McNeill & Sedinha Teßendorf (eds.), *Body – Language – Communication. An International Handbook on Multimodality in Human Interaction. (Handbooks of Linguistics and Communication Science 38.1.)*, 1098–1125. Berlin/ Boston: De Gruyter Mouton.

Bressem, Jana & Cornelia Müller. 2014a. The family of Away gestures: Negation, refusal, and negative assessment. In Cornelia Müller, Alan Cienki, Ellen Fricke, Silva H. Ladewig, David McNeill & Jana Bressem (eds.), *Body – Language – Communication. An International Handbook on Multimodalityin Human Interaction (Handbooks of Linguistics and Communication Science 38.2.)*, 1592–1604. Berlin/Boston: De Gruyter Mouton.

Bressem, Jana & Cornelia Müller. 2014b. A repertoire of recurrent gestures of German. In Cornelia Müller, Alan Cienki, Ellen Fricke, Silva H. Ladewig, David McNeill & Jana Bressem (eds.), *Body – Language – Communication. An International Handbook on Multimodality in Human Interaction (Handbooks of Linguistics and Communication Science 38.2.)*, 1575–1591. Berlin/Boston: De Gruyter Mouton.

Bressem, Jana & Cornelia Müller. 2017. The "Negative–Assessment–Construction"–A multimodal pattern based on a recurrent gesture? *Linguistics Vanguard* 3(s1).

Bressem, Jana, Nicole Stein & Claudia Wegener. 2015. Structuring and highlighting speech – Discursive functions of holding away gestures in Savosavo. *GESPIN 4*. Nantes.

Brookes, Heather 2001. O clever 'He's streetwise' When gestures become quotable: When gestures become quotable. *Gesture* 1(2). 167–184.

Brookes, Heather. 2004. A repertoire of South African quotable gestures. *Journal of Linguistic Anthropology* 14(2). 186–224.

Brookes, Heather. 2005. What gestures do: Some communicative functions of quotable gestures in conversations among Black urban South Africans. *Journal of Pragmatics* 32. 2044-2085.

Brookes, Heather. 2015. The social nature of cognitive-semiotic processes in the semantic expansion of gestural forms. In: Gaelle Ferre & Mark Tutton (eds.) *Gesture and Speech in Interaction - 4th edition (GESPIN 4)*. Nantes, France.

Butterworth, Brian, Geoffrey Beattie, Campbell Robin N. & Smith Philip T. 1978. Gesture and silence as indicators of planning in speech. In Robin N. Campbell & Philip T. Smith (eds.), *Recent Advances in the Psychology of Language: Formal and Experimental Approaches*, 347–360. New York: Plenum Press.

Butterworth, Brian & Uri Hadar. 1989. Gesture, speech, and computational stages: A reply to McNeill. *Psychological Review* 96(1). 168–174.

Calbris, Geneviève. 1990. *The Semiotics of French Gestures*. Bloomington: Indiana University Press.

Calbris, Genevieve. 2003. From cutting an object to a clear-cut analysis. Gesture as the representation of a preconceptual schema linking concrete actions to abstract notions. *Gesture* 3(1). 19–46.

Calbris, Genevieve. 2011. *Elements of Meaning in Gesture*. Amsterdam: John Benjamins Publishing Company.
Chafe, Wallace L. 1987. Cognitive constraints on information flow. In Russel S. Tomlin (ed.), *Coherence and Grounding in Discourse*, 21–51. Amsterdam: John Benjamins.
Chafe, Wallace L. 1994. *Discourse, Consciousness, and Time: The Flow and Displacement of Conscious Experience in Speaking and Writing*. Chicago: University of Chicago Press.
Chafe, Wallace L. 1996. How consciousness shapes language. *Pragmatics & Cognition* 4. 35–54.
Channon, Rachel. 2002. *Signs are single segments: Phonological Representations and Temporal Sequencing in ASL and Other Sign Languages*. Maryland: University of Maryland.
Chang, Nancy. 2008. *Constructing Grammar: A Computational Model of the Emergence of Early Constructions*. Berkeley: University of California at Berkeley.
Cienki, Alan. 1997. Some properties and groupings of image schemas. *Lexical and Syntactical Constructions and the Construction of Meaning*. 3–15.
Cienki, Alan. 1998a. Straight: An image schema and its transformations. *Cognitive Linguistics* 9. 107–149.
Cienki, Alan. 1998b. Metaphoric gestures and some of their relations to verbal metaphorical expressions. In J.-P. König (ed.), *Discourse and Cognition: Bridging the Gap*, 189–204. Stanford, CA: Center for the Study of Language and Information.
Cienki, Alan. 2005. Image schemas and gesture. In Beate Hampe (ed.), *From Perception to Meaning: Image Schemas in Cognitive Linguistics*, 421–441. Berlin, New York: Mouton de Gruyter.
Cienki, Alan. 2012. Usage events of spoken language and the symbolic units (may) abstract from them. In Krzysztof Kosecki & Janusz Badio (eds.), *Cognitive Processes in Language*, 149–158. Frankfurt: Peter Lang.
Cienki, Alan. 2013. Gesture, space, grammar, and cognition. *Space in Language and Linguistics: Geographical, Interactional, and Cognitive Perspectives*. Berlin: Walter de Gruyter. 667–686.
Cienki, Alan. 2015a. Spoken language usage events. *Language and Cognition* 7(04). 499–514.
Cienki, Alan. 2015b. Repetitions in view of talk as variably multimodal. *Vestnik of Moscow State Linguistic University* 6(717). 625–634.
Cienki, Alan. 2017. Utterance Construction Grammar (UCxG) and the variable multimodality of constructions. *Linguistics Vanguard* 3(s1).
Cienki, Alan & Olga K. Iriskhanova (eds.). 2018. *Aspectuality across Languages: Event Construal in Speech and Gesture*. John Benjamins Publishing Company.
Cienki, Alan & Irene Mittelberg. 2013. Creativity in the forms and functions of spontaneous gestures with speech. *Creativity and the Agile Mind: A Multidisciplinary Study of a Multifaceted Phenomenon*, Berlin: De Gruyter. 231–252.
Cienki, Alan & Cornelia Müller (eds.). 2008. *Metaphor and Gesture* (Gesture Studies). Amsterdam: Benjamins.
Clark, H. Herbert. 1996. *Using Language*. Cambridge: Cambridge University Press.
Condon, William S. & William D. Ogston. 1967. A segmentation of behavior. *Journal of Psychiatrical Research* 5. 221–235.
Cooperrider, Kensy. 2017. Foreground gesture, background gesture. *Gesture* 16(2). 176–202.

Coulter, Geoffrey R. 1990. Emphatic stress in ASL. In Susan D. Fischer & Patricia Siple (eds.), *Theoretical Issues in Sign Language Research, Vol. 1: Linguistics*, 109-125. Chicago, IL: University of Chicago.

Crasborn, Onno. 2001. *Phonetic implementation of phonological categories in sign language of the Netherlands*. Utrecht: LOT.

Croft, William. 1990. A conceptual framework for grammatical categories (or, a taxonomy of propositional acts). *Journal of Semantics* 7. 245–279.

Croft, William. 2002. *Typology and Universals*. Cambridge University Press.

Croft, William. 2001. *Radical Construction Grammar: Syntactic Theory in Typological Perspective*. Oxford: Oxford University Press.

Croft, William & D. Alan Cruse. 2004. *Cognitive Linguistics*. Cambridge: Cambridge University Press.

De Beaugrande, Robert–Alain & Wolfgang Dressler. 1981. *Einführung in die Textlinguistik*. Tübingen: Niemeyer Tübingen.

de Ruiter, Jan Peter. 1998. *Gesture and Speech Production* Nijmegen: Katholieke Universiteit Nijmegen PhD Thesis.

de Ruiter, Jan Peter. 2000. The production of gesture and speech. In David McNeill (ed.), *Language and Gesture*, 284–311. Cambridge: Cambridge University Press.

Deppermann, Arnulf. 2006. Construction Grammar-Eine Grammatik für die Interaktion. *Grammatik und Interaktion*. 43–65.

Dressler, Wolfgang, Katarzyna Dziubalska–Kołaczyk, Natalia Gagarina & Marianne Kilani–Schoch. 2005. Reduplication in child language. In Bernhard Hurch (ed.), *Studies on Reduplication*, 454–474. Berlin u.a.: de Gruyter.

Duncan, Susan. 1996. Grammatical Form and 'Thinking-for-Speaking' in Mandarin Chinese and English: An Analysis *based on Speech-Accompanying Gestures*. Chicago, Illinois: University of Chicago PhD Thesis.

Duncan, Susan. 2005. Gesture in signing: A case study in Taiwan Sign Language. *Language and Linguistics* 6(2). 279–318.

Efron, David. 1972 [1941]. *Gesture, Race and Culture*. Paris/ The Hague: Mouton.

Eisenberg, Peter. 1999/2001. *Grundriß der deutschen Grammatik: Der Satz*. Weimar: Metzler.

Eisenstein, Jacob. 2008. *Gesture in Automatic Discourse Processing*. PhD Thesis.

Ekman, Paul & Wallace V. Friesen. 1969. The repertoire of nonverbal behavior: Categories, origins, usage and coding. *Semiotica* 1. 49–98.

Ekman, Paul & Wallace V. Friesen. 1972. Hand Movements. *The Journal of Communication* 22. 153–374

Ekman, Paul. 1972. Universals and Cultural Differences in Facial Expressions of Emotion. In James Cole (ed.), *Nebraska Symposium on Motivation, 1971 Vol. 19*, 207–283. Lincoln, NE: University of Nebraska Press.

Enfield, N.J. 2009. *The Anatomy of Meaning: Speech, Gesture, and Composite utterances*. Cambridge University Press.

Engberg–Pedersen, Elisabeth. 2011. Cognitive foundations of topic–comment and foreground–background structures: Evidence from sign languages, co-speech gesture and homesign. *Cognitive Linguistics* 22(4). 691–718.

Engle, Randi A. 2000. *Toward a Theory of Multimodal Communication: Combining Speech, Gestures, Diagrams, and Demonstrations in Instructional Explanations*. Stanford: Stanford University PhD Thesis.

Evans, Vyvyan, Benjamin K. Bergen & Jörg Zinken. 2007. *The Cognitive Linguistics Reader*. London; Oakville: Equinox.

Fillmore, Charles. 1982. Frame semantics. *Linguistics in the Morning Calm*. 111–137.

Fillmore, Charles J, Paul Kay & Mary Catherine O'Connor. 1988. Regularity and idiomaticity in grammatical constructions: The case of let alone. *Language*. 501–538.

Fischer, Susan D. 1973. Two processes of reduplication in the American Sign Language. *Foundations of language*. 469–480.

Frishberg, Nancy. 1975. Arbitrariness and iconicity: Historical change in American Sign Language. *Language* 51(3). 696–719.

Fornel, Michel de. 1992. The return gesture: Some remarks on context, inference, and iconic gesture. In Peter Auer & Aldo di Luzio (eds.), *The Contextualization of Language*, 159–176. Amsterdam / Philadelphia: John Benjamins.

Freedman, Norbert. 1977. Hands, words and mind: On the structuralization of body movements during discourse and the capacity for verbal representation. In Norbert Freedman & Stanley Grand (eds.) *Communicative Structures and Psychic Structures. The Downstate Series of Research in Psychiatry and Psychology*, vol 1. 109–132.Springer, Boston, MA.

Fricke, Ellen. 2007. *Origo, Geste und Raum: Lokaldeixis im Deutschen*. Berlin: Walter de Gruyter.

Fricke, Ellen. 2010. Phonaestheme, Kinaestheme und multimodale Grammatik: Wie Artikulationen zu Typen werden, die bedeuten können. *Sprache und Literatur* 41(1). 70–88.

Fricke, Ellen. 2012. *Grammatik multimodal: Wie Wörter und Gesten zusammenwirken*. Berlin: Mouton de Gruyter.

Fricke, Ellen. 2013. Towards a unified grammar of gesture and speech: A multimodal approach. In Cornelia Müller, Alan Cienki, Ellen Fricke, Silva H. Ladewig, David McNeill & Sedinha Teßendorf (eds.), *Body – Language – Communication. An International Handbook on Multimodality in Human Interaction. (Handbooks of Linguistics and Communication Science 38.1.)* 733–754. Berlin, Boston: De Gruyter Mouton.

Fricke, Ellen. 2014a. Kinesthemes: Morphological complexity in co-speech gestures. In Cornelia Müller, Alan Cienki, Ellen Fricke, Silva H. Ladewig, David McNeill & Jana Bressem (eds.), *Body – Language – Communication. An International Handbook on Multimodality in Human Interaction (Handbooks of Linguistics and Communication Science 38.2.)*, 1618–1629. Berlin/Boston: De Gruyter Mouton.

Fricke, Ellen. 2014b. Syntactic complexity in co-speech gestures: Constituency and recursion. In Cornelia Müller, Alan Cienki, Ellen Fricke, Silva H. Ladewig, David McNeill & Jana Bressem (eds.), *Body – Language – Communication. An International Handbook on Multimodality in Human Interaction (Handbooks of Linguistics and Communication Science 38.2.)*, 1650–1661. Berlin/Boston: De Gruyter Mouton.

Fricke, Ellen. 2014c. Between reference and meaning: Object-related and interpretant-related gestures in face-to-face interaction. In Cornelia Müller, Alan Cienki, Ellen Fricke, Silva H. Ladewig, David McNeill & Jana Bressem (eds.), *Body – Language – Communication. An International Handbook on Multimodality in Human Interaction (Handbooks of Linguistics and Communication Science 38.2.)*, 1788–1802. Berlin/Boston: De Gruyter Mouton.

Fricke, Ellen. 2014d. Towards a unified grammar of gesture and speech: A multimodal approach. In Cornelia Müller, Alan Cienki, Ellen Fricke, Silva H. Ladewig, David McNeill & Jana Bressem (eds.), *Body – Language – Communication. An International Handbook on Multimodality in Human Interaction (Handbooks of Linguistics and Communication Science 38.2.)*, 733–754. Berlin/Boston: De Gruyter Mouton.

Furuyama, Nobuhiro. 2002. Prolegomena of a theory of between-person coordination of speech and gesture. *International Journal Human-Computer Studies* 57. 347–374.
Gerwing, Jennifer & Meredith Allison. 2009. The relationship between verbal and gestural contributions in conversation: A comparison of three methods. *Gesture* 9. 312–336.
Gibbs, Raymond W. 2006. *Embodiment and Cognitive Science*. Cambridge: Cambridge University Press.
Gil, David. 2005. From repetition to reduplication in Riau Indonesian. In Bernhard Hurch (ed.), *Studies on Reduplication*, 31–63. Berlin u.a.: de Gruyter.
Goldberg, Adele E. 1995. *Constructions: A Construction Grammar Approach to Argument Structure*. Chicago: University of Chicago Press.
Goldberg, Adele E. 2006. *Constructions at Work: The Nature of Generalization in Language*. Oxford University Press on Demand.
Goldberg, Adele E. 2013. Constructionist approaches. In Thomas Hoffmann & Graeme Trousdale (eds.), *The Oxford Handbook of Construction Grammar*, 15–31. Oxford: Oxford University Press.
Goldin-Meadow, Susan. 2003. *Hearing Gesture: How Our Hands Help Us Think*. Cambridge: Belknap Press of Harvard University.
Goldin-Meadow, Susan, Howard Nusbaum, Spencer D. Kelly & Susan Wagner. 2001. Explaining math: Gesturing lightens the load. *Psychological Science* 12(6). 516–522.
Gonda, Jan. 1950. The functions of word duplication in Indonesian languages. *Lingua* 2. 170–197.
Goodwin, Charles. 2000. Action and embodiment within situated human interaction. *Journal of Pragmatics* 32. 1489–1522.
Gülich, Elisabeth. 1994. Formulierungsarbeit im Gespräch. In Světla Čmejrková, František Daneš & Eva Havlová (eds.), *Writing vs Speaking: Language, Text, Discourse, Communication. Proceedings of the Conference held at the Czech Language Institute of the Academy of Sciences of the Czech Republic, Prague, October 14–16,1992*, 77–95. Tübingen: Gunter Narr.
Gullberg, Marianne. 2011. Thinking, speaking and gesturing about motion in more than one language. In Aneta Pavlenko (ed.), *Thinking and Speaking in Two Languages*, 143–169. Bristol, Buffalo, Toronto: Multilingual Matters.
Gumperz, John J. 1982. *Discourse Strategies*. Cambridge: Cambridge University Press.
Gut, Ulrike, Karin Looks, Alexandra Thies & Dafydd Gibbon. 2002. Cogest: Conversational gesture transcription system version 1.0. *ModeLex Technical Report* 1.
Hadar, Uri & Robert Krauss. 1999. Iconic gestures: The grammatical categories of lexical affiliates. *Journal of Neurolinguistics* 12. 1–12.
Haiman, John. 1985. *Iconicity in Syntax: Proceedings of a Symposium on Iconicity in Syntax, Stanford, June 24–6, 1983*. Amsterdam; Philadelphia: J. Benjamins.
Harrison, Simon. 2009. *Grammar, Gesture, and Cognition: The Case of Negation in English*. Université Michel de Montaigne, Bourdeaux 3 PhD Thesis.
Harrison, Simon. 2010. Evidence for node and scope of negation in coverbal gesture. *Gesture* 10(1). 29–51.
Harrison, Simon. 2018. *The Impulse to Gesture – Where Language, Minds, and Bodies Intersect*. Cambridge: Cambridge University Press.
Haspelmath, Martin. 2002. *Understanding morphology*. New York: Oxford University Press.
Hassemer, Julius, Gina Joue, Klaus Willems & Irene Mittelberg. 2011. Dimensions and mechanisms of form constitution: Towards a formal description of gestures. *2nd Workshop on Gesture and Speech in Interaction- GESPIN*. Bielefeld.

Helbig, Gerhard & Joachim Buscha. 1998. *Übungsgrammatik Deutsch*. Verlag Enzyklopädie.
Hinnell, Jennifer. 2018. The multimodal marking of aspect: The case of five periphrastic auxiliary constructions in North American English. *Cognitive Linguistics* 29(4). 773–806.
Holler, Judith & Geoffrey Beattie. 2003. How iconic gestures and speech interact in the representation of meaning: Are both aspects really integral to the process? *Semiotica* 146(1–4). 81–116.
Holzrichter, Amanda S. & Richard P. Meier. 2000. Child-directed signing in American sign language. In Charlene Chamberlain, Jill P. Morford & Rachel I. Mayberry (eds.), *Language Acquisition by Eye*, 25–40. Mahwah, NJ: Lawrence Erlbaum.
Hurch, Bernhard. 2000. Zur Kategorie des Intensiv im Tarahumara. In Andreas Bittner, Dagmar Bittner & Klaus Michael Köpcke (eds.), *Angemessene Strukturen: Systemorganisation in Phonologie, Morphologie und Syntax*, 63–77. Hildesheim: Olms.
Hurch, Bernhard (ed.) 2005. *Studies on Reduplication* (Empirical Approaches to Language Typology 28). Berlin u.a.: Mouton de Gruyter.
Hurch, Bernhard & Veronika Mattes. 2005. Über die Entstehung von partieller Reduplikation. In Gertraud Fenk-Ozclon & Christian Winkler (eds.), *Sprache und Natürlichkeit–Gedenkband für Willi Mayerthaler*, 137–156. Tübingen: Narr.
Inkelas, Sharon & Cheryl Zoll. 2005. *Reduplication: Doubling in Morphology*. Cambridge: Cambridge University Press.
Jakobson, Roman. 1966. Quest for the essence of language. *Morphology, Critical Concepts in Linguistics* 2004.
Jantunen, Tommi & Ritva Takkinen. 2011. Syllable structure in sign language phonology. In Diane Brentari (ed.), *Sign Languages*. 312–331. Cambridge: Cambridge University Press.
Jewitt, Carey. 2014. *The Routledge Handbook of Multimodal Analysis*, 2. edn. London [u.a.]: Routledge.
Johnson, Robert E. & Scott K. Liddell. 2011. Toward a Phonetic Representation of Signs: Sequentiality and Contrast. *Sign Language Studies* 11(2). 241–274.
Joo, Jungseock, Francis F. Steen & Mark Turner. 2017. Red Hen Lab: Dataset and tools for multimodal human communication research. *KI–Künstliche Intelligenz* 31(4). 357–361.
Kappelhoff, Hermann & Cornelia Müller. 2011. Embodied meaning construction. Multimodal metaphor and expressive movement in speech, gesture, and in feature film. *Metaphor and Social World* 1. 121–153.
Karlsson, Fred. 2010. Syntactic recursion and iteration. In van der Harry Hulst (ed.), *Recursion and Human Language*, 43–67. Berlin/New York: Mouton de Gruyter.
Kendon, Adam. 1972. Some relationship between body motion and speech In Aaron Seigman & Benjamin Pope (eds.), *Studies in Dyadic Communication*, 177–216. Elmsford, New York: Pergamon Press.
Kendon, Adam. 1980. Gesticulation and speech: Two aspects of the process of utterance. In Key Mary Ritchie (ed.), *Nonverbal Communication and Language* 207–227. The Hague: Mouton.
Kendon, Adam. 1983. Gesture and speech: How they interact. In John M. Wiemann (ed.), *Nonverbal Interaction*, 13–46. Beverly Hills, California: Sage Publications.
Kendon, Adam. 1987. On gesture: Its complementary relationship with speech. In Aaron W. Siegman & Stanley Feldstein (eds.), *Nonverbal Behavior and Communication*, 65–97. Hillsdale: Lawrence Erlbaum Associates.
Kendon, Adam. 1992. Some recent work from Italy on quotable gestures (emblems). *Journal of Linguistic Anthropology* 2(1). 92–108.

Kendon, Adam. 1995. Gestures as illocutionary and discourse structure markers in Southern Italian conversation. *Journal of Pragmatics* 23. 247–279.
Kendon, Adam. 2003. Some uses of the head shake. *Gesture* 2. 142–183.
Kendon, Adam. 2004a. *Gesture: Visible Action as Utterance.* Cambridge: Cambridge University Press.
Kendon, Adam. 2004b. Contrasts in gesticulation. A Neapolitan and a British speaker compared. *The Semantics and Pragmatics of Everyday Gestures.* Berlin: Weidler.
Kendon, Adam. 2008. Some reflections on the relationship between 'gesture' and 'sign'. *Gesture* 8 (3). 348–366.
Kettebekov, Sanshzar. 2004. Exploiting prosodic structuring of coverbal gestures. *International Conference on Multimodal Interfaces.*
Kimmelman, Vadim. 2018. Reduplication and repetition in Russian Sign Language. In Rita Finkbeiner & Ulrike Freywald (eds.), *Exact Repetition in Grammar and Discourse*, 91–109. Berlin: De Gruyter.
Kinsella, Anna R. 2010. Was recursion the key step in the evolution of the human language faculty? In Harry van der Hulst (ed.), *Recursion and Human Language.* 177–192. De Gruyter Mouton.
Kipp, Michael. 2004. *Gesture Generation by Imitation: From Human Behavior to Computer Character Animation.* Boca Raton, Florida.: Dissertation.com.
Kita, Sotaro. 1990. *The Temporal Relationship between Gesture and Speech: A study of Japanese–English Bilinguals.* Chicago: University of Chicago.
Kita, Sotaro. 2000. How representational gestures help speaking. In D. McNeill (ed.), *Language and gesture*, 162–185. Cambridge: Cambridge University Press.
Kita, Sotaro. 2003. *Pointing: Where Language, Culture, and Cognition Meet.* Hillsdale: L. Erlbaum Associates.
Kita, Sotaro & Asli Özyürek. 2003. What does cross–linguistic variation in semantic coordination of speech and gesture reveal? Evidence for an interface representation of spatial thinking and speaking. *Journal of Memory and Language* 48. 16–32.
Kita, Sotaro, Asli Özyürek, Shanley Allen, A. Brown, R. Furman & T. Ishizuka. 2007. Relations between syntactic encoding and co–speech gestures: Implications for a model of speech and gesture production. *Language and cognitive processes* 22(8). 1212–1236.
Kita, Sotaro, Ingeborg van Gijn & Harry van der Hulst. 1998. Movement phases in signs and co–speech gestures and their transcription by human encoders. *Gesture, and Sign Language in Human–Computer Interaction. Proceedings of the International Gesture Workshop, Bielefeld, Germany, September 17–19.* 23–35.
Kita, Sotaro, Ingeborg van Gijn & Harry van der Hulst. 1998. Movement phases in signs and cospeech gestures and their transcription by human encoders. In Ipke Wachsmuth & Martin Fröhlich (eds.), *Gesture and Sign Language in Human–Computer Interaction*, 23–35. Berlin: Springer.
Kiyomi, Setsuko. 1995. A New Approach to Reduplication: A Semantic Study of Noun and Verb Reduplication in the Malayo–Polynesian Languages'. *Linguistics* 33. 1145–1167.
Klima, Edward S. & Ursula Beluggi. 1979. *The Signs of Language.* Cambridge: Harvard University Press.
Koffka, Kurt. 1962. *Principles of Gestalt Psychology.* London: Routledge & Kegan Paul.
Köhler, R., G. Altmann & R.G. Piotrovskiĭ. 2005. *Quantitative Linguistics.* Walter de Gruyter.
Köhler, Wolfgang. 1935. *Gestalt Psychology.* New York: Liverlight.

Kok, Kasper. 2016. The grammatical potential of co-speech gesture: A Functional Discourse Grammar perspective. *Functions of Language* 23(2). 149–178.

Kok, Kasper. 2016. *The Status of Gesture in Cognitive–Functional Models of Grammar*. Utrecht: LOT.

Kok, Kasper, Kirsten Bergmann, Alan Cienki & Stefan Kopp. 2016. Mapping out the multifunctionality of speakers' gestures. *Gesture* 15(1). 37–59.

Kok, Kasper I & Alan Cienki. 2016. Cognitive Grammar and gesture: Points of convergence, advances and challenges. *Cognitive Linguistics* (27(1)). 67–100.

Kolter, Astrid, Silva H. Ladewig, Michela Summa, Sabine Koch, Thomas Fuchs & Cornelia Müller. 2012. Body memory and emergence of metaphor in movement and speech. An interdisciplinary case study. In Sabine Koch, Thomas Fuchs & Cornelia Müller (eds.), *Body Memory, Metaphor, and Movement*, 202–226. Amsterdam & Philadelphia: John Benjamins.

Kopp, Stefan, Paul Tepper & Justine Cassell. 2004. Towards an integrated microplanning of language and iconic gesture for multimodal output. *ICMI 04 October 13–15*. Pennsylvania, USA: State College.

Kotschi, Thomas. 2001. Formulierungspraxis als Mittel der Gesprächsaufrechterhaltung. In Klaus Brinker (ed.), *Text–und Gesprächslinguistik: Ein internationales Handbuch zeitgenössischer Forschung*, 1340–1348. Berlin: Walter der Gruyter.

Kouwenberg, Silvia. 1994. *A Grammar of Berbice Dutch Creole*. Berlin: Walter de Gruyter.

Kouwenberg, Silvia. 2003. *Twice as Meaningful: Reduplication in Pidgins, Creoles and other Contact Languages*. London: Battlebridge Publications.

Krahmer, Emiel & Marc Swerts. 2007. Hearing and seeing beats: The influence of visual beats on the perception of prominence. *Journal of Memory and Language* 57 (3). 396–414.

Krauss, Robert M., Chen Yihusiu & Chawla Purnima. 1996. Nonverbal behavior and nonverbal communication: what do conversational hand gestures tell us? In M. Zanna (ed.), *Advances in Experimental Psychology*, 389–450. San Diego: Academic Press.

Ladd, D. Robert. 1996. *Intonational Phonology*. Cambridge: Cambridge University Press.

Ladewig, Silva H. 2010. Beschreiben, suchen und auffordern – Varianten einer rekurrenten Geste. *Sprache und Literatur* 41(1). 89–111.

Ladewig, Silva H. 2011. Putting the cyclic gesture on a cognitive basis. *CogniTextes* 6.

Ladewig, Silva H. 2012. *Syntactic and Semantic Integration of Gestures into Speech: Structural, Cognitive, and Conceptual Aspects*. Frankfurt (Oder): European University Viadrina PhD Thesis.

Ladewig, Silva H. 2014a. Recurrent gestures. In Cornelia Müller, Ellen Fricke, Alan Cienki, Silva H. Ladewig, David McNeill & Jana Bressem (eds.), *Body – Language – Communication. An International Handbook on Multimodality in Human Interaction (Handbooks of Linguistics and Communication Science 38.2.)*, 1558–1574. Berlin/ Boston: De Gruyter Mouton.

Ladewig, Silva H. 2014b. The cyclic gesture. In Cornelia Müller, Ellen Fricke, Alan Cienki, Silva H. Ladewig, David McNeill & Jana Bressem (eds.), *Body – Language – Communication. An International Handbook on Multimodality in Human Interaction (HSK 38.2)*, 1605–1618. Berlin, Boston: De Gruyter Mouton.

Ladewig, Silva H. 2014c. Creating multimodal utterances. The linear integration of gestures into speech. In Cornelia Müller, Ellen Fricke, Alan Cienki, Silva H. Ladewig, David McNeill & Jana Bressem (eds.), *Body – Language – Communication. An International Handbook on Multimodality in Human Interaction (Handbooks of Linguistics and Communication Science 38.2.)*, 1662–1677. Berlin/ Boston: De Gruyter Mouton.

Ladewig, Silva H. 2020. *Integrating Gestures – Cognitive Grammar Multimodal*. Berlin, Boston: De Gruyter Mouton.

Ladewig, Silva H. & Jana Bressem. 2013. New insights into the medium 'hand': Discovering recurrent structures in gestures. *Semiotica* 197. 203–231.
Lakoff, George. 1987. *Women, Fire, and Dangerous Things: What Categories Reveal about the Mind*. Chicago: University of Chicago Press.
Langacker, Ronald. 1987. *Foundations of Cognitive Grammar. Vol. 1: Theoretical Prerequisites*. Stanford: Standford University Press.
Langacker, Ronald. 1999. *Grammar and Conceptualization*. Mouton de Gruyter.
Langacker, Ronald. 2000. *Grammar and Conceptualization*. Berlin; New York: Mouton de Gruyter.
Langacker, Ronald. 2001. Dynamicity in grammar. *Axiomathes* 12. 7–33.
Langacker, Ronald. 2008. *Cognitive Grammar: A Basic Introduction*. Oxford: Oxford University Press, USA.
Langacker, Ronald W. 2009. Cognitive (Construction) Grammar. *Cognitive Linguistics* 20(1). 167–176.
Lanwer, Jens Philipp. 2017. Apposition: A multimodal construction? The multimodality of linguistic constructions in the light of usage-based theory. *Linguistics Vanguard* 3(s1).
Lapaire, Jean-Remí. 2006. Negation, reification and manipulation in a cognitive grammar of substance. In Stephanie Bonnefille & Sebastian Salbayre (eds.), *La Négation* (35), 333–349. Tours.
Lascarides, Alex & Matthew Stone. 2006. Formal semantics for iconic gesture. In David Schlangen & Raquel Fernandez (eds.), *brandial'06 Proceedings*, 64–71. Potsdam: Potsdam University Press.
Latoschik, Marc Erich. 2000. *Multimodale Interaktion in Virtueller Realität am Beispiel der virtuellen Konstruktion*. Bielefeld: Technische Universität Bielefeld PhD Thesis.
Lausberg, Hedda & Han Sloetjes. 2009. Coding gestural behavior with the NEUROGES-ELAN system. *Behavioral Research Methods* 41(3). 841–849.
Lempert, Michael. 2011. Barack Obama, being sharp: Indexical order in the pragmatics of precision-grip gesture. *Gesture* 11(3). 241–270.
Leroy, Marie & Aliyah Morgenstern. 2005. Reduplication before two years old. In Bernhard Hurch (ed.), *Studies on Reduplication*, 478–494. Berlin: Mouton de Gruyter.
Loehr, Dan 2004. *Gesture and Intonation*. Washington, D.C.: Georgetown University PhD Thesis.
Loehr, Daniel. 2007. Aspects of rhythm in gesture and speech. *Gesture* 7(2). 179–214.
Lücking, Andy. 2013. *Ikonische Gesten*. Berlin: De Gruyter.
Marantz, Alec. 1982. Re Reduplication. *Linguistic Inquiry* 13. 435–482.
Mattes, Veronika. 2014. *Types of Reduplication a Case Study of Bikol*. Berlin: Mouton de Gruyter.
Martell, Craig. 2005. *FORM: An Experiment in the Annotation of the Kinematics of Gesture*. Pennsylvania: University of Pennsylvania PhD Thesis.
Mayerthaler, Willi. 1980. Ikonismus in der Morphologie. *Zeitschrift für Semiotik* 2. 19–37.
McClave, Evelyn Z. 1991. *Intonation and Gesture*. Washington DC: Georgetown University PhD Thesis.
McClave, Evelyn Z. 1994. Gestural beats: The rhythm hypothesis. *Journal of psycholinguistic research* 23(1). 45-66.
McCullough, Karl Erik. 2005. *Using Gestures during Speaking: Self-generating Indexical Fields*. Chicago: Chicago University PhD Thesis.

McNeill, David. 1985. So you think gestures are nonverbal? *Psychological Review* 92(3). 350–371.

McNeill, David. 1992. *Hand and Mind. What Gestures Reveal About Thought*. Chicago: University of Chicago Press.

McNeill, David. 2000. Catchments and contexts: Non–modular factors in speech and gesture production. In David McNeill (ed.), *Language and gesture*, 312–328. Cambridge: Cambridge University Press.

McNeill, David. 2002. Gesture and Language Dialectic. *Acta Linguistica Hafniensia* 34(1). 7–37.

McNeill, David. 2005. *Gesture and Thought*. Chicago: University of Chicago Press.

McNeill, David. 2007. Gesture and thought. In A. Esposito, M. Bratanic, E. Keller & M. Marinaro (eds.), *Fundamentals of Verbal and Nonverbal Communication and the Biometric Issue*, 20–33. Amsterdam: IOS Press.

McNeill, David & Susan Duncan. 2000. Growth points in thinking-for speaking. In David McNeill (ed.), *Language and Gesture*, 141–161. Cambridge: Cambridge University Press.

McNeill, David, Francis Queck, Karl-Erik Mccullough, Susan Duncan, Nobuhiro Furuyama, Robert Bryll & Rashid Ansari. 2001. Catchments, prosody and discourse. *Gesture* 1. 9–33.

McNeill, David & Elena Tevy Levy. 1982. Conceptual representations in language activity and gesture. In J. Jarvella & Wolfgang Klein (eds.), *Speech, Place, and Action. Studies in Deixis and Related Topics*, 271–295. Chichester: John Wiley.

McNeill, David, Elena T. Levy & Susan D Duncan. 2015. Gesture in discourse. *The Handbook of Discourse Analysis, 2*. 262–289.

McNeill, David, Francis Queck, Karl-Erik Mccullough, Susan Duncan, Nobuhiro Furuyama, Robert Bryll, Xf Ma & Rashid Ansari. 2002. Dynamic imagery in speech and gesture. In D. Granström, D. House & I. Karlsson (eds.), *Multimodality in Language and Speech Systems*, 27–44. Dordrecht, The Netherlands: Kluwer Academic Publishers.

Meir, Irit. 2012. Morphology. In Roland Pfau, Markus Steinbach & Bencie Woll (eds.), *Sign Languages*, 77–112. Berlin/Boston: De Gruyter Mouton.

Mittelberg, Irene. 2006. *Metaphor and Metonymy in Language and Gesture: Discoursive Evidence for Multimodal Models of Grammar*. PhD Dissertation, Cornell University. Ann Arbor, MI: UMI.

Mittelberg, Irene. 2008. Peircean semiotics meets conceptual metaphor: Iconic modes in gestural representations of grammar. In Alan Cienki & Cornelia Müller (eds.), *Metaphor and Gesture*, 145–184. Amsterdam: Benjamins.

Mittelberg, Irene. 2010a. Interne und externe Metonymie: Jakobsonsche Kontiguitätsbeziehungen in redebegleitenden Gesten. *Sprache und Literatur* 41(105). 112–143.

Mittelberg, Irene. 2010b. Geometric and image–schematic patterns in gesture space. In Vyv Evans & Paul Chilton (eds.), *Language, Cognition, and Space: The State of the Art and New Directions*, 351–385. London: Equinox.

Mittelberg, Irene. 2013. The exbodied mind: Cognitive-semiotic principles as motivating forces in gesture. In Cornelia Müller, Alan Cienki, Ellen Fricke, Silva H. Ladewig, David McNeill & Sedinha Teßendorf (eds.), *Body–Language–Communication. An International Handbook on Multimodality in Human Interaction. (Handbooks of Linguistics and Communication Science 38.2.)*, 755–784. Berlin/Boston: De Gruyter Mouton.

Mittelberg, Irene. 2014. Gestures and iconicity. In Cornelia Müller, Alan Cienki, Ellen Fricke, Silva H. Ladewig, David McNeill & Jana Bressem (eds.), *Body – Language – Communication. An International Handbook on Multimodalityin Human Interaction*

(Handbooks of Linguistics and Communication Science 38.2.), 1712–1732. Berlin/Boston: De Gruyter Mouton.

Mittelberg, Irene. 2017. Multimodal existential constructions in German: Manual actions of giving as experiential substrate for grammatical and gestural patterns. *Linguistics Vanguard* 3(s1).

Mittelberg, Irene & Linda Waugh. 2009. Multimodal figures of thought: A cognitive-semiotic approach to metaphor and metonymy in co-speech gesture. In Charles Forceville & Eduardo Urios-Aparisi (eds.), *Multimodal Metaphor*, 329–356. Berlin/New York: Mouton de Gruyter.

Mittelberg, Irene & Alexander Gerner (eds.). in preparation. *Body Diagrams: On the Epistemic Kinetics of Gesture*. Amsterdam: John Benjamins.

Montredon, Jacques, Aderrahim Amrani, Marie Paule Benoit–Barnet, Emanuelle Chan You, Régine Llorca & Nancy Peuteuil. 2008. Catchment, growth point and spatial metaphor: Analysing Derrida's oral discourse on deconstruction. In Alan Cienki & Cornelia Müller (eds.), *Metaphor and Gesture*, 171–194. Amsterdam, New York: John Benjamins.

Moraycsik, Edith A. 1978. Reduplicative constructions. In Joseph Greenberg (ed.), *Universals of Human Language: Word Structure*, 297–334. Stanford: Stanford University Press.

Morris, Desmond. 1979. *Gestures, their origins and distribution*. Stein & Day Pub. Neumann, Ranghild. 2004. The conventionalization of the ring gesture in German discourse. In Cornelia Müller & Roland Posner (eds.), *The Semantics and Pragmatics of Everyday Gestures*, 217–223. Berlin: Weidler.

Morrel-Samuels, Palmer & Robert M. Krauss. 1992. Word familiarity predicts temporal asynchrony of hand gestures and speech. *Journal of Experimental Psychology: Learning, Memory, and Cognition* 18(3). 615–622.

Mosher, Joseph A. 1916. *The Essentials of Effective Gesture for Students of Public Speaking*. New York: The Macmillan Company.

Müller, Cornelia. 1998. Beredte Hände. Theorie und Sprachvergleich redebegleitender Gesten. In Thomas Noll & Caroline Schmauser (eds.), *Körperbewegungen und ihre Bedeutung*, 21–44. Berlin: Arno Spitz.

Müller, Cornelia. 2000. Zeit als Raum. Eine kognitiv–semantische Mikroanalyse des sprachlichen und gestischen Ausdrucks von Aktionsarten. In W. B. Hess-Lüttich Ernest & H. Walter Schmitz (eds.), *Botschaften verstehen. Kommunikationstheorie und Zeichenpraxis. Festschrift für Helmut Richter*, 211–228. Frankfurt a.M.: Peter Lang.

Müller, Cornelia. 2004. Forms and uses of the Palm Up Open Hand. A case of a gesture family? In Cornelia Müller & Roland Posner (eds.), *Semantics and Pragmatics of Everyday Gestures*, 233–256. Berlin: Weidler Verlag.

Müller, Cornelia. 2007. A dynamic view on metaphor, gesture and thought. In Susan Duncan, Justine Cassell & Elena T. Levy (eds.), *Gesture and the Dynamic Dimension of Language. Essays in Honor of David McNeill*, 109–116. Amsterdam/Philadelphia: John Benjamins.

Müller, Cornelia. 2008. *Metaphors. Dead and Alive, Sleeping and Waking. A Dynamic View*. Chicago: University of Chicago Press.

Müller, Cornelia. 2009. Gesture and Language. In Kirsten Malmkjaer (ed.), *Routledge's Linguistics Encyclopedia*, 214–217. Abington/New York: Routledge.

Müller, Cornelia. 2010a. Mimesis und Gestik. In Gertrud Koch, Martin Vöhler & Christiane Voss (eds.), *Die Mimesis und ihre Künste*, 149–187. Paderborn, München: Fink.

Müller, Cornelia. 2010b. Wie Gesten bedeuten. Eine kognitiv–linguistische und sequenzanalytische Perspektive. *Sprache und Literatur* 41(1). 37–68.

Müller, Cornelia. 2013. Gestures as a medium of expression: The linguistic potential of gestures. In Cornelia Müller, Alan Cienki, Ellen Fricke, Silva H. Ladewig, David McNeill & Sedinha Teßendorf (eds.), *Body – Language – Communication. An International Handbook on Multimodality in Human Interaction. (Handbooks of Linguistics and Communication Science 38.1.)*, 202–217. Berlin, Boston: De Gruyter Mouton.

Müller, Cornelia. 2014. Gestures as "deliberate expressive movement". In Mandana Seyfeddinipur & Marianne Gullberg (eds.), *From Gesture in Conversation to Visible Action as Utterance*, 127–152. Amsterdam: John Benjamins.

Müller, Cornelia. 2017. How recurrent gestures mean: Conventionalized contexts-of-use and embodied motivation. *Gesture* 16(2). 276–303.

Müller, Cornelia, Jana Bressem & Silva H. Ladewig. 2013. Towards a grammar of gesture: A form-based view. In Cornelia Müller, Alan Cienki, Ellen Fricke, Silva H. Ladewig, David McNeill & Sedinha Teßendorf (eds.), *Body – Language – Communication. An International Handbook on Multimodality in Human Interaction. (Handbooks of Linguistics and Communication Science 38.1.)*, 707–733. Berlin/ Boston: De Gruyter Mouton.

Müller, Cornelia, Jana Bressem & Silva H. Ladewig. in preparation. *Gesture and language*. Routledge: Taylor & Francis Group.

Müller, Cornelia, Alan Cienki, Ellen Fricke, Silva H. Ladewig, D. McNeill & Sedinha Teßendorf (eds.). 2013. *Body – Language – Communication. An International Handbook on Multimodality in Human Interaction (Handbooks of Linguistics and Communication Science 38.1.)*. Berlin, Boston: De Gruyter Mouton.

Müller, Cornelia, Silva H. Ladewig & Jana Bressem. 2013. Gesture and speech from a linguistic point of view. In Cornelia Müller, Alan Cienki, Ellen Fricke, Silva H. Ladewig, David McNeill & Sedinha Teßendorf (eds.), *Body – Language – Communication. An International Handbook on Multimodality in Human Interaction. (Handbooks of Linguistics and Communication Science 38.1.)*, 55–81. Berlin, Boston: De Gruyter Mouton.

Müller, Cornelia & Gerald Speckmann. 2002. Gestos con una valoración negativa en la conversación cubana. *DeSignis* 3. 91–103.

Müller, Cornelia & Susanne Tag. 2010. The dynamics of metaphor: Foregrounding and activating metaphoricity in conversational interaction. *Cognitive Semiotics* 6. 85–120.

Muntigl, Peter. 2004. Modelling multiple semiotic systems: The case of gesture and speech. In Eija Ventola, Cassily Charles & Martin Kaltenbacher (eds.), *Perspectives on Multimodality*, 31–50. Amsterdam: John Benjamins Publishing Co.

Neumann, Ranghild. 2004. The conventionalization of the ring gesture in German discourse. In Cornelia Müller & Roland Posner (eds.), *The Semantics and Pragmatics of Everyday Gestures*, 217-223. Berlin: Weidler.

Nguyen, Thu & John Ingram. 2006. Reduplication and Word Stress in Vietnamese. In Paul Warren & Catherine I. Watson (eds.), *11th Australian International Conference on Speech Science & Technology*, 187–192. Canberra: Australian Speech Science & Technology Association Inc.

Nguyen, Phu-Phang. 1997. Reduplication and Affixation in Vietnamese. *Actes du 16é Congrés International des Linguistes*.

Niepokuj, Mary. 1997. *The Development of Verbal Reduplication in Indo-European*. Washington: Institute for the Study of Man.

Ningelgen, Jana & Peter Auer. 2017. Is there a multimodal construction based on non-deictic so in German? *Linguistics Vanguard* 3(s1).

Nöth, Winfried. 2008. Semiotic foundations of natural linguistics and diagrammatic iconicity. *Naturalness and Iconicity in Language*. John Benjamins, Amsterdam, Philadelphia. 73–100.
Oakley, Todd. 2004. Elements of attention: a new approach to meaning construction in the human sciences. http://www.mind-consciousnesslanguage.com.
Oakley, Todd. 2009. *From Attention to Meaning: Explorations in Semiotics, Linguistics, and Rhetoric*. New York: Peter Lang.
Park-Doob, Mischa Alan. 2010. *Gesturing Through Time: Holds and Intermodal Timing in the Stream of Speech*. Berkeley: University of Berkeley PhD Thesis.
Parrill, Fey. 2007. Metagesture: An Analysis of Theoretical Discourse about Multimodal Language. In Susan D. Duncan, Justine Cassell & Elena T. Levy (eds.), *Gesture and the Dynamic Dimension of Language*, 82–89. Amsterdam/Philadelphia: John Benjamins.
Parrill, Fey. 2008. Subjects in the hands of speakers: An experimental study of syntactic subject and speech-gesture integration. *Cognitive Linguistics* 19(2). 283–299.
Payrató, Luis. 1993. A pragmatic view on autonomous gestures: A first repertoire of Catalan emblems. *Journal of Pragmatics* 20. 193–216.
Payrató, Luis. 2014. Emblems or quotable gestures: Structures, categories, and functions. In Cornelia Müller, Alan Cienki, Ellen Fricke, Silva H. Ladewig, David McNeill & Jana Bressem (eds.), *Body – Language – Communication / Körper – Sprache – Kommunikation. Handbücher zur Sprach- und Kom munikationswissenschaft / Handbooks of Linguistics and Communication Science*. Berlin/Boston: Mouton de Gruyter.
Peirce, Charles S. 1960. *Collected Papers of Charles Sanders Peirce (1931–1958). Vol. I.: Principles of Philosophy, Vol. II: Elements of Logic*. Cambridge: The Belknap Press of Harvard University Press.
Pfau, Roland & Markus Steinbach. 2005. Backward and sideward reduplication in German Sign Language. In Bernhard Hurch (ed.), *Studies on Reduplication*, 568–593. Berlin u.a.: de Gruyter.
Pfau, Roland & Markus Steinbach. 2006. Pluralization in sign and in speech: A cross-modal typological study. *Linguistic Typology* 10(2). 135–182.
Pike, Kenneth 1971. *Language in Relation to a Unified Theory of the Structure of Human Behavior*, 2nd edn. Den Haag: Mouton.
Posner, Roland. 1980. Ikonismus in den natürlichen Sprachen. *Zeitschrift für Semiotik* 2. 1–6.
Pott, Friedrich. 1862. *Dopplung (Reduplikation, Gemination) als eines der wichtigsten Bildungsmitel der Sprache beleuchtet aus Sprachen aller Weltteile*. Lemgo/Detmold: Verlage der Meher'schen Hofbuchhandlung.
Prieto, Pilar, Alice Cravotta, Olga Kushch, Patrick Rohrer & Ingrid Vilà-Giménez. 2018. Deconstructing beat gestures: a labelling proposal. *Proceedings from the 9th International Conference on Speech Prosody*.
Pusch, Claus D. 2001. Ikonizität. In Martin Haspelmath, Ekkehard König & Wulf Österreicher (eds.), *Language Typology and Language Universals /Sprachtypologie und sprachliche Universalien /La Typologie des Langues et les Universaux Linguistiques. An International Handbook /Ein internationales Handbuch /Manuel International*, 369–384. Berlin, New York: De Gruyter.
Queck, Francis, David McNeill, Robert Bryll, Susan Duncan, Xin-Feng Ma, Cemil Kirbas, Karl E. McCullough & Rashid Ansair. 2002. Multimodal Human Discourse: Gesture and Speech. *ACM Transactions on Computer–Human Interaction* 9(3). 171–193.

Renwick, Margaret, Hufnagel Shattuck, Stefanie & Yelena Yasinnik. 2004. The timing of speech-accompanying gestures with respect to prosody. *Journal of Acoustical Society of America* 115. 2397.

Rubino, Carl. 2005. Reduplication: Form, function and distribution. In Bernhard Hurch (ed.), *Studies on Reduplication*, 11–29. Berlin u.a.: de Gryuter.

Ruth-Hirrel, Laura & Sherman Wilcox. 2018. Speech-gesture constructions in cognitive grammar: The case of beats and points. *Cognitive Linguistics* 29(3). 453–493.

Sager, Svend F. 2001. Probleme der Transkription nonverbalen Verhaltens. In Klaus et al. Brinker (ed.), *Text und Gesprächslinguistik. Ein internationales Handbuch zeitgenössischer Forschung. HSK 16.2*, 1069–1085. Berlin/New York: de Gruyter.

Sager, Svend F. & Kristin Bührig. 2005. Nonverbale Kommunikation im Gespräch – Editorial. In Kristin Bührig & Sven F. Sager (eds.), *Osnabrücker Beiträge zur Sprachtheorie 70: Nonverbale Kommunikation im Gespräch*, 5–17.

Sato, Manami, Amy J. Schafer & Benjamin K. Bergen. 2013. One word at a time: mental representations of object shape change incrementally during sentence processing. *Language and Cognition* 5(4). 345–373.

Sapir, Edward. 1921. *An Introduction to the Study of Speech*. New York: Harcourt, Brace.

Saussure, Ferdinand de. 1966. *Course in General Linguistics*. First published [1916] edn. New York/Toronto: McGraw-Hill.

Schegloff, Emanuel A. 1984. On some gestures' relation to talk. In Maxwell J. Atkinson & John Heritage (eds.), *Structures of Social Action*, 266–296. Cambridge: Cambridge University Press.

Scherer, Klaus R. 1979. Die Funktionen des nonverbalen Verhaltens im Gespräch. In K. R. Scherer & H. G. Wallbott (eds.), *Nonverbale Kommunikation: Forschungsberichte zum Interaktionsverhalten*, 25–32. Weinheim: Beltz.

Schindler, Wolfgang. 1991. Reduplizierende Wortbildung im Deutschen. *Zeitschrift für Phonetik, Sprachwissenschaft und Kommunikationsforschung* 44. 597–613.

Schneider, Jan Georg. 2015. Syntaktische Schemabildung – zeichentheoretisch betrachtet. In Christa Dürscheid & Jan Georg Schneider (eds.), *Satz – Äußerung – Schema* (Reihe Sprachwissen, Band 1), 167–194. Berlin/Boston: de Gruyter.

Schoonjans, Steven. 2014. *Modalpartikeln als multimodale Konstruktionen. Eine korpusbasierte Kookkurrenzanalyse von Modalpartikeln und Gestik im Deutschen*. Berlin/Boston: de Gruyter.

Schoonjans, Steven. 2017. Multimodal Construction Grammar issues are Construction Grammar issues. *Linguistics Vanguard* 3(s1).

Schoonjans, Steven, Geert Brône & Kurt Feyaerts. 2015. Multimodalität in der Konstruktionsgrammatik: Eine kritische Betrachtung illustriert anhand einer Gestikanalyse der Partikel ‚einfach'. In Jörg Bücker, Susanne Günthner & Wolfgang Imo (eds.), *Konstruktionsgrammatik V – Konstruktionen im Spannungsfeld von sequenziellen Mustern, kommunikativen Gattungen und Textsorten*, 291–308. Tübingen: Stauffenburg Verlag.

Schwaiger, Thomas. 2011. 'Zur Struktur von Reduplikanten: Vereinfachung in der Reduplikation'. *Wiener Linguistische Gazette* 75. 126–140.

Scullen, Mary Ellen. 2002. New insights into French reduplication. *Amsterdam Studies in the Theory and History of Linguistic Science Series* 4. 177–190.

Selting, Margret, Peter Auer, Dagmar Barth-Weingarten, Jörg Bergmann, Pia Bergmann, Karin Birkner, Elizabeth Couper-Kuhlen, Arnulf Deppermann, Peter Gilles, Susanne Günther, Martin Hartung, Friederike Kern, Christine Mertzlufft, Christian Meyer, Miriam Morek,

Frank Oberzaucher, Jörg Peter, Uta M. Quasthoff, Wilfried Schütte, Anja Stukenbrock & Susanne Uhmann. 2009. Gesprächsanalytisches Transkriptionssystem 2 (GAT 2). *Gesprächsforschung–Online Zeitschrift zur verbalen Interaktion* 10. 353–402.

Seyfeddinipur, Mandana. 2006. *Disfluency: Interrupting Speech and Gesture*. Nijmegen: U. Nijmegen PhD Thesis.

Shattuck-Hufnagel, Stefanie & Ada Ren. 2018. The prosodic characteristics of non-referential co-speech gestures in a sample of academic-lecture-style speech. *Frontiers in Psychology* 9.

Slama-Cazacu, Tatiana 1976. Nonverbal components in message sequence: "Mixed syntax". In W. C. McCormack & S. A. Wurm (eds.), *Language and Man: Anthropological Issues*, 217–227. The Hague: Mouton.

Sowa, Timo. 2005. *Understanding Coverbal Iconic Gestures in Object Shape Descriptions*. Berlin: Akademische Verlagsgesellschaft Aka GmbH Phd Thesis.

Sparhawk, Carol. 1978. Contrastive-Identificational Features of Persian Gesture. *Semiotica* 24(1/2). 49–86.

Steen, Francis & Mark B. Turner. 2013. Multimodal Construction Grammar. In Michael Borkent, Barbara Dancygier & Jennifer Hinnell (eds.), *Language and the Creative Mind*, 1–19. Stanford, CA: CSLI Publications.

Stefanowitsch, Anatol. 2007. Wortwiederholungen im Englischen und Deutschen: eine korpuslinguistische Annährerung. In Andreas Ammann & Aina Urdze (eds.), *Wiederholung, Parallelismus, Reduplikation: Strategien der multiplen Strukturanwendung*, 29–45. Bochum: Brockmeyer Verlag.

Stetter, Christian. 2005. *System und Performanz symboltheoretische Grundlagen von Medientheorie und Sprachwissenschaft*, 1. Aufl. edn. Weilerswist: Velbrück Wiss.

Stjernfelt, Frederik. 2007. *Diagrammatology: An Investigation on the Borderlines of Phenomenology, Ontology, and Semiotics*. Springer Science & Business Media.

Stokoe, William. 1960. *Sign Language Structure*. Buffalo, NY: Buffalo Univ. Press.

Stokoe, W.C. 1991/2001. Semantic phonology. *Sign Language Studies* 71. 107–114.

Stolz, Thomas. 2007a. Das ist doch keine Reduplikation! Über falsche Freunde bei der Suche nach richtigen Beispielen. In Andreas Ammann & Aina Urdze (eds.), *Wiederholung, Parallelismus, Reduplikation: Strategien der multiplen Strukturanwendung*, 47–81. Bochum: Brockmeyer.

Stolz, Thomas. 2007b. Re: duplication: Iconic vs counter-iconic principles (and their correlates). In Paolo Ramat & Elisa Roma (eds.), *Europe and the Mediterranean as Linguistic Areas*, 317–350. Amsterdam: Benjamins.

Stolz, Thomas. 2008. Grammatikalisierung ex nihilo. Totale Reduplikation – ein potentielles Universale und sein Verhältnis zur Grammatikalisierung. In Thomas Stolz (ed.), *Grammatikalisierung und grammatische Kategorie*, 83–109. Bochum: Brockmeyer.

Stolz, Thomas, Cornelia Stroh & Aina Urdze. 2011. *Total Reduplication: The Areal Linguistics of a Potential Universal*. Walter de Gruyter.

Streeck, Jürgen. 1988. The significance of Gesture: How it is established. *IPrA Papers in Pragmatics* 2(1/2). 60–83.

Streeck, Jürgen. 1990 Gesture as communication I: Its coordination with gaze and speech London Routledge.

Streeck, Jürgen. 2002. Grammars, words, and embodied meanings: On the uses and evolution of so and like. *The Journal of Communication* 52(3). 581–596.

Streeck, Jürgen. 2005. Pragmatic aspects of gesture. In Jacob Mey (ed.), *International Encyclopedia of Languages and Linguistics*, 275-299. Oxford: Elsevier.

Streeck, Jürgen. 2006. Gestures: Pragmatic aspects. In Keith Brown (ed.), *Encyclopedia of Language & Linguistics*, 71–76. Oxford: Elsevier.
Streeck, Jürgen. 2008. Depicting by gesture. *Gesture* 8 (3). 285–301.
Streeck, Jürgen. 2009. *Gesturecraft. The Manu-facture of Meaning*. Amsterdam: John Benjamins.
Streeck, Jürgen. 2016. Gestische Praxis und sprachliche Form. In Arnulf Deppermann, Helmuth Feilke & Angelika Linke (eds.), *Sprachliche und kommunikative Praktiken*, 57–79. Berlin: De Gruyter Mouton.
Streeck, Jürgen & Ulrike Hartge. 1992. Previews: Gestures at the transition place. In Peter Auer & Aldo di Luzio (eds.), *The contextualization of language*, 138–158. Amsterdam: John Benjamins.
Stukenbrock, Anja. 2015. *Deixis in der face-to-face-Interaktion*. Walter de Gruyter GmbH & Co KG.
Supalla, Ted & Elissa Newport. 1978. How many seats in a chair? The derivation of nouns and verbs in American Sign Language. In Patricia Siple (ed.), *Understanding Language through Sign Language Research*, 91–132. New York: Academic Press.
Sutton-Spence, Rachel & Bencie Woll. 1998. *The Linguistics of British Sign Language*. Cambridge: Cambridge University Press.
Sweetser, Eve. 1998. *Regular Metaphoricity in Gesture: Bodily-Based Models of Speech Interaction*. Elsevier.
Talmy, Leonard. 1983. How language structures space. In Herbert L. Pick & Linda P. Acredolo (eds.), *Spatial Orientation: Theory, Research, and Application*, 225–282. New York: Plenum Press.
Talmy, Leonard. 2000. *Toward a Cognitive Semantics*. Cambridge, Mass.: MIT Press.
Talmy, Leonard. 2007. Attention phenomena. In Dirk Geeraerts & Hubert Cuyckens (eds.), *Handbook of Cognitive Linguistics*, 264–293. New York/Oxford: Oxford University Press.
Tannen, Deborah. 2007. *Talking Voices: Repetition, Dialogue, and Imagery in Conversational Discourse*. Cambridge University Press.
Ternes, Elmar. 1999. *Einführung in die Phonologie*. Darmstadt: Wiss. Buchges.
Teßendorf, Sedinha. 2014. Pragmatic and metaphoric gestures– combining functional with cognitive approaches in the analysis of the "brushing aside gesture". In Cornelia Müller, Alan Cienki, Ellen Fricke, Silva H. Ladewig, David McNeill & Jana Bressem (eds.), *Body – Language – Communication. An International Handbook on Multimodality in Human Interaction (Handbook of Linguistics and Communication Science 38.2.)*, 1540–1558. Berlin/ Boston: De Gruyter Mouton.
Teßendorf, Sedinha. 2016. Actions as sources for gestures. In Konstanze Jungbluth & Marta Fernández-Villanueva (eds.), *Beyond Language Boundaries Multimodal Use in Multilingual Contexts*. 34–54. Berlin/ Boston: de Gruyter/Mouton.
Tomlin, Russel S. 1997. Mapping conceptual representations into linguistic representations: The role of attention in grammar. In J. Nuyts & E. Pederson (eds.), *Language and Conceptualization*, 162–189. Cambridge: Cambridge University Press.
Trubetzkoy, Nikolaj S. 1939. *Grundzüge der Phonologie*. Göttingen: Vandenhoeck & Ruprecht.
Tuite, Kevin 1993 The production of gesture. *Semiotica* 93 (1–2). 83–105
Tutton, Mark. 2015. *Locative Expressions in English and French: A Multimodal Approach*. Berlin New York: de Gruyter.
Uspensky, Boris A. 1972. Subsystems in language, their interrelations and their correlated universals. *Linguistics* 10(88). 53–71.

Välimaa-Blum, Riitta. 2005. *Cognitive Phonology in Construction Grammar: Analytic Tools for Students of English*. Berlin, New York: Mouton de Gruyter.

Vater, H. 2001. *Einführung in die Textlinguistik: Struktur und Verstehen von Texten*. München: Fink.

Webb, Rebecca. 1996. Linguistic features of metaphoric gestures. In Lynn Messing (ed.), *Proceedings of WIGLS. The Workshop on the Integration of Gesture in Language and Speech. October 7–8, 1996*, 79–95. Delaware: Applied Science and Engineering Laboratories Newark.

Wehling, Elisabeth. 2018. Discourse management gestures. *Gesture* 16(2). 245–276.

Wertheimer, Max. 1925. *Über Gestalttheorie*. Erlangen: Philosophische Akademie.

Wiese, Richard. 1990. Über die Interaktion von Morphologie und Phonologie – Reduplikation im Deutschen. *Zeitschrift für Phonetik, Sprachwissenschaft und Kommunikationsforschung* 43. 603–624.

Wilbur, Ronnie B. 1973. *The Phonology of Reduplication*. Urbana–Champaign: University of Illinois at Urbana–Champaign.

Wilbur, Ronnie B. 2005. A reanalysis of reduplication in American Sign Language. In Bernhard Hurch (ed.), *Studies on Reduplication*, 594–623. Berlin u.a.: de Gruyter.

Wilbur, Ronnie B. & Susan Bobbitt Nolen. 1986. The duration of syllables in American Sign Language. *Language and Speech* 29(3). 263–280.

Wilcox, Sherman. 2007. Routes from gesture to language. In Elena Pizzuto, Paola Pientrandrea & Raffaele Simone (eds.), *Verbal and Signed Languages: Comparing Structures, Constructs and Methodologies*, 107–131. Berlin, New York: Walter de Gruyter.

Wilcox, Sherman, Paolo Rossini & Elena Pizuto Antinoro. 2010. Grammaticalization in sign languages. In Diane Brentari (ed.), *Sign Languages*, 332–355. Cambridge: Cambridge University Press.

Wilcox, Sherman & André Nogueira Xavier. 2013. A framework for unifying spoken language, signed language, and gesture. *Todas as Letras–Revista de Língua e Literatura* 15(1). 88–110.

Wittenburg, Peter, Hennie Brugman, A. Russal, A. Klassmann & Han Sloetjes. 2006. ELAN: A professional framework for multimodality research. *Proceedings of LREC 2006, Fifth International Conference on Language Resources and Evaluation*.

Wrobel, Ulrike. 2007. *Raum als kommunikative Ressource. Eine handlungstheoretische Analyse visueller Sprachen*. Frankfurt/ Main: Peter Lang

Wu, Suwei. 2018. *Multimodality of Constructions in Construction Grammars: Transitivity, Transitivity Alternations, and the Dative Alternation*. Vrije Universiteit Amsterdam.

Wundt, Wilhlem 1921. *Völkerpyschologie: Eine Untersuchung der Entwicklungsgesetze von Sprache, Mythus und Sitte. Erster Band. Die Sprache*.

Yasui, Eiko. 2013. Collaborative idea construction: Repetition of gestures and talk in joint brainstorming. *Journal of Pragmatics* 46(1). 157–172.

Ziem, Alexander. 2017. Do we really need a Multimodal Construction Grammar? *Linguistics Vanguard* 3(s1).

Ziem, Alexander & Alexander Lasch. 2013. *Konstruktionsgrammatik: Konzepte und Grundlagen gebrauchsbasierter Ansätze*. Berlin: Walter de Gruyter.

Zima, Elisabeth. 2014. Gibt es multimodale Konstruktionen? Eine Studie zu [V (motion) in circles] und [all the way from X PREP Y]. *Gesprächsforschung – Online Zeitschrift zur verbalen Interaktion* 15. 1–48.

Zima, Elisabeth. 2017. On the multimodality of [all the way from X PREP Y]. *Linguistics Vanguard* 3(s1).

Zima, Elisabeth & Alexander Bergs. 2017. Multimodality and construction grammar. *Linguistics Vanguard* 3(s1).

Zlatev, Jordan. 2005. What's in a schema? Bodily mimesis and the grounding of language. In Beate Hampe (ed.), *From Perception to Meaning: Image Schemas in Cognitive Linguistics*, 313. Berlin, New York: Mouton de Gruyter.

Index

Aktionsarten 7, 78–79, 107, 111–112, 123, 169, 178, 192
aspect 1, 8, 26–27, 30, 43–44, 139, 181–182

Cognitive Grammar 10, 120, 149
complex unit 18, 21, 38, 45–46, 54, 56, 82, 84, 86
complexity 2, 6–7, 9, 38, 41, 45, 60
conceptualization 3, 5, 11, 78–79, 82, 86, 89, 108, 110, 115, 121, 146, 154, 158, 165, 167–170, 173, 177, 190, 192, 194, 197
construal 10, 75, 82, 86, 120, 139, 177
construction 2, 10, 29, 47, 56, 63, 82, 84, 113, 134–135, 138–144, 146, 148, 150, 176–180, 189–191
– gestural construction 54
– verbo-kinesic construction 137, 143–144, 146–148
– multimodal construction 114, 136, 140, 146
Construction Grammar 3, 10, 20, 133–135, 141, 194
conventionalization 70, 142, 146–148, 152, 179

depiction 40–41, 50–51, 53–54, 56, 68, 75, 77–80, 86, 91–92, 94, 105, 124–125, 129–130, 138, 144, 168, 178, 184

embodiment 146
entrenchment 9–10, 46, 120, 134, 139–142, 144, 146, 148, 152, 179

Figure-Ground 2, 20, 46, 153–154, 157–158, 166, 171–172, 174, 180, 182, 186–187
focus of attention 2, 24, 31, 46, 110, 156, 158–159, 163–164, 166, 169–171
– activation cost 166, 170
– scale of attention 169–170
– scope of attention 167–170
foregrounding 112, 156–158, 164, 171, 173–174, 178

– foregrounding technique 158, 160–161, 165, 170, 186

Gestalt 7, 14, 21, 36, 38, 65, 69, 73, 82, 85–86, 112, 172, 177, 182, 185–188, 195
– Gestalt principles 112, 185–188, 195
gestural adverb 20, 132–133, 150–151
gestural attribute 9, 20, 45, 53, 107, 116–117
gestural modes of representation 6, 15, 17–18, 50, 70, 73–74, 78, 83, 85–86, 125, 149, 177
grammar of gesture 18, 195
grammaticalization 2, 6, 31, 182, 191

iconicity 27, 158, 161, 189–190
– diagrammatic iconicity 11, 21, 60, 181–182, 190–192, 195
integration 8–9, 20, 60, 99, 116–118, 121, 127–128, 148, 151–152, 171, 179, 194, 196
– cataphoric integration 127, 129, 149
– positional integration 129, 151
– semantic integration 20, 60, 88, 93, 99, 112, 114, 121, 151, 153, 178–179
– temporal integration 151, 179
intensification 23, 27, 30–31, 42–44, 83, 135, 181, 191–192
iteration 2, 44, 128, 192
– iteration in gestures 19–20, 39, 45–46, 49–54, 60–65, 67, 73–78, 80, 83–88, 93–95, 98–99, 104–108, 110–112, 122–133, 149–153, 158–165, 167–170, 172–174, 176–181, 183, 185, 187, 189, 191, 193–195
– iteration in speech 22–23
– iterations in signed languages 32, 36
iterativity 2, 19–20, 26–27, 40, 43–44, 52, 55–56, 78–79, 86, 105, 107, 110, 113, 123, 169, 177, 182, 184, 190–191, 195

https://doi.org/10.1515/9783110697902-017

metonymy 11, 181
motivation 11, 14, 70, 136, 146, 190, 192
– relative motivation 182
Multimodal Construction Grammar 148, 152
multimodal grammar 8–9, 20, 39, 88, 114, 117–118, 151, 179–180, 195–196

plural 1–2, 19–20, 28, 34, 59, 181–182, 191
plurality 7, 26–27, 30, 32, 43–44, 59, 82–83, 86, 108–111, 142, 169, 177–178, 182, 190–195

reduplication 2, 22, 44, 60, 189, 191–194
– reduplication in gestures 46, 56–57, 63, 65, 73, 79–82, 84–85, 88, 93, 99, 112, 123–124, 169, 176–178, 181–182, 187, 195
– reduplication in signed languages 1, 32, 34–37
– reduplication in speech 23–31, 37, 181
repetition 2–3, 22, 27, 44, 46, 192–194, 211

– repetition in gestures 15, 18–19, 41–43, 45, 50, 52–55, 59, 62–64, 66, 77, 79–82, 84–86, 88, 92–93, 98–99, 105, 108, 112, 121, 123–125, 128–131, 133, 151, 159, 161, 164, 166–167, 173–174, 176–178, 182, 185, 187–188, 193–194, 196
– repetition in signed languages 36–37, 63, 193
– repetition in speech 1, 22–23, 24, 25, 29–31, 123, 181

salience 20, 46, 98, 110, 153, 155–159, 169–171, 174, 180, 186–187
schema 14, 19, 54, 83–84, 86, 109, 138, 141–143, 152, 179, 190
scope 20, 65, 120, 153–154, 159, 174, 180, 188
semantization 2, 9, 117, 146

www.ingramcontent.com/pod-product-compliance
Lightning Source LLC
Chambersburg PA
CBHW031424150426
43191CB00006B/387